THE
STORM LEOPARD

The
Storm Leopard

Martyn Murray

Whittles Publishing

Published by
Whittles Publishing,
Dunbeath,
Caithness KW6 6EG,
Scotland, UK

www.whittlespublishing.com

© 2010 Martyn Murray

ISBN 978-184995-004-6

Printed and bound in the UK by J F Print Ltd., Sparkford, Somerset

To the Bushmen of the Kalahari and
those who care about the wild

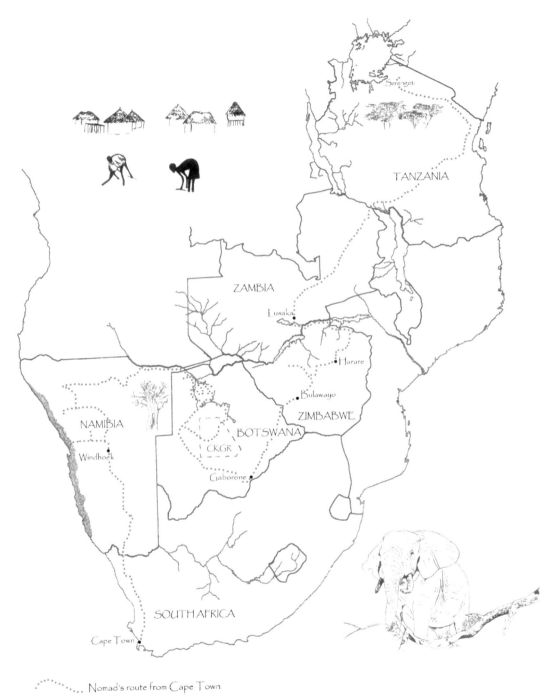

TANZANIA

Serengeti

ZAMBIA

Lusaka

Harare

Bulawayo

ZIMBABWE

NAMIBIA

BOTSWANA

Windhoek

CKGR

Gaborone

SOUTH AFRICA

Cape Town

········· Nomad's route from Cape Town

0   500   miles

0   800   kilometres

Contents

ACKNOWLEDGEMENTS

Many people helped me along the road and some have become characters in the story for which I offer my sincere thanks and apologies. I would like to thank the following for their help and hospitality: Geoff and Sue Ritson for the best possible start and end to my safari, Mrs Strauss for showing me the 'hunter', Debbie and Colin for providing a base in Windhoek, Flip Stander for the invitation to join him in the field, Eileen Drotsky for providing a guest cabin at their camp, Roy Sesana and Bulanda Thamae for opening a window into the lives of mobile Bushmen, Philip Marshall for insights into Kalahari management planning, Peter and Verity Mundy for their warm hospitality and friendship, Christmas Dube for accompanying me back into the world of impala, Dave and Meg Cumming for friendship and support, John and Beverley Hargrove for a much-needed half-way tonic, Guy Parker for showing me his study area, John Cavallo and Mr Kileo for fascinating conversations about our ancestors, and Justin Hando and Emily Kisamu for opening up the Serengeti to me once more. And then there is Stu – thanks man, what a brilliant ride. To them and all the others, may your African dreams come true.

At home in Scotland I thank my parents, Greer and Wendy, for a lifetime of love that has borne me up and over some desperate obstacles and filled me with laughter in-between. This book is dedicated to them. I thank Isla for agreeing to board for 10 long weeks – without a moment's hesitation – so that I could make my dream come true and, as an older teenager, for loosening up the dialogue. I thank Torran for giving me the happiest few days of my safari. This book is dedicated to them also. Robin and Diana, my brother and sister-in-law, provided vital backup all the way along.

In gratitude for kindness, assistance and information, I mention Andrew and Alison Johnson, Bonnie Schuman, Carole Gale, Derek Albertson, Elaine Carney,

Elspeth Parry, Françoise Wemelsfelder, Fumi Mizutani, Fungai Muroki, Ivan Baehr, Jay Gedir, Jim Aitken, John Hanks, Jonathan Scott, Karim and Stella Hirji, Kevin Dunham, Morris Gosling, Neil Munro, Norman Monks, Paul Sheller, the late Richard Bell, Richard Hoare, Richard Quixley, Sandy Gall, Sarah Cleveland, Simon Alan and Zaccheus Mahlangu.

Warm thanks are due to those who helped one way or another during the book's long gestation: Alan Barnard for discussions on the history of the Bushman peoples, David Baird for his deft touch in the problem areas of the manuscript, Harry Bingham for expounding on the art of creative writing, Lorrie Collins for loosening up the writing style, Julian Derry who called for boldness in style and elegance in presentation, Robert Hitchcock for bibliographic information on Bushman studies and helpful contacts, Lucy Odling-Smee for patiently editing the entire manuscript in its roughest form, Kirk Olson for demanding greater precision and wanting even more, Linda Philips who knew I would have to go back to the beginning, Linda Proud for her wonderful literary criticism, Frans Prins for discussions on rock painting and Bushman culture, the late Lucinda Tweedie for her help with book presentation and sparkling wit, Douglas Williamson for sharing his Kalahari memories and Jacqueline Yelland for incisive and poetic insights that enriched the story. I would also like to thank Aubrey Manning, George Schaller and Peter Matthiessen for their early endorsements. Catherine Munro drew and illustrated the map. All other sketches are by Isla Bell Murray.

Two organisations that aim to help the Bushman in various ways are: First People of the Kalahari, P.O. Box 173, Ghanzi, Botswana; and Kalahari Peoples Fund, P.O. Box 7855, University Station, Austin, TX 78713-7855, USA.

PREFACE

Sometimes you just have to do it. No reasoning, no accounting, no planning, you simply jump… and pray the landing is soft.

That day began like any other: alarm chirps at 6.30, shower, exercise routine, wake Isla from her coma, yoghurt and toast for breakfast, into the car and off to school. It was hot though, unusual for coastal Scotland, and the air was muggy. A few hours later I was checking the pressure in the tyres of my Ford Mondeo at the local Esso station – the hiss of air, the smelly haze of petrol, the wilted daisies by the litter bin, trying to make a go of life – when I thought of Africa. I noticed the sheen on my shoes, polished for the meeting. When did I do that? This morning? Yesterday evening? Sometime in a routine series of mechanical preparations for another pitch for another contract to save wildlife. How many reports have I written? How many academic papers? Have they made the slightest difference? The hiss of air, the smell of petrol, the darkening sky, a heavy roll of thunder, and Africa bloomed in my memory.

A small but insistent voice whispered, 'Now is the right time… You can do it… This may be your one chance.' Do what? Go back to Africa without a project. Go back to Africa with no purpose other than to know, to feel, to understand. Go back to meet the man I once was and question his assumptions. Go back to face my old adversary. I could see that younger me on the forecourt, bush hat lifted at the front, safari shirt half unbuttoned, one eyebrow raised in a mocking challenge. That younger guy seemed to merge with the voice in my head, pushing me, almost taunting me, as if in some playground dare. 'If you don't go back now, you might as well turn away forever.'

For a moment I thought about my one-man wildlife consultancy business. It had taken 10 years to build up. Ten years of fighting for contracts, assisting faltering projects in remote corners of the globe, holding evaluation teams together and writing interminable reports. The work was highly competitive and just keeping afloat consumed every spare moment. I couldn't afford the time away. Worse, this journey would put my future job prospects at risk. But one by one the objections were overturned, vanishing from sight like tent pegs plucked out the sand by a gathering storm. Eventually only one peg held firm and I might have guessed what she would say.

'You've got to go for it Dad. My friends think it's so cool. And I'll be happy boarding.' Isla seemed positively excited at the prospect, perhaps expecting that boarding for a term would be like some awesome sleepover party. I really hoped so. At 15 years old it would be her first taste of independence. Not a bad thing, but we were used to sorting things out together, more like a team than a dependency. And if one of us was down, the other jumped in to lend support. I told myself that she would be fine and that, after all, the journey was for her and her generation, but it didn't make it any easier. Once the last peg had pulled itself out, with a hop, skip and a jump, the tent gathered itself up and flew off with the winds, arriving in Africa a few weeks later.

1

NOMAD

Table Mountain

The breakfast table was covered with pancakes and Cape oranges, the sort of combo which would make no sense at home in Scotland, but makes the best possible sense when stretched over a linen-covered table in the shade of a South African verandah on a warm September's morning. Sue, an old friend and my host for a few days, was taking command of me as usual.

'We will go to the mall, buy some cappuccino and a copy of the *Cape Ads*. You will find a car, then I can pick up some groceries, and by the way we need to be home by 10.30 a.m.'

'Finding the right car will take time,' I said and began to tell Sue the reasons why I wouldn't be able to buy a suitable four-wheel drive by 10.30 that morning. Plenty of reasons: things to do with extra ground clearance, twin-cab models, torsion bars, mileage limits, model types.

Sue nodded, but clearly wasn't listening. Her expression told me all I needed to know – roughly, 'Yes, dear, but if we don't go to the mall right now and get that four-wheel drive of yours, we're going to be hard pushed to be back here at 10.30.'

I sighed, reckoning up the weeks that it would take to organise the safari. Van der Post took two months to outfit for his expedition to the central Kalahari, not that I intended telling Sue that. For now, I thought I might as well just fall into line. Sue hustled me away from the breakfast table (me feeling a bit the way Isla must have felt every morning for her last 15 years), got me into her car, a beat-up Toyota, and drove down to the shiny new urban mall that could be a symbol of the modern South Africa.

The mall was built in the traditional Cape Dutch style with white stucco gables shaped like jaunty Dutch hats and long cool verandahs. A line of cypresses ran down one side of the car park. Above them, clouds were riding high over Table Mountain. Sue swept me quickly past the flower sellers that flanked the main entrance and into a bustling café, filled with the wonderfully natural post-apartheid mix of black, white and every shade in between. Sue got us some coffees whilst I bought a copy of *Cape Ads*, the local free-ad newspaper, from a kiosk outside; then she installed us at a corner table and settled down to her own newspaper. I busied myself with the ads. Nothing looked at all promising. The one good 4×4 was way out of budget. The cheap ones were dire. As I reflected on the injustices of life, I remembered a time when an earlier passion had been thwarted. I was six. Every time I passed the toy shop my eyes were drawn to a beautiful wooden yacht, sails hoisted, rigging and fittings perfect down to the smallest detail. But the price was astronomical relative to my pocket money. The word hopeless hovered not far from reach.

I'm not usually a groaner, but I must have let out something, because Sue looked at me sharply and asked what the matter was.

'Oh, nothing,' I said, 'there doesn't seem to be much here, that's all.'

'Go and talk to the café owner,' she ordered, and buried her head back in the paper.

Again I was baffled, wondering what Sue could be thinking. After all, I did know something about buying secondhand four-wheel drives, having owned a variety of them at different times and driven one across Africa. You found them by combing the paper for weeks, or by contacting four-wheel drive clubs, or visiting specialist garages, or even by hanging out with overlanders at their favourite campsites. If you were lucky, someone at the end of an international contract would be selling up before leaving the country, and a friend of a friend would put you in touch. There were in fact lots of ways to find a reliable secondhand 4×4, but they all took time and none of them had anything to do with the local café owner. But then there was something about Sue, events seemed to fall into line around her, as if by magic. She had life pretty much sorted out, I decided. And it was really quite relaxing to be told what to do, so I pushed back my chair and went looking for the proprietor.

'He's over at the counter,' called Sue.

I found the café owner next to the till attending to some accounts and put my question to him.

'I would try Richard Quixley,' he said, half looking up.

I blinked a couple of times. 'Would you happen to have a telephone number?' I asked.

But Sue was already at my elbow. 'It's only a mile down the road,' she assured me. 'Come on, time to go.'

We drove down to the main street of Constantia, turned left, continued for another 200 metres, and there on the opposite side of the street was 'Nomad'. She was an Isuzu 4×4 twin cab, standing prim and proper on the forecourt, unpretentious but business-like. I hurried across the street and walked right round her, trying to be circumspect but unable to hide my interest, a bit like one dog getting to know another. Richard came over from the desk, aware that I was hooked, but too polite to say so. We started swapping yarns about cars we had owned and loved. It transpired that Richard's real passion in life was racing souped-up performance saloons, and by all accounts (at least by all of *his*) he frequently got the chequered flag. He told me that Nomad had belonged to one previous owner, a farmer, who used her once a week to drive into Cape Town. She was low mileage, reliable and cheap. We agreed the price at 55,000 Rand. Job done.

Sue was waving frantically from her car across the street; I ran back over and jumped in.

'How did it go?' she asked.

'Sorted,' I replied.

She laughed as we took off down the high street with a screech of rubber and headed for the supermarket. Half an hour later, we were back home with several bags of shopping. I glanced at the clock in the kitchen: it was 10.30 a.m. exactly. I turned to thank Sue for her fantastic help, but she was already on the telephone. To my mental list marked 'Ways to buy a 4×4 in Africa' I added one more: know Sue.

The rest of that day was spent doing car-related things with Geoff, Sue's resourceful yet easygoing husband and one of my mates from uni. Back then we had spent more time rebuilding classic cars than studying. Once again it stood us in good stead. We sorted out the safari modifications, arranging for a dual battery system (so I could run a laptop and lights in camp without depleting the car's battery), tyres that would be suitable for brutal off-road driving, 'high lift' jacking points for when I got stuck in deep mud, and much, much else.

Among the chores that day was heading over to the AA office in downtown Cape Town, to secure a *carnet de passage* that would enable me to drive across Africa, importing and exporting the car at each border. The very capable manageress took on the job and was soon talking animatedly on the telephone as she nudged a bank guarantee down the line from North Berwick, my home town in Scotland, to London to Johannesburg to Cape Town. She was alternately friendly and efficient, outraged, drippingly formal, deeply concerned and sweetly seductive. I was slightly in awe of the way she seamlessly combined the roles of businesswoman, actress and sympathetic human being in conducting the everyday affairs of her office. At one point she almost lost her patience whilst debating some technicality with a bank clerk in Johannesburg. 'But my client is driving to *Africa!*' she expostulated. '*Africa!*'

I didn't say anything, but the oddity of the word made itself felt. Here was a local African, in Africa, talking to another African who himself was located in a not too distant African city. But towns are towns, and the coast is the coast. Africa, the real Africa, the one of my imagination and hers, lay well outside Cape Town's cosmopolitan limits.

The moment reminded me forcibly of another place and time.

It was the summer of 1970 and it seemed a long way off now, almost a different me. That younger me had been happy-go-lucky, more in the here and now, but lacking in purpose. I'd had no direction, no compass to steer by, other than a fascination with wild animals and far-off places. I'd ended up in Kenya on a 10-week trip, by accident almost. After travelling all over the country, gazing at wild African animals by day and camping under the stars at night, I'd fallen under the spell of the place, completely and for life. One Sunday towards the end of my visit, I was invited to lunch by a safari operator who had retired years earlier, but still undertook the occasional expedition. The invitation brought me to his home, which turned out to be a plot of land with a vehicle workshop, a solid-looking storehouse, and two spacious safari tents. There was no house. The old-timer looked after the catering himself, barbecuing steak and onions over an open fire and serving them up on freshly baked rolls with green salad. Inevitably, the conversation turned to wildlife and the far-flung corners of Africa. Sitting beside me, the old-timer started to talk of Kenya as it had been in the 1920s, with remote mountains, untouched forests and endless plains teeming with game. Much of it was now gone having been turned under the plough, overrun with livestock, or converted to forestry plantations, even where the land had supposedly been protected from development. The litany of woes continued for some time.

'People are plain greedy,' the old-timer concluded, 'and nothing is going to change that.'

'Not everyone,' I protested. 'Some people do care about wildlife. They can make a difference.'

I said it. I meant it. Back then, I really believed in the power of positive change.

The old guy gazed at me a moment in silence. I don't know what he was thinking, but then out they came, 10 words spoken slowly and deliberately, with all the finality of the closing lines in a Shakespearean tragedy: 'You mark my words: *they will all disappear one day. Every single wild place.*'

Then and there, in that bustling AA office, with the manageress now busy with some other bureaucratic problem to chase down, I realised why I had come. I needed to face up to that old-timer's challenge. The end of the wild. Was he right? Was he wrong? I was here to find out.

2

DOWN THE RABBIT HOLE

Guinea fowl at Kirstenbosch

Arranging Nomad's modifications had taken a week of hectic activity but at last they were done. In between chasing up suppliers and ferrying Nomad between specialist workshops I'd found time to explore. One morning I'd hiked up a steep path to the top of Table Mountain and sat for a few minutes in the heather. A veil of white clouds drifted beneath the leaden sky, dissolving and evolving, conjuring a fairyland from the glistening cliffs and tree-clad ravines. On my descent, I'd entered the botanical gardens of Kirstenbosch passing through one hidden glade after another – a bed of heathers, a grove of cycads, a blazing border of Cape daisies where guinea fowl clucked and scratched, a mountain vista framed by yellowwood trees, a secluded dell with mysterious sculptures and finally a dark avenue of Morton Bay figs. The contrast between wild heights and carefully tended gardens could not have been greater. It had made me think. Care can smother as well as nurture. How does one care for a wild spirit?

Now that I was free to roam across Africa, free to leave my carefully tended lifestyle behind, I was oddly reluctant to go. I decided on a test run and drove down the Cape Peninsula to a lighthouse on the outermost tip of the Cape of Good Hope. Here I climbed down the rocks to a cove of yellow sand where the ocean swell, which travels unimpeded around the southern latitudes, drives up against the unyielding spur of Africa. Waves lifted as they rode over the rising beach, sucked in their breath, and thundered onto the shore; sand hissed under the tug of the backwash. One deep inhalation followed another in this, the first song of Africa. I threw off my socks and shoes and ran down to the edge of the ocean to paddle about, enjoying the rush of water over my feet. Looking back later, there was a solitary line of footprints emerging from the sea, beginning their long journey across the land.

Not knowing how to answer the old-timer's premonition, I could not settle on a plan. Conservationists had looked at the value of the wild from umpteen different viewpoints – its beauty, biological wonder, natural wealth of animal and plant products, and the services it provided in protecting water and soil. But for some reason it didn't hang together and the wild kept slipping away. I wanted to find some glue on this trip, an eco-epoxy that would bond the different pieces into a coherent whole. Right now, I didn't even know where to go. It had been puzzling me all week. Once again my mind filled with a host of alluring alternatives. If I stopped to look for desert elephants in Namibia, would there be time to visit the Luangwa Valley in Zambia with its dense game concentrations? But should the rains arrive early there, I could be stuck for weeks. Taking the longer route north by Lake Malawi would give me the chance to swim with flocks of cichlid fish. And what about Gombe Stream on the shores of Lake Tanganyika? As our closest relatives, might not chimpanzees provide some important clues? Perhaps if I reached Kenya in time, Isla and her brother Torran could join me on the coast for Christmas. Then, oh what a tempting thought, I could surely find another four weeks to continue the safari into January.

These thoughts washed over me, like the salt water rushing over my bare feet. Those words, about driving into Africa, swirled in the ocean's backwash, making a mockery of my attempts to plan forwards. I remembered reading about a nineteenth century Bushman called //Kabbo who, when released from hard labour on the Table Bay breakwater, sat down, doing nothing, waiting. (That '//' notation indicates a clucking sound, of the sort you might use to urge on a horse. More of that in a little while.) When asked by his guardian, a noted linguist, what he was waiting for, the man replied, 'Thou knowest that I sit waiting for the moon to turn back for me, that I may return to the places of my home … for when a man has travelled along a road, and goes and sits down, he waits for a story to travel to him, following him along the same road…'

//Kabbo was, I realised, spot on. I needed to do the same. All the attempted planning for my trip was getting me nowhere whilst //Kabbo's philosophy offered an alternative. It was less rigid, more intuitive, the kind of left-of-centre approach that might uncover something unexpected. I resolved to listen for stories and allow them to draw me hither and thither across the face of the continent. That seemed to be the right approach for my other journey too, for the question I was asking – Why are we so destructive of nature? – had not yielded to logical attack, at least not by me. Perhaps the deeper answer was to be found in the preferences and biases that evolved in our remote past, or maybe in the institutions that lie at the heart of modern society, or maybe in something else entirely. I decided then and there to feign disinterest in the big question. In that way, I would be free to follow my nose, to look into any oddities that came my way and to explore new terrain wherever I found it. And once it was off-guard, I would sneak up on the big question from behind and catch it unawares.

Leaving the ocean's roar behind, I clambered to the top of the cove, feeling the wet sand on my feet turn quickly dry on the warm rocks. I got back to the lighthouse, elated. Nomad was cooling off in the sea breeze. I checked the odometer – 76,316 kilometres. On the drive back to Cape Town, I watched for any signs of future trouble – odd noises, dropping oil pressure, uneven handling – but Nomad behaved perfectly the whole day. We were both ready for safari.

At first light Nomad and I slipped out of Cape Town, heading north for Africa and the hinterland. Multi-storey offices gave way to suburban bungalows, then patches of open country, vineyards and farms. Soon Table Mountain was only a smudge on the horizon and even pinching my arm failed to convince me this was for real. In no time, we were cruising along a small country road deep in the Western Cape, the new all-terrain tyres humming on the tarred surface. Willow trees massed with yellow flowers traced the line of a stream on the left, contrasting with the monotonous regularity of commercial farmland on the right. I mentally took stock of the safari gear one more time. The seats behind were packed with clothes, books, my laptop, camera equipment and a solar lamp, all covered in a thick blue blanket. The rear lock-up section was crammed with assorted travel equipment: a tent, jerry cans, canvas chair, water containers, tools, spares and three wooden boxes with plates and food – in fact everything from sand ladders to rusks. Not that I had any teething infants to look after, but Geoff assured me they were *de rigueur* for camping trips in South Africa.

Regimented wheat fields yielded to a large orchard where I pulled into a garage forecourt with a heavenly scent of orange blossom wafting amongst the pumps. Boxes of fruit and other local produce were stacked up inside the office where I bought a jar of homemade apricot jam. Homemade jam has been a favourite of mine since my early years at boarding school where I had subsisted on dishwater soup and potted hough that was so disgusting none could finish it. Starvation was warded off by copious quantities of strawberry jam which, though thin and runny, had tasted like nectar to me. A little further on, Nomad nosed off the highway onto a dirt road that led to the Cederberg, a craggy mountainous range some 200 kilometres to the north of Cape Town. The hills were now shorn of cedar trees but as we left the patchwork of farms behind, a magical landscape of gnarled and weathered rocks unfolded. My senses pricked up as we climbed into the first bit of wild Africa. Some of those rocks might conceal Bushman paintings.

Before their disastrous contact with the West, the Bushman people enjoyed an intimate relationship with wildlife that enabled them to occupy the greater part of southern Africa for several thousand years without causing the extinction of any game species. Maybe longer, for Stone Age peoples with anatomical features like the Bushmen of today lived in this region from as early as 120,000 years ago. The almost symbiotic relationship between Bushmen and wildlife intrigued me. Was it really true that they had restrained themselves and lived within the limits of their environment? If so, it ran contrary to much of the rest of human history with its well-known tales of warfare and agricultural expansionism, and more recent accounts of collapsing civilizations that had outstripped their resource base.[1] Humans are not supposed to rein themselves in, yet there were persistent stories about the Bushmen doing just that. I was hooked. Could the Bushmen provide a remedy to the relentless loss of wild places in the modern world and, beyond that perhaps, an insight into the central enigmas of sustainable living and environmental balance? I knew from my previous work on African mammals that a number of large animals had disappeared from the Cape region of Africa, the giant forms of buffalo and zebra as recently as 10,000 years ago. But since then and until historical times, Bushmen had apparently coexisted continuously with a diverse fauna of large mammals. In contrast when Europeans arrived at the Cape, the bluebuck (a relative of the roan antelope), quagga (a relative of the mountain zebra), and Cape lion were all wiped out within 200 years, whilst the bontebok, blesbok, black wildebeest, red hartebeest, Cape buffalo, mountain zebra and southern population of elephants only just escaped a similar fate.

Some have argued that the survival of wildlife in southern Africa was fortuitous: animals were spared because the human population was small, itself a consequence of the harsh landscape, unpredictable climate and want of advanced technology. But the anthropologist, George Silberbauer, who studied the ecology of Bushman bands living in the central Kalahari from 1958 to 1966, refutes this notion. He concluded that the G/wi people could easily have overhunted their prey populations with their poisoned arrow technology but chose not to.[2] If he is right then there must have been some unique feature in their relationship with nature that differed from ours. Would it be visible still in modern times with the mobile Bushmen taking their last faltering stand in the Kalahari? I wanted to find out. First I decided to begin by looking at rock paintings in the Western Cape, which spoke of a time prior to any contact with Europeans. Most researchers considered that the still visible paintings of the Cederberg were created within the last 7,000 years. This was to be my starting point, the period when Bushmen coexisted with African wildlife, and I would avert my Western eye in the interest of slipping into the mind of the Bushman.

A jingle from my cellphone announced the arrival of a text message. It was from Isla:

> I just wanna make sure u know that im behind u 100% and im so proud of u...

Looking out the window at the strange landscape, it felt for a few seconds as if she was right there beside me. I thought about her starting a new life in Edinburgh. How did it feel when the bell went at the end of the day and the others went home, laughing and shouting? She must think about them heading back to their mums and dads, their irritating brothers, the pets who understood them, and the sanctuary of their own rooms. I told myself to stop fretting. Some of her school friends were boarding too and her uncle, aunt and cousins were just down the road.

Nomad and I descended through a series of tight curves into a wide valley in the heart of the Cederberg. At the bottom I took the turning signposted to Traveller's Rest, a private farm reputed to have a rich collection of Bushman art. Stopping outside the homestead, I walked over to the front door, greeting several large dogs on the way. Before I reached it the owners Mr and Mrs Strauss appeared at the door, calling to the dogs and smiling a formal welcome. Mr Strauss walked over. 'Can I help?' he asked in halting English. Although I had rung in advance, he seemed slightly surprised to see me. But as I chatted on about Bushmen and rock art, the awkwardness passed and soon Mrs Strauss was leading the way in her pickup to Sevilla Cottage. I followed her down the rutted track running alongside a ravine with a bright, tumbling stream. After a couple of miles we pulled up at a picturesque two-roomed cottage. I looked up at the rocky cliffs on either side that could have hidden a hoard of hunter-gatherers, and then followed Mrs Strauss inside. The low doorways and handmade furnishing gave the cottage a homely feel. Mrs Strauss pointed out the hotplate, fridge and antiquated shower and made sure I had all the supplies that I would need. The fire in the living room was laid with pine logs, and someone had reproduced a rock-art painting of a Bushman hunter on the mantelpiece. Another of two women dancers was on the doorway leading into a cosy bedroom. Mrs Strauss smiled at my interest and seemed to relax. I was delighted with the cottage. It was exactly what I'd wanted; the perfect base from which to launch my explorations. As I watched Mrs Strauss drive off, I hoped I would be able to find the real

Bushman paintings on my own and that this time they would communicate something more.

The first time I'd discovered one of their paintings was when I was studying the impala antelope of the Zambezi Valley. It had been set on a vertical slab under an overhanging rock in amongst a crowd of enormous boulders. There was a line of blood-red hunters carrying bows and quivers; two had paused, arrows at the ready, to face a huge crocodile lying belly up above them. I remember looking closely at the detail and wondering about the crocodile – some totem animal perhaps? At the time I was a postgraduate student out to prove my academic prowess. My mind was racing with scientific ideas about the impala. Did the females choose their companions according to levels of kinship? Could the rutting behaviour of males be predicted by game theory? I found nothing in the painting that connected with the subtle Western concepts of sociobiology. It was animalistic, foreign, arising out of another realm of existence. It was just a quirky oddity and well to the side of my scientific adventuring. But now as I mulled over the fundamental issues of people and their environment, I had a completely different feeling about them.

After a cheese and tomato roll for lunch, I set off to find the kloof at Salmanslaagte. Turning off the main road, Nomad bumped along a rough track which led to a barren rocky dead-end. The kloof turned out to be a deeply cut gorge providing both permanent water and concealment from unfriendly eyes. I clambered down a short goat track to a stream at its base and followed this further downhill, squeezing through gaps between large boulders, until finding myself under a 30-foot-long rock shelter overhanging the streambed. By the look of its smooth walls, it had been carved out by swiftly flowing waters fed by mountain storms. The pale sandstone walls were awash with yellow sunlight reflecting off the rocks below.

Beneath the arching roof I spied a line of dancing women filling the canyon with energy and joy. Hands waved and breasts swung as the women shuffled along to the throbbing, pulsating rhythms that filled the shelter. I could almost imagine them returning to the shelter that evening. The dancing women had large buttocks and fat calves. Perhaps the artist was rejoicing in a bountiful summer in a country where hunger was never far away. They bobbed along in a human snake. I grinned at the happy band, nearly ready to join in. Yet I also felt the pathos in that day of merriment and laughter, at a time of peace and wellbeing before the Bushman's troubles really began, before tragedy befell them.

Stepping back from the ladies, I could see that the line of dancers was superimposed on four enormous yellow elephants that had congregated on the face of the creamy rock. Comedy and tragedy seem to walk hand in hand with these extraordinary people. The different pigments used by the artists came from sandstone rocks: shades of red, brown and yellow derived from the oxides of iron, white from zinc oxide and black from manganese oxide. Eyewitness accounts described how this ochre was prepared by heating it over a fire until it was red hot, whence it was ground between stones and made ready for mixing and binding with animal fat, egg yolk and fresh blood.[3] I guessed that the artist had prepared his paints under the light of a full moon as it was a ceremonial occasion full of symbolism and spiritual energy. He would apply the paints with brushes made from the stiff tail hairs of gnus, neatly tied with tendon to a thin reed. I admired his skill again. He had no paper or bits of old canvas on which to practise, and there was no room for error. He had just the one shot at it. If the brush was too coarse for the finer details, he would have reached for the quill of a porcupine. The exquisite painting had bonded well to the rock surface and had already lasted hundreds of years.

Scrambling out the bottom of the gorge, I climbed to higher ground finding an easier route back to Nomad. Looking down, the kloof no longer felt barren, in fact it was humming with hidden life. What it meant, and how it connected to the lives of contemporary Bushmen, I couldn't even guess. But for some reason the humming from the belly of the kloof had got me humming along. Back on the main road, I drove the short distance to the start of the Sevilla trail. The sketch map showed this as a squiggly route that more or less followed the same stream that ran in front of my cottage, but on the other side. It was hard to find the start of the trail. There were no intrusive signposts or litter bins or other hints, and there was nothing in the rocky valley before me to suggest that it contained an open-air art gallery. Eventually I spotted a child-sized footprint painted in white, and another maybe 30 feet beyond it. Pulling on my daypack, I followed the faded footprints along a trail that wound its way along narrow ledges, in amongst flowering bushes, and past mysterious caverns. By now it was late afternoon, quiet and peaceful, and the heat of the day was beginning to subside providing ideal conditions for walking. I lengthened my stride, anxious to see as much as possible before night fell.

Quite suddenly I spotted the first painting set in a small shelter next to an exposed rock face: an ostrich with two very human legs sticking out. It made me laugh. When stalking the quagga and other game animals, the southern Bushmen were said to have disguised themselves in ostrich skins using a long pliant stick run through the neck to keep the head erect. They were expert at imitating the actions of the living bird, directing the mock ostrich to pick at bushes, preen itself and gaze about, as they crept up on their quarry.[4] One day, I would love to try that.

I walked a little further along, searching every rock face, scanning each dimple for clues. Under a shallow overhang, and partially hidden by an ancient wild olive tree, I found a Bushman archer. He strode forward, bow raised, bowstring pulled back, ready to fire. His arrow was of the type still used by

Bushmen today to inject poison into their prey. Several kinds of poison are concocted, derived from beetle grubs, snake venoms and certain pods and roots: all are highly toxic and fast acting. //Kabbo recounted the story of a man who was accidentally shot with a poisoned arrow.[5] He was with a group of hunters who came across a large herd of springbok, and in the dust and confusion of the hunt he was hit by a friend's arrow. In the account, he felt no anger: 'I did not see the arrow. I could have avoided it and prevented our brother's fear … The dust was dense because there were many springbok. We did not see that we were shooting at each other because we were shooting in the dust.' But the poison soon took effect: 'I burn with pain, because the wound swells, it swells greatly. Therefore I am bloated. The swelling throbs. That is why my heart is falling.' The hunter passed on that night. He had lived and died so close to nature, almost a part of it.

By now the light was beginning to fade and I walked even faster along the narrow trail, passing between two huge flattened rocks like a mouse scampering between enormous stone pillows lying on a giant's bed. At the far end of the pillows was a shallow overhang too exposed to be used as a sleeping place, but nevertheless covered in figures. One tableau contained three fantastical monsters. I felt my spine tingling. To my eye, it showed the transformation of a semi-human, shamanistic figure into a giant four-legged beast with an enormous clawed head. Close by were two human figures one bent forward, the other crouching, both in postures that living Bushmen associate with the entry into trance. Had the shamanic artist undergone a terrible transformation? Was this a 'bad trip' or had he summoned some powerful spirit? I shook myself free of the thought. One of the great discoveries of prehistoric art is the symbolic nature of the Bushman's painting. Rather than simple portrayals of people and animals, they are now recognised as visual expressions of a spiritual world that held deep meaning for the artists.[6] In the Bushman's stories, people slip easily from their daily lives into the spiritual realm where humans and animals can converse freely with one another and even change identity. It seems unreal to many of us in the West who tend to stick to the physical realm. Maybe there is an important difference here?

Tragically we cannot ask the Bushman about his art and its meaning. The last known artist was shot in 1866 whilst hiding amongst the rocks and caves of his mountain fastness in what is now the Witteberg Nature Reserve in Lesotho. We can tell he was an artist from the ten small horn pots hanging from his belt, each with a different coloured paint,[7] but we know nothing of his paintings.[8] We are ignorant of his name. Even his belt of colours is lost. All that is told by the posse who cornered him is that he successfully rustled some horses. Thus ended the great era of rock painting, smashed against a cultural barrier of ignorance and prejudice.

It was growing dark by the time I turned to head back towards Nomad. The cool scented air added to my sense of exhilaration as I trotted happily down the trail, backpack swaying from side to side with the weight of cameras, camcorder, notebooks and water bottle. In the gathering gloom, I lost my way several times, finally reaching Nomad just after nightfall, helped along at the end by the light of a two-thirds moon. Back at Sevilla cottage, I lit the fire and rummaged around for a tin of ratatouille. Soon the flames were crackling in the hearth and a sweet smell of herbs and vegetables pervaded the tiny living room.

Next morning, I packed up Nomad, bid farewell to Sevilla cottage and drove down to the farmhouse. I wanted to ask Mrs Strauss for permission to visit one of the restricted sites on their land. Some rock-art paintings are considered especially sensitive, either because they have unique significance or because of their vulnerability to collectors and vandals, and access to them is controlled. I found Mrs Strauss outside the house talking to one of the farm workers. She walked over to Nomad with a smile. 'How was your night?' she asked.

'Wonderful, thanks,' I replied with gusto, continuing more cautiously. 'I was hoping to visit one other site on your farm.'

'Which one were you thinking about?'

There was one in particular I was curious to see. 'The Hunter,' I replied.

'Ja,' she nodded. 'That should be okay.' She paused for a moment, frowning. 'But I don't think it is safe for you. You have to drop down a tiny hole, ja? There's only a narrow ledge to land on.' She suppressed an involuntary shudder. 'You really need help and I can't spare anyone just now.'

Seeing my chances beginning to slip, I leapt in quickly without thinking of the danger. 'I'll take care, don't worry.'

'Ja, but even if you manage to get down on your own, you might not get out again. There's no step up to the exit hole.'

I paused, imagining a dark cave with an exit hole high above my outstretched arms where the light of day waxed and waned as day turned to night. I keep myself reasonably fit and can scramble up a hill as well as the next person, but I'm no rock climber. What I do know is that a single step on a Scottish mountain can take you from safety to extreme exposure and another to beyond the point of easy return. 'I'll bring a rope. I'll be fine,' I replied with more confidence than I felt, taking a private bet it wouldn't be as bad as she made out.

'I hope so,' she said with a frown.

I smiled reassuringly whilst cursing myself for not including a light rope amongst Nomad's emergency gear. A few minutes later, as I rummaged in the back for something that might do, Mrs Strauss reappeared with one of the farmhands.

'It will be safer if you take a guide,' she said, smiling at my obvious relief. The farmhand had a creased friendly face, just like a Bushman's. He was short and slender, skin tanned to dark cinnamon, and above the three deep wrinkles on his forehead was a scattering of peppercorn hair. Perhaps he was a Khoekhoe,[9] herding people closely related to Bushmen who settled on farms after their land was seized by European settlers. Unfortunately we shared no common language but I nodded to him, and gave him a thumbs-up, and was rewarded by a grin.

As we made our way up the flank of a broad hill where flaxen grass rippled in the breeze, a second Khoekhoe, rangy and taller, sauntered up to join us. I tried to work out from my companions' reactions whether this had been a prearranged rendezvous, but after a few moments put my European anxieties to one side. Who cared, anyway? We grinned at each other, laughed at nothing, and continued on in our little group of three. The two Khoekhoe chattered away with numerous clicks and pops.

It was cheering to be with such carefree companions; we strolled along the side of a field, passed through a gate and across an area of stony scrubland before reaching a line of low cliffs. At this juncture, my two guides bounded up the rocks like a pair of klipspringers and disappeared from sight. Panting with the climb and heat and frustrated at my slower speed, I followed them up reaching the top a minute or more behind them. I found myself on a flat ridge of pockmarked limestone about 40 metres wide with an occasional stunted bush. Looking about I found no sign of my Khoekhoe companions. It was puzzling: surely they wouldn't have deserted me. I walked along the ridge the way I guessed they had gone and halloed a couple of times but there was no response. A little further on, I came across a hollow in the floor of the rock platform. It was shaped like a funnel with sides that steepened into a round hole just large enough for a body to squeeze through. The hole led straight underground. I walked on a little way in case my guides were waiting even further along the ridge, but they were nowhere to be seen. I returned to the hole. This must be it. The thought of getting stuck in a tunnel underground was unappealing but there seemed little option. I needed to enter the inner world of the Bushman. I lowered myself slowly into the unknown, swinging my feet from side to side to locate a foothold. There was none. For a second or two my feet dangled in space. Now I knew how Alice must have felt, when poised on the edge of the rabbit hole. I held myself up for a moment longer realising this was foolhardy. Then, with an inner shrug I let myself go and dropped about three feet onto a rough stone floor. Landing awkwardly I lurched to one side: the edge of a cliff dropped away from my startled gaze to the veldt far below.

A jumble of broken rocks and thorn bushes were scattered about at the base. I realised that I was in a cave that was open on one side, and that side happened to be in the wall of a sheer cliff. I edged back inside. My companions were sitting on the floor nearby, happily chatting together and quite unaware of my rapidly beating heart. Beyond them, the rock shelter stretched for a further 30 feet. I skirted past the pair to examine the far end, which had a smooth wall of white alabaster. Three tiny figures in deep chocolate red were in motion on this massive rock canvas. In the centre was a Bushman hunter, racing forward across the plains, right arm stretched back and ready to launch a heavy throwing stick; the left arm carried low, thrusting a small spear forward. Every detail could be seen down to the bangle on his right thigh. Nearly a metre in front was a tiny rhebok[10] lamb, fleeing for its life, the little scut of a tail lifted and ears pricked, as if hearing the alarm cry of its mother. She was behind the hunter, staring at the unfolding scene, panic in her breast, but unable to respond because of a broken hind leg.

The painting was so fresh I could imagine it had just been finished. Perhaps it was fashioned on a spring day, like today, at the height of the rhebok lambing season, to record the first successful hunt of a young man. He had followed the rhebok mother to where her infant was hiding, awaiting its next feed. If her leg had not been broken, the pair might have fled together and escaped. Did he regret killing these animals, I wondered.

Sitting down and looking out over the rugged valley below, dotted with olive green bushes and distorted black rocks, I reflected on how I might have felt. If it were today, I would regret killing this pair but then my survival is not in question, nor am I concerned about finding my next meal. It is different for Bushmen who depend on wild animals for their food and seldom harbour sentimental attitudes. In her moving account of the mobile Bushman bands living in the northern Kalahari, Elizabeth Marshall Thomas recalled how the people laughed and joked when a partly eviscerated springbok jumped and kicked before it died.[11] She also told of one father who gutted and cooked a still-living tortoise for his infant son. Her mother, the renowned anthropologist Lorna Marshall, mentioned that they showed no concern for wounded creatures and no remorse for the pain they might be causing them.[12] Children were not prevented from pulling legs off live grasshoppers and on one occasion a group of them were permitted to play with a baby hare until they had killed it. But a hundred years earlier, another Bushman child, the son-in-law of //Kabbo the dreamer, also played with a baby hare and he did not want to kill it. 'I was not willing to kill the leveret, because I felt that nothing acted as prettily as it did, when it was gently running, gently running along. It did in this manner (showing the motion of its ears), while it was gently running along, nothing acted as prettily as it did; and it went to sit down … And I went to fetch water; then, they killed my leveret for me, while I was at the water. They killed my leveret for me; and then I came and cried about the leveret … which I had meant to let alone, so that it might live on in peace'.[13]

It reminded me of an old Bushman story about the Early Race, set at a time when humans and animals had not yet diverged. In this story Pishiboro, the trickster-god of the G/wi Bushmen, and his younger brother were sleeping alongside Pishiboro's elephant wife who was making the two men uncomfortable by rolling them between her thighs.[14] They decided to get up and slip away whilst it was still dark. Next morning, the younger brother saw the elephant wife coming after them and urged Pishiboro to run on whilst he stayed behind to divert her attention. He talked to her in a friendly way, winning her confidence, only to pierce her in the heart with a long thorn. In a show of complete indifference, he cut off her breast and roasted it, then climbed onto her back and ate the meat, whilst enjoying the splendid view. And that is where Pishiboro found his brother when he returned. 'Ah, can it be that my younger brother has killed my wife and is sitting on her body?' Pishiboro was wildly angry. But his younger brother handed him some of the roasted meat, and said in a voice filled with scorn: 'Oh, you fool. You lazy man. You were married to meat and you thought it was a wife.' Pishiboro saw that this was true and helped his brother to get on with the skinning.

It's a strange story but I think that serves to emphasise its message that animals should be considered primarily as meat. This is what the Bushman's God has decided: that they must brush aside sentimentality and enjoy a square meal. On the other hand, the very existence of such a fable indicates that they, like us, recognise the conflict existing between their love of animals and their need for food. It is just that in living closer to nature, their pragmatism is brought to the forefront.

My Khoekhoe guide coughed politely. I turned and scrambled to my feet, realising that I'd been sitting for some time gazing out at the view. With a happy grin he pointed to the rabbit hole. It was time to go. He gave his companion a leg-up, and received a hand-up in turn. I quickly went to the base of the hole and grasped his outstretched arm. With a heave and a scramble I was out. A few minutes later we arrived back at the homestead where I thanked Mrs Strauss for her help. Pulling out from the driveway at Traveller's Rest, I waved goodbye to her and my two companions before heading westwards towards the coastal highway, which runs all the way north to Namibia. Ideas about our substantial need for meat and our spiritual need for nature were buzzing about my head. I hoped to find some living Bushmen to discuss them with.

3

FIELD OF BLACK RAGS

Dancing ostrich

The crisp dawn air at Ai-Ais camp on the Fish River carried a wonderful fragrance of wild herbs, spring blossoms and desert sands. In Africa I just can't sleep in. The early morning air is invigorating and there are discoveries to be made around the camp – nocturnal rodents may have left tiny trails in the sand, a dainty dik-dik could have walked past in the dead of night, or there may be signs of night prowlers. Africa has the greatest number of large wild animals on Earth and dawn is its most revealing time. Those journeying across the land need to rise even earlier as travelling is never entirely predictable. Floods, sandstorms, collapsed bridges, checkpoints and breakdowns far from town, can surprise the best organised safari. So if there is a journey to be made, it's best to start before sunup. Nomad and I were on the road at first light.

After leaving Mrs Strauss yesterday, I had cruised along the coastal highway crossing the mountainous landscapes of the Northern Cape gloriously decked out in spring flowers. I kept pushing on north trying to get away from the farms and fences to wilder country. Nomad was like a horse scenting lush meadows ahead; I hardly had to touch the accelerator. As the day wore on, the countryside had become noticeably drier, eventually turning into a desert landscape as we arrived in Namaqualand. Even here feathered flowers thrust from the sand in white and yellow clumps, and even here fences ran along the side of the road. Realising I could make the Namibian border before nightfall, I had given Nomad free rein. We had made it, reaching Ai-Ais at dusk and that had given me a chance to reach Windhoek today. I was looking forward to seeing my son, Torran, who was at school there. I would also be able to arrange a rendezvous with Stu, a journalist friend from Edinburgh, who was flying out to join the safari.

The road north from Ai-Ais had a loose marram surface, but was well maintained. Nomad hummed along leaving a 10-mile plume of fine dust in her wake; it hung in the still morning air, barely moving. I was glad to be the first car on the road. An hour later I joined the main highway and continued cruising north to Keetmanshoop stopping at a petrol station to fill up. I got out to clean the windscreen which was caked in dust. When I'd finished, a guy, who had been sitting on the edge of the forecourt watching, approached and asked for some money to clean the car. There was no smile on his face and for a few seconds he wouldn't take no for an answer. In town I was harangued by several beggars when I stopped to pick up a local SIM card for my cellphone. I wasn't prepared and beat a hasty retreat to Nomad. On my way out of town, I decided against picking up a rough-looking hitchhiker. I got a fist shake. Three trivial incidents perhaps, but they caused me to reflect on the problems of urban poverty and social injustice in Africa. Local conditions must be worse here than in South Africa.

The road continued through endless flat horizons of desert scrub whitened by the glaring sun. Just north of the next town, my eye was caught by a field of black rags on the other side of a railway line. On second glance I thought it might be the remnants of meat from a slaughterhouse, hung up to dry. Now I realised that it was a huge ostrich farm with hundreds, no thousands, of hen ostriches. Fenced into paddocks devoid of vegetation, shade or water, they were drifting about listlessly in crowds like so many inmates of a POW camp. Looking at the nearest birds through my binoculars, I could see that they were panting in the heat, mouths gaping, feathers dishevelled and lacklustre. I gritted my teeth and scanned with binoculars back across the mob. There was nothing here to remind me of the magnificent wild ostriches that roamed across the wide roof of Africa. As a young field biologist, I had sometimes stumbled upon gangs of 10 or 20 chicks scuttling about under the feet of their gigantic parents, like fluffy grey puffballs on stilts. When older, the gangly ostriches joined other broods of similar age which soon struck out on their own. Alert, handsome and fleet-footed, they wandered huge distances. On one occasion, I came across a group of 50 teenagers out on their own in the vast Serengeti plains miles from anywhere; the forest of ostrich heads followed my every move. These ragged animals, by contrast, lacked all curiosity. Even when I approached the electrified fence, they ignored me. I remembered how the wild males danced, necks and feet flushed coconut-pink offsetting their glossy black backs and fluffy white hips. They swayed and bowed and fanned each other with wings of jet, and boomed warnings from their throats. Meanwhile the females sat brooding on their clutches, protecting the eggs from jackals, mottled grey feathers blending with the patchy savannah grasses.

Looking at these pens stretching away into the distance, I wondered what one person could want with 5,000 ostriches. At one time I wouldn't have graced such ponderings with an answer. I used to ignore the economic motivation behind commercial wildlife farming. It was alien to me. In my youthful eyes, wild creatures had a high intrinsic value that placed them in a sacred place beyond the reach of an accountant's pen. My holy grail was to understand their behaviour and ecology. I believed that knowledge about wild places and their inhabitants was inspirational. It was the one true antidote to the old-timer's fatalism. So I ignored the farms and ranches that were spreading across the land. They were an irrelevance. Today I recognise this as naivety, if not hubris, and am ready to answer my question. Presumably it is the profit that comes from selling feathers and satisfying the demand for low cholesterol meat in the diet-conscious markets of the West. Fine! I also like to earn a profit and enjoy a bit of luxury. But there was precious little understanding of wild ostriches, or the needs of captive ones, apparent in this ostrich ghetto and that concerned me. Where does callous exploitation begin and cautious utilisation end? For that matter, how do any of us strike the right balance between making a profit and caring for nature? I wondered whether the last nomadic Bushmen, now forcibly settled in their own depressing ghettos, would be able to answer these deeper questions? Surely it was expecting too much.

Starting at Cape Point, I had traversed the whole of South Africa and a good part of Namibia, travelling 1,700 kilometres across what would have been prime game country not so long ago. In all this distance I had come across one wild animal, a dik-dik spotted yesterday near the Fish River canyon. I had encountered 5,000 ostriches but no wildlife. There were no Bushman hunters either, and that was surely no coincidence. Writing a century ago, the historian, George Stow[1] recounted how Bushmen 'were driven out of their own country, the vast herds of game which once afforded them abundance of food ruthlessly destroyed, their children seized and carried into slavery...' Some of my countrymen were amongst the worst offenders. The oppression of Bushmen by other races did not stop with the publication of Stow's book: to this day Bushmen remain without legal rights to any part of their traditional lands.[2] The last refuges where they might have continued their traditional way of life are under pressing threat. The story of their systematic persecution has been likened to over 300 years of persistent genocide.[3]

Angered by these injustices I drove on fast, reaching the outskirts of Windhoek, the capital of Namibia, in the late afternoon. I passed through the prosperous suburbs and into the modern centre with its odd mix of tall office blocks, shopping centres and colonial buildings with tin roofs extending over wide verandahs that serve as a reminder of the not-so-distant past.

4

JACKAL AND TIDE

Black-backed jackal

Torran made the passing and dribbling look easy, loping along on long teenage legs, tawny hair flopping about above a broad forehead. I wondered if the others in his team were as nuts about football as him; even I was beginning to catch the bug. He had gone out to Africa some eight years earlier at the age of five when his mum decided to emigrate. Torran's sister Isla stayed with me, and we'd worked hard to make sure the two of them could spend their holidays together, rotating between Namibia and Scotland. Even so I never felt I had enough time with Torran. Part of me was dismayed to be picking him up from a strange school in a foreign country where he lived without my guidance or help; another part found the whole thing quite normal. I was simply fetching him from school: one of the most common occurrences of everyday family life.

He ran over at the end of the game clutching a small holdall and jumped into Nomad with a grin stretching from cheek to freckled cheek.

'Let's go Dad,' he yelled in excitement, switching to a studied air of nonchalance as he noticed some schoolkids watching.

'Engaging warp drive,' I confirmed as we accelerated out of the school grounds. We shared a whoop of exhilaration as Nomad hit the empty street at speed. It reminded me of the last day of term at my own school when the old bus took us down the drive on a countdown to 'freedom'. Today there was the added relief of escaping from the curious stares of parents and staff. Not that they were unsympathetic. The headmaster had made a particular effort to be friendly and helpful. As we joined the main road leading north out of Windhoek, I glanced over at Torran feeling contentment settle over me like the mantle of an oyster round an awkwardly shaped pearl.

We drove north on the highway to Okahandja and then west towards the coast, passing through a vast scrubby wilderness. The only habitation was at Karibib, a small mining town on the edge of the Namib Desert. We stopped in front of a general purpose store. Outside the street lacked definition – bleached by the naked energy of the sun – but inside, as if in compensation, the shutters were closed and it was almost too dark to see. A bunch of kids aged about 12 or 13 were hanging out near the chest freezer. To my amazement, one of them recognised Torran and came over. It turned out they had been classmates together at the local primary school. That felt even more bizarre. But I was happy to buy them ice-lollies and to down a soft drink myself. It was so dry here the sweat evaporated before your skin had a chance to grow moist.

School life and the bringing home of school friends were a part of Torran's upbringing that I had missed. In some important areas, I hardly knew him. And I couldn't help but wonder what he thought of me. We really needed some time together, on his turf.

'C'mon Dad, let's go,' said Torran tugging at my arm.

'What's the hurry?' I asked downing the last of my drink.

'We won't make the Skeleton Coast if we don't go now.'

Torran had set his heart on camping on the beach tonight. We walked into the furnace outside and clambered into Nomad. I started her up quickly to get the air-con working. 'What's it like?' I asked. 'Is it spooky?'

'No,' Torran shook his head. 'It's fun. You'll see.'

On the western side of Karibib, it was even drier. The scrub thinned out leaving just the occasional broken line of thorn bushes to mark the edge of an empty watercourse. Torran was enjoying a novel, *The Power Of One*, and read a passage aloud as we drove along. It was about a young boy growing up in South Africa who had been orphaned and ended up as the only English pupil in an Afrikaans boarding school. The boy is given a rough induction but from this experience he develops a passion for changing the world. Listening to his voice set against the wild landscapes of his adopted country, I wondered about the deeper currents stirring within him. Close-up the sun shimmered on the dark tarmac. In the distance, liquid hills floated above the heat haze, the nearest in brick pink and the furthest in slate blue.

Karibib had stirred deep currents before. A pair of German geologists, Henno Martin and Hermann Korn, camped in this inhospitable region rather than face internment during the Second World War. Loading up their geological truck with provisions in Windhoek, they drove along the same route that we had taken, turning off the main road at Karibib and disappearing from sight for two and a half years. They lived as hunter-gatherers using Bushman rock shelters to escape the sun; finding scarce supplies of water and game animals in the sandy canyons and rocky desert outcrops. Henno Martin's account[1] of their travails is one of the finest real life adventure stories written; in many ways it is a sister book to *Seven Years in Tibet* by Heinrich Harrer whose spur to journey into hidden lands was also an escape from British internment. And it provides one more insight into the intimate relationship of the hunter – the real subsistence hunter who lives off the land – and his prey.

The geologists learnt how to shoot the local game animals – springbok, gemsbok and zebra – using either a light pistol or a shotgun. As they possessed only a few hundred rounds of old ammunition for the pistol and a handful of cartridges for the shotgun, this meant ambushing their intended prey at close quarters to ensure that each shot was effective. Their preferred range was about the same as that of a Bushman hunter with bow and poisoned arrow. It was difficult to get so close and they missed constantly. Soon they were on the edge of starvation.

Henno and Hermann were pushing themselves hard: their focus on life was closely defined by their need to survive. They lived on the edge, unprotected by either Western welfare or African community. They watched their prey intently, hunger sharpening their powers of observation, and they began to understand the habits of the wild animals, even to predict their behaviour. 'We learnt to recognise their mood and intentions from the way they held their heads, or set their hooves, or from the swishing of their tails or the flicking of their ears. We got to understand them and their behaviour as you get to understand your friends without the need of speech.' Here was another similarity with the Bushman hunters who can classify individual animals according to more than 18 categories of personality and character, enabling them to reject those animals judged to possess too much courage or contrariness[2] for easy hunting. Modern day field biologists have not even approached this level of differentiation.[3]

Hermann confessed to trembling with eagerness 'like a dog' when a gemsbok came near enough for a shot and Henno remarked that he became tremendously keyed up when hunting for food on an empty stomach, and afterwards when the animal was killed, the release of tension was correspondingly great. Yet despite their best efforts, the two were constantly hungry.

They tried all kinds of food from berries to wild onions, and from smoked carp to casseroled quail, but most of all they craved the large game animals, not just for their meat but for the tallow-like fat and soft marrow dripping. With such intensity of observation and purpose, it is not surprising to find that animals also featured in the dreams of the geologists, to the extent that animal and human identities began to mingle. Perhaps Henno dreamt of being a gemsbok in its handsome black-on-fawn coat with a pair of deadly sabre-like horns, pacing along the sandy canyon floor behind his friend, or of being a leopard, hungry in the night, ready to leap for his kill.

I turned to ask Torran if he had ever dreamt of being an animal but he was fast asleep. One minute wide awake, the next oblivious to everything; kids are good at being in the present. I concentrated on staying awake. Even with the air-con full on, it was uncomfortably hot in the cab and I was determined to ensure a safe weekend. I felt hugely happy just to be travelling in Africa with Torran and absurdly proud of being his dad. Back home in Scotland, I had grown accustomed to his long absences, and to fending off the constant questions about how he was doing, which I couldn't really answer. I'd walled it off in the way one walls off the pain from a persistent sore. Now, almost accidentally, we were together. It was as if some unknown nurse had applied a healing balm whilst I slept. When I awoke the next morning the sore place had gone, and in its place was a feeling of lightness.

Looking about I noticed that the countryside had become pure desert. There was nothing but sand and rock in every direction as far as the eye could see, surely a sign that we were entering the coastal zone. I pressed on, conscious that I was grinning with pleasure, like a well-fed meerkat.

Folklore from all over the world contains stories of humans who can turn into animals and *vice versa*. Our own European mythology has tales of wolves and werewolves, and of seals and silkies. Henno suggested that this common heritage in Man's mythology may have arisen from dreams such as his. Under conditions of absolute necessity, the pursuit of meat becomes an all-consuming central purpose to life, so much so that the hunter's spiritual identity begins to mingle with that of his quarry. Would such deep attachment to one's prey help to curb excessive hunting?

There is much to learn from the experiences of these two remarkable men as regards hunting and survival in the desert, but I would not want to leave them sitting with their stash of dried meat by a campfire in the Namib without making mention of another side to their adventure – their tireless debates on the origins of human nature. These continued throughout the whole period of their isolation and some of the conclusions they reached were remarkable.

The first Stone Age artist to trace the outline of an antelope in the sand consciously created something new. Henno and Hermann recognised that the tracing of an antelope was no random event. Life had not been waiting for that million-to-one mutation that produced an artist where none had been before; rather, they argued, the early humans were beginning to use their minds to create new possibilities, driving the process of evolution before them. The geologists' idea is not contrary to Darwinian evolution. Before there were artists, the human line must have been ready to produce them: the opposable thumb, tight eye-to-hand coordination and sophisticated pattern recognition of the brain, all pre-adapted humans for art. And following its advent, the standing of those individuals with artistic talent might have risen in their bands, and no doubt their survival and reproduction would consequently also have benefited. The genes that helped shape good artists would surely spread in the population. But within this thread of thought is the novel idea that imagination might have played a pre-eminent role in human evolution. The mind recognises new possibilities; perhaps it sees the image of an animal marked on a rock where no such thing has ever occurred, so impelling an early attempt at rock painting which eventually leads to a classical process of natural selection for artistic aptitudes. It has been suggested that the physical variety we find amongst modern peoples would not have evolved without the ingenuity shown by our ancestors in creating new technology. Throwing sticks and ocean-going canoes created new opportunities, new niches for our human ancestors to occupy, and these carried their own selective pressures that ended up shaping us.[4] If the human mind has been at the centre of human evolution, it is a potent tool indeed.

My daydreams had helped to pass the time on the hot drive to the coast. Right on cue, Torran woke up as we entered the pretty seaside town of Swakopmund with its oasis of flowers and palms. We already had plenty of fresh food in the cool box but I stopped at a shop selling sports gear and found just what I was looking for. Climbing back into Nomad, I tossed the football over to Torran with a challenge. 'Now we'll see who's the best goal kicker round here.'

Torran had no doubts about the outcome. 'Sure Dad, get ready for total annihilation.'

We followed the Atlantic seaboard northwards out of town, and began looking for a place to camp. A number of 4×4s passed us going in the opposite direction, sporting up to seven fishing rods fastened vertically to the front bumper. It appeared that shore-fishing was a popular weekend pastime in this isolated community. All along the road were little markers set on the verge – an empty beer can, a broken wooden post, a couple of stones – each with a track in the sand that led the way to the beach and somebody's favourite fishing spot. Many an evening must be whiled away with a case of beers and the pounding surf for company. As the miles slipped by, the markers began to thin out, eventually disappearing altogether; only then was Torran satisfied. We turned off the road and made our own way across the desert. On reaching the shore, I engaged four-wheel drive and Nomad ploughed along the beach to a fine sandy point jutting out into the ocean.

A never-ending stream of cormorants was flying southwards past the point whilst others sat in rafts about 50 metres from shore, rising and falling in the swell on the outer edge of the breakers. The sea was streaked with foam and spindrift and the beach scarred with lines of weed and oceanic debris. Torran was first down to the tide's edge with his football, kicking it repeatedly up the steep bank of the sandy terrace where Nomad was sitting. As the sun set, the wind began to rise. I called him over to help put up the big red tent. The first time with a tent is always the hardest and we battled in the wind trying to work out where the poles went and what the guy ropes did, succeeding finally by lashing the guys to Nomad on the windward side and to jerry cans of petrol on the downwind side. Torran found some long sticks which he sharpened with a sheath knife, digging them deep into the sand to hold down the groundsheet. After helping with the tent, he searched about for some large stones to make a fireplace, and then went off to gather in some driftwood. Returning with a large armful, he stacked up the wood carefully and, without needing any encouragement, set about coaxing a fire into life. It was good to have him around, pulling his weight without being asked, being onside without question. In a short while, the smoky smell of *boerewors* permeated the camp. This was my first go with Geoff and Sue's *braaivleis* grill which trapped a spiral of spiced sausage between two mesh frames, enabling the whole thing to be turned over quicker than a marshmallow could drip. Reinvigorated by barbecued sausage and a mug of orange juice, we set off to explore. First we went back to the edge of the sand terrace to look at the ocean some 15 metres beyond. All light from the west had now gone but a rising full moon lit up the beach in silvery relief, and there, at the edge of the ocean, was a huge Cape Fur Seal sitting up on its front flippers. Torran was transfixed. 'Look at him Dad. Do you think he's seen us?' I pulled out my torch and we approached cautiously. Halfway over, it let out a few grunts and lunged towards us; we turned and ran up the beach whooping with excitement. The seal lumped off into the waves and disappeared, wearing an annoyed expression.

The edge of the water was receding fast as the tide ebbed causing me to worry that it might turn and rise equally fast in a few hours time. With a full moon we could expect a spring tide which might bring the sea flooding inland. Torran had picked up an announcement on the car radio that high tide would be at four o'clock in the morning. As a precaution we walked along the beach with Nomad's rechargeable lantern to map out the highest line of retreat; satisfied, we retired to the tent and climbed into our sleeping bags. Torran went out like a light. I set my digital watch alarm for 2 a.m. and lay awake thinking over the marvellous day but worrying about the vast ocean just a few metres away. Miraculously, I awoke to the tinny jingle. Steeling myself against further sleep, I unzipped a panel in the tent and peered outside. The moon was now riding high, shining a soft grey light over the desert sands. Thankfully the onshore gale had died down but in its place was the roar of ocean waves. They sounded close. Extricating myself from the sleeping bag, I slipped out of the tent and walked over to the sand ledge.

Woh! The waves were crashing in and reaching right to the top of the ledge; with two more hours of rising tide, our camp was about to be inundated. I ran back to Nomad, unlocked all the doors, threw down the tailgate and began untying the guy ropes. Then in a mounting frenzy, I grabbed jerry cans, water containers, *braaivleis* machine, food boxes, cool box, cups, plates, camp chair, bedding and more, throwing them into the back of Nomad, before pulling out tent pegs and finally rousing Torran. As I collapsed the tent and thrust it unceremoniously into the back of the cab, Torran ran over to check the sandy ledge. 'Dad! The waves are coming over the edge. They're right here!' he yelled back.

'Quick,' I ordered, 'into the car!' Hands fumbling, I pushed the ignition key into the lock and turned it. Nothing happened; just a click and the ignition light went out. Oh horror! The battery must have gone flat from leaving the lights on in the evening. Fortunately there was that second battery which was wired into the ignition system in Cape Town for just such an eventuality as this. Blessing my foresight, I hoped against hope that it would work as it should. Out I jumped, threw open the bonnet, turned the heavy lever that pointed at battery one over to battery two, slammed shut the bonnet, glanced at the oncoming sea over my shoulder, jumped back into the car, and hastily turned the ignition key. There was another click. The ignition light went out. Surely impossible, I wailed. But there it was; the red ignition light was out indicating a second dead battery. And unlike the old Land Rovers that could be cranked into life with a bit of muscle power, the new breed of off-road vehicle was entirely dependent on charged batteries. I was stunned. Over towards the coast road, it was inky black. Even though we were a mile away, we should have seen the headlights of any vehicles driving past. But nothing was moving at 2.30 in the morning along the Skeleton Coast. The impending horror of our situation began to sink in. Without help, the tide would soon race past Nomad, sucking her deeply into the soft sand. And that would be that. End of weekend. End of safari. End of all those dreams. I dragged myself back to the problem in hand; Torran must not see that I was worried. 'No problemo,' I said lightly. 'I'll just try something else.' Leaping out again, I turned the heavy lever midway to bring both batteries into circuit, knowing even as it clicked into place that this was almost certainly a futile gesture. Then I jumped back into the cab, and at the same time forced my mind to slow down and concentrate on what little I knew of electrical circuitry. Suddenly the penny dropped. In my haste to escape the sea, I had forgotten to press the anti-disabling button dangling on the key chain. Small wonder the car wouldn't start – the ignition circuit was being broken by a security device, something else that I had fitted in Cape Town. Swiftly I pressed the button. The ignition light clicked on. What a relief! I screwed round the starter key. Instantly Nomad fired up and we were off, tanking through the soft sands at high revs in low wheel ratio. Some 250 metres later, we lurched up onto a high terrace, swung round to face inland and continued for another hundred metres just to be safe.

As I manoeuvred the car to create a windbreak, I noticed something else was abroad on the otherwise deserted strand. 'Hey Torran, did you see that?' A black-backed jackal hobbled along the rotting tidemark, momentarily baring its teeth as it turned from the headlights. We watched it for a few seconds. No doubt it was searching for the carcass of a dead bird or seal. The night was too far advanced to bother with a tent, and so we hastily arranged two camp beds in the lee of Nomad. We took out blankets to place on top of the sleeping bags to keep off the cold sea breeze, then settled down for the second half of the night, this time under the stars as Torran had originally wanted. I dozed fitfully at first, finally dropping into a heavy sleep in which I had the most vivid dream. A jackal approached me, coming up to my bed and grabbing my hand with its sharp teeth. As this happened, I realised that I was still sleeping and in extreme danger. I yelled with the utmost urgency to my other self, 'Wake up! Wake up! Wake up! For Christ's sake Wake up!' And my other self responded, pushing back the deep waves of sleep, at first so slowly, but then more strongly and I began to rise from the depths of slumber to the light of consciousness. And all the while, I was aware that this was taking too much time, much too much time. 'Wake up! Wake up now!' Just as I reached the edge of wakefulness, the sense of crisis in my dream subsided for no apparent reason. I fell back into an easy dream where I showed my hand, complete with bite marks, to various friends.

The sea breeze continued to blow strange stories down the coast, and at length the long night drew to a close. Torran surfaced first to be greeted by a cold grey dawn and the reassuringly distant sound of ocean waves. He was soon out of his bag and ferreting about. 'Look Dad,' he said. 'There are jackal prints all around your camp bed, and see, he walked right up to your head.'

Despite our troubled night, Torran and I were in high spirits as we headed north to take a look at a colony of fur seals. On the way, we stopped to breakfast on 'Weet-Bix', long-life milk and dry brown bread covered in the glorious homemade apricot jam that I had purchased from the sweetest-smelling-filling-station-in-the-world, all washed down with coffee and fruit juice. It was time for Torran to beat his personal world record of 'keepie uppies', tapping the football into the air without letting it hit the ground. This morning he reached 51 but clearly wasn't satisfied. On arriving at the rocky shoreline where the seal colony was located, Torran held his hands over my eyes. 'Walk forward slowly Dad, and don't look until I tell you.' He steered me along until my feet touched something hard. The rotting marine aroma and cacophony of noise were hefty clues as to what to expect. When he took his hands away, I found myself surrounded by hundreds of fur seals – bellowing, arguing, mewing and wailing – a bit of Antarctica right there in Africa. The noise and excitement were infectious. I tried a few sea lion barks which quickly turned into a full scale seal performance. Torran, the famous wildlife filmmaker, captured these antics for posterity on miniDV. We ended up giggling so hard that the action came to a helpless standstill. Meanwhile our furry audience bellowed their amusement and grunted in disdain.

We spent a couple of hours gazing hypnotically at fur seals as they romped in the ocean surf or dragged themselves onto rocks to proclaim their territory. The seal maidens used each other as pillows as they nursed their young, and the adolescents lurched about at our feet. Setting off about midday, we headed inland making for the Erongo Mountains, enjoying the sensation of cruising at speed along a sand-covered highway. We were rocking across the Namib Desert to the sounds of 96.7 FM on the car radio. I glanced over at Torran, 'What do you reckon, good music?' I got an emphatic thumbs-up. He was evidently enjoying the trip as much as me. It seemed a pity that Isla couldn't be with us. Though close as anything, she and Torran were quite different. He was easygoing yet thoughtful, carried little gear on holiday, was tidy, self-contained and happy to fit in with whatever was going on. He loved animals and I was beginning to realise that he had a tough inner core and a natural affinity for life in the bush. His sister was the untidiest person in the world with loads of clothes and other gear accumulated from endless shopping expeditions. She was brimming over with social confidence and liked to organise her weekends well in advance, filling them with sleepovers, swimming parties, cinema and pizza gatherings. She also liked to organise the family but I had a feeling that Torran wouldn't be letting her organise him for much longer.

Our road snaked past the isolated massif of Spitzkoppe, a steep-sided 1,800-metre mountain where prospectors had discovered many gemstones – amethyst, aquamarine, topaz and green tourmaline. This Tolkienesque mountain looked to me like a colossal lion, its head raised in commanding pose. It dominated the desert plains, luring generations of adventurers with its promise of hidden treasure.[5] We stopped at a roadside stand where I bought a smoky amethyst from a desperate-looking woman wrapped in a dirty shawl. In its flawed depths was a perfect silver bubble floating within an invisible liquid bed. So curious – I considered the small price to be a bargain but Torran, who knew the real price of imperfect gems from his years in Karibib, told me it was extortionate. A man at the stand showed us two huge aquamarine crystals, one alone barely fitted onto his large gnarled hand. He had discovered them that morning in a cave on the side of the mountain. 'God smiled on me today,' he said in a strong Afrikaans accent. 'One of these will buy me a new bakkie.'[6] He and Torran chatted away in Afrikaans. Torran told me later that the prospector had asked him to pass on a message about his find to the gemstone dealer in Otjiwarongo, Torran's home town. Initially I had been dismayed when Torran was given Afrikaans as a foreign language at school. I carried a knee-jerk antiapartheid response to anything associated with the Afrikaners as a nation. The warmth and hospitality of those I had met on this trip had gone a long way to allaying these fears. I realised it had been a mistake to demonize a whole people. And secretly I was proud that Torran was so well integrated in Africa. Two miles further down the road, I stopped again to give five vagabonds some petrol for their broken-down Land Rover. Torran cautioned me that it was a common trick, but that weekend I was happy, and happy to spread happiness around. Later when I heard about the hijacking and murder of a tourist at this spot, I determined to be more careful.

Whilst in Windhoek I had poured over the map working out several possibilities for the second part of our weekend, finally opting for a night at the Erongo Wilderness Lodge. A deciding factor had been the mention of a Bushman's cave. In the late afternoon we wound our way up a steep rough track that led to the lodge, halting on the brow of a hill to look around. The air was still and dry but the occasional sonorous chirp from an unseen bird indicated that the true desert was behind us. On both sides were enormous whale-back *kopjes*; their naked tops streaked by weathering and their boulder-strewn bottoms fringed by leafless bushes. The track took us between the *kopjes* and down into an enclosed amphitheatre surrounded by mountains. We barely had time to take in the tented chalets hidden amongst the towering rock-clad hillsides or the thatched restaurant high above, when the proprietor appeared at my door side and whisked us into a waiting safari truck. Gerson, our grinning guide, was at the wheel dressed in a green safari uniform offset by white sneakers and baseball cap. We set off at once on the evening's game drive.

The truck wound its way in and out of the granite leviathans where wild figs clung to cracks in sheer walls, and bulbous trees balanced leafless on minute ledges. All life was dormant, awaiting the summer rains. I felt dormant too: tired and in need of nourishment. Shortly after crossing a dry streambed we pulled up at the base of one of the great *kopjes*. It was time to proceed on foot. Taking a deep breath, I followed the others along a small track leading upwards. At the top, Torran sat down with Gerson to enjoy a chilled soda whilst I wandered off to investigate the nearby cave.

At first the smooth granite sloped gently but as I approached the cave it fell away steeply. My desert boots had a fair grip but a slip here would send me tumbling down the side to the valley below. I looked about for a better route, moving cautiously up to where the gradient was shallower. I clambered warily along to the cave entrance which was shaped like a teardrop on the point of falling. It was concealed at the front by thorny shrubs and from either side by the rounded contours of granite. I walked past the shrubs and stood at the opening which was twice my height.

On one wall I noticed several figures painted in red ochre playing musical instruments. From there the sides shelved steeply inwards to a darkened recess at the furthest point. It was an awesome cave. Irresistibly, I found myself drawn to the small opening at its far end. Without pausing to think, I ducked in under the mantel and stood up. Inside it was pitch black, as if one were standing within the massive chimney of a Georgian manor house. There was a smell of bat droppings and a peaceful sense of distant humming. I was enjoying the feeling of enclosed space and blackness above, when the humming changed note. With a shock I realised it was being made by bees. Instantly, I ducked back out into the main chamber, but one bee was already buzzing about my head and others were coming in hot pursuit. As I stumbled down the cave, I was stung hard on the right ear. I increased my speed, flying out of the entrance and along the shoulder of the *kopje*. Luckily this satisfied the other bees which gave up the chase. Gerson came over, his face a picture of concern, and insisted on removing the sting before it could pump a full sac of poison into my ear. I felt chastened, as if given a sound clipping by the spirit of a Bushman hunter offended at my thoughtless intrusion into his sacred place.

Back at the lodge, Torran and I took a hot shower in our tented cabin before donning fresh clothes. On the way out Torran picked up his football, bounced it up and down a couple of times and tucked it under his arm. I suggested that it might be okay to leave it behind, seeing as how it was now dark and we were only going for dinner. He placed it carefully on his bed. We strolled across the rockbound amphitheatre following an illuminated trail to the dining room which was set on top of the facing kopje. The owner came over to chat about the possibility of re-introducing game animals to the area and creating a private reserve with neighbouring ranches. It was a great idea but we were starving and too intent on eating to do the subject justice. Finally over crêpes and ice-cream, we slowed down. Torran was curious about last night's visitor on the beach.

'Dad, do you think he wanted to eat you?'

'He was dribbling at the mouth.'

'Be serious! Do you think you smelt his rotten breath and that gave you the dream?'

This one was harder. 'Maybe.'

'Was it your guardian angel that was trying to wake you up?'

I didn't have any clear answer to that but I could see that Torran needed some kind of explanation.

'Sometimes you see things more vividly in dreams...' I paused trying to work out an answer he might understand, '...they give you a clue to something deeper. Last night, the warning was unmistakable but I don't know how it came to me.'

Although it was now late, the night air remained warm from the heat radiating off the surrounding rocks. We walked slowly back to our luxury tent. I opened up the flaps on both sides but it was too hot inside even for sheets, let alone blankets. Torran was soon fast asleep. I lay awake thinking over our second day of adventures and the teardrop cave. Outside, all was quiet. My right ear throbbed from the bee sting. Those Bushmen were beginning to talk to me. Perhaps their subconscious world, the world of dreams and intuitions, was tuned to their conscious world. It could act like a sensitive barometer, indicating change in their environment from the earliest signs.

In the morning we were up early for breakfast, ready to catch the guided walk. On our way up the *kopje*, Gerson pointed out some slivers of rock lying about on the bare granite surface. They varied in size from saucer-sized shards to tabletops several inches thick that must have weighed quarter of a ton. They were constantly being shed from the giant whaleback hills, helped by baboons which broke them off in the hunt for scorpions and snakes. We didn't see baboons or any other large animals but, stopping next to the path, Torran scooped up a handful of dusty soil. He sprinkled it onto the ground, searching for some inhabitant in his hand. On the second scoop he found an antlion. These little round larvae build conical pits in the sand to trap ants which they pierce and suck dry through fanglike jaws. I hadn't seen one fully exposed before. Being taught a little bush lore by Torran made me realise how much I'd missed teaching him the bits of natural history I'd picked up over the years. He and Prongo, the lodge-owner's English Pointer pup, bounded up to the top of the *kopje* where both sat down to look out over the vista of round hills, scrub-filled valleys and dry sand rivers. Sitting upright on the rock, backs straight, eyes taking in every detail, they made a great pair.

It was getting late for our departure as Torran needed to be back at school in the evening. We packed up quickly and drove fast down the empty highway to Windhoek, neither wanting to spoil the day by talking about farewells. As we entered the city, Torran asked if we could go on a long safari together when he finished school. It brought a lump to my throat. I nodded emphatically. He guided me to a private hostel in a nearby side-street which served as a makeshift dormitory during the week. I watched him walk through the door with his small holdall. It felt worse than going back to school myself. Suddenly he darted out again and thrust the football into my arms. 'It's for you Dad.'

5

DREAM POOLS AND RAIN CREATURES

Desert tree

Stu arrived at Windhoek Airport smack on time, managing a happy-go-lucky grin from behind the tangle of hair and beard in spite of his missing backpack, tent and guitar. Like me he had started his career in zoology, though his had centred round a passion for creepy-crawlies, and gory ones at that, such as *Nicrophorus*, a beetle remarkable for making an underground crypt out of a dead mouse and feeding her larvae on the decaying carcass. Now he combined two of his other great passions into one chaotic lifestyle – in the daytime a journalist charting the undercurrents of science in erudite columns that he embellished with below-the-belt humour; in the night time a singer-songwriter with his fledgling band, Peggy Vestas. Needing a break from it all, he decided to join the expedition for a month. At the lost luggage counter, the clerk told him that his luggage would turn up the next day.

'That would be a bonus,' he muttered, eyebrow raised in mock surprise. Beneath the unruly hair were two steely blue eyes that missed little and behind those the acerbic wit of a stand-up comic. We headed into town where I was staying with friends.

There was no sign of his luggage the next day, or on the day after that. Losing a guitar is a particular blow to a band leader, so we gave the airline one last chance, electing to make a start on our travels but to stop for a night whilst still in range of the airport. We ended up at a small hotel in Otjiwarongo, a farming town about two hours drive to the north of Windhoek. The next morning Stu rang the airport but there was still no news of his things; we discussed our options over a late breakfast.

'Let's give it one more day,' I said, eyeing up the rumpled cotton shirt and baggy yellow trousers now greeting their fourth unwashed morning. 'You can't smell any worse than you do already.'

'No,' replied Stu emphatically. 'Sod the gear. I'll pick up some clothes in town and we can be on our way.' He headed off with a list of essentials whilst I looked around for camping supplies. It was mid-morning but outside the sun was pounding the streets of Otjiwarongo with glaring energy, causing shoppers to retreat under awnings and loiter in narrow corridors of shade. I put on my bush hat and began to hunt about. In a small wooden shack just off the main square I found a shop almost completely empty, but for a collection of short-handled axes and a bewilderingly large stock of Omo detergent. I bought an axe but passed on the detergent. A short while later we rendezvoused at the car park in the main centre. Stu was carrying a modest bundle of T-shirts, toothbrush and a neat silver tent; in addition to the axe, I had two cans of sparkling granadilla. Back in the cab there was a smell of hot plastic from melting seats; we turned the air-con to max and set off for Twyfelfontein.

Driving westwards, we quickly dropped off the tarmac onto an unsurfaced road but continued at good speed with stones rattling off the wheel arches. The scrubby bushveld of central Namibia gradually gave way to a semi-desert of rocky hills and sandy plains. Stu was quiet, perhaps dumbstruck by the awesome landscape. It was quite a contrast to the soggy streets of Edinburgh. After two hours, we entered a narrow canyon with burnt-orange cliffs where a single tree survived, branches bunched towards the sky in a naked fist. The road was rougher here and we were forced to slow down. It was like driving through an oven. It occurred to me that this wasn't a good place for a breakdown. After a few miles, the canyon took a wide turn before opening out into a sandy bay where the track petered out in front of an information board. We were surrounded by a semicircle of cliffs with huge boulders scattered all about. It was primeval. I felt an intruder in somebody else's realm.

Not the only intruder. A group of teenage girls was sitting under a thatched shelter nearby, talking and laughing amongst themselves like a flock of brightly coloured parakeets. They told us it was mandatory to have a guide to visit the rock engravings, but as it was late none of them wanted to take us. Eventually Stella was chosen as the unlucky volunteer. She walked quickly down a dusty track and into the boulders, leaving us with occasional glimpses of her red T-shirt and white shorts in amongst the megaliths. We followed along, scrambling up 20 metres to a large stone slab that faced out across the valley like a Stone Age cinema. Carved on the screen was a menagerie of rock etchings – giraffe, rhino, wildebeest, warthog, a lizard, and a big baggy elephant that you just had to grin at. Stella was anxious to move on but this was art that you couldn't hurry. It contained hidden messages. Some of the engravings were crudely done but others had been skilfully pecked with a piece of hard stone, catching something of the feel of the animal. All were in profile. With time the patina of engravings and surrounding rock had blended to the same colour, making the animals hard to make out except when the angle of the sun cast a deep shadow. Strangely there were no etchings of people but one engraving in particular caught my attention. It was a manic-looking lion with a large head, frothing mouth and elongated tail that was held high with its tip in the shape of a large pugmark. Unlike the other animals, which looked like simple portrayals, this one appeared to represent something more. The !Kung Bushmen of the northern Kalahari have a word which translates as 'pawed-creature' but can also mean 'to go on out-of-body travel in the form of a lion.'[1] Perhaps this lion symbolised a shaman surveying the animals that he might hunt.

On the underside of another rock, I found a delicate painting of a gemsbok looking as if it had been plucked yesterday from the artist's brush. I admired the graceful lines of the haunch and tail. By comparison to this painting, the engravings were blunter, more monumental, like the great boulders on which they were set, and because of their physicality they would endure for longer. Our guide showed little interest in the engravings or in us; it was obvious that she wanted to be somewhere else. I suggested she join her friends at the shelter, and this she did, missing her lift as we found out later, and having to walk the four miles to camp on her own. Stu and I felt sorry for these girls. They were stuck in the middle of nowhere, living in a desolate camp without any chance of a social life; hardly surprising if they sniped at each other from time to time.

With Stella gone I could at least relax, but try as I might I couldn't capture the atmosphere of nomadic hunters living in Twyfelfontein. My mind was too crowded with other things – what Torran was up to, what Isla was doing, whether Stu would cope with my peculiar way of travelling, how good an ice-cold beer would taste, in fact anything other than the here and now. Rather than persevere whilst in the wrong mood, I climbed down the hill and walked across to Nomad. Stu joined me after a few minutes and we decided to set up camp nearby and take a fresh look in the morning. By now the sun had dipped below the canyon wall and the air was cooling rapidly. A light breeze was stirring. We drove a few hundred metres further up the valley to find a sandy spot in the lee of a thick succulent shrub. As we unpacked our gear, the breeze picked up. Soon half a gale was blowing straight up the canyon, no doubt fuelled by hot air convecting upwards from the sun-baked cliffs. Stu's silver tent went up a treat but my big red monster blew about like a spinnaker in a storm. Finally we brought it under control using the system pioneered by Torran. A short trip along the banks of a nearby streambed secured several armfuls of deadwood which we placed in the lee of a thick bush. As the twilight faded Stu lit the fire; soon a spiral of tomato-flavoured *boerewors* was sizzling in Geoff and Sue's marvellous *braaivleis* machine.

A large sausage fly – harmless, but resembling a lethal hornet – crashed into Stu's plate causing minor hysterics. Usually nothing gave Stu greater pleasure than close encounters of the creepy-crawly kind, and his surprise soon turned to fascination. He placed a lantern on top of the cool box to cast light on the buzzing creature – in fact the male reproductive caste of the safari ant.

'Flippin' 'eck,' he said. 'What a geezer!'

'They taste good when dipped in beer, you know.'

'On you go, then.'

A couple of beers later and the mood was mellow. Stu had just demonstrated his levitation trick, almost fooling me, when a large hairy spidery thing with huge jaws raced in from the night making straight for him.

'What the shittin' fuck is that?' yelled Stu.

'That's a testicle-seeker,' I shouted, as the solifuge tore under Stu's canvas stool and headed back into the encircling night. Stu almost fell over backwards for the second time in an hour.

'What did you call them?' he asked, having regained a vertical position.

'The Bushmen call them testicle-seekers,' I replied. 'Except they would probably say, //testicle ⊙ seeker.' I made a clumsy attempt to add in a couple of clicks.

In fact, most Bushman words contain chucks and pops which are represented by an agreed notation. For instance ⊙ is the kiss-click which is produced by sucking air between the lips; ! is a loud pop as used by English-speakers to imitate the sound of horses' hooves; / is the sound made by a British person who is irritated 'tsk'; // is like the clucking used to urge on a horse as mentioned earlier in relation to //Kabbo; and ≠ is a click similar to but harder than //. I can just about manage an individual click or pop, but get hopelessly stuck when trying to combine them with other bits of a word.

There was hardly time to recover before the '! ⊙ seeker' was back, rushing erratically here and there, powerful jaws raised and ready.

'Help! It's carnage,' cried Stu. 'This ! ≠bleeder means business.'

Much laughter and joking followed for as Stu well knew, once his frontal lobes reasserted control, these sun spiders are also harmless. Feeling a bit sheepish perhaps, he decided to take a closer look at the desert micro-life. Donning a caver's torch, he set off on a nocturnal hunt; the bobbing light soon disappeared from view. Occasionally I heard distant exclamations of surprise and delight.

Long before the sun had risen above the canyon walls I was up and scanning the surrounding rocks through binoculars. Tons and tons of loose stones and scree were strewn over the lower slopes and scattered amongst the debris were enormous rust-red boulders, some as much as 12 metres across, that had detached from the cliffs and tumbled down to their precarious resting places. A few had sheared in half creating perfectly flat, smooth faces – ideal surfaces for Stone Age artists. Engravings have been found all over the rock-strewn slopes, more than 2,000 in all; some are reckoned to be 6,000 years old. Although unprotected from the wind or rain and catching the full force of the midday sun, they show little sign of deterioration.

Moving further down the canyon, I started to climb up the broken slopes enjoying the earthy smells of dawn and the sense of solitude. Midway up I came across the remains of a Stone Age dwelling, looking something like the stone circles found on a hill near my home in Scotland. Passing this, I edged round a large boulder teetering on the edge of a steep fall down to the canyon below and came face to face with the giant head of a leopard – an overhanging rock with jaws wide open in a defiant snarl big enough to walk through. Surely others could not fail to have recognised her. Perhaps she was a storm leopard, the mythical Bushman animal that can kill a herd or destroy a camp. I felt an immediate contact with the artists who had worked these rocks. Walking between the jaws, I looked about on the other side. Nearby was a smooth rock face with a solitary engraving of a hartebeest, perfectly executed with two simple curves revealing the exact proportions of belly and thigh. Another rock had a small herd of antelope laid out in a diagonal across the cut face; the one at the top had a raised tail and long thin spirals emerging from the back of the head extending about twice the animal's height, and with twice the number of twists as the horns of a fully mature kudu bull. Attached to the nose of this strange creature was a curving horn like that of a rhinoceros. But if this seemed weird, it was nothing compared with the adjacent scene.

Next to the snarling leopard, where the slope of the canyon eased into a flat narrow ledge, was a rectangular slab of stone about two metres across. A profusion of circles and abstract designs was cut into its unusual slate-grey patina. In the centre was a mythological figure. It had a person's head set directly above two arms that were held outwards: the upper arms were muscular and powerful whilst the lower parts were elongated and rope-like. They in turn were set upon a long curving neck that attached to an antelope body, possibly that of a kudu judging by the modestly bushy tail. It was a centaur-like creature. Or was it. In a blink, the upper part changed from human to kudu, the human head and upper arm becoming two round kudu ears, the lower arm its face. I wondered if some Stone Age shaman had taken on the form of this supernatural figure.

In Bushman mythology, the people of the Early Race were nearly like men and women but many had animal characteristics and were called by animal names. At some point in the distant past, the old world changed into the present one; then some of these early people were given their animal shape and others became ordinary humans. It was the end of the magical time. One of Wilhelm Bleek's Bushman informants in Cape Town recalled this legendary era: 'We, who are Bushmen, were once springbucks and the Mantis shot us, and we really cried, like a little child. Then the Mantis said we should become a person, become people, because we really cried.'[2]

The Bushmen also believed that a woman is filled with power during her first menstruation, and if she does not comply with strict rules of confinement, then men will be transformed into trees, or frogs.[3] One rock painting near to Traveller's Rest showed a line of tree-like human figures with arms that turned into branches. Human-animal and -plant transformations were evidently a central part of the Bushman's belief system, and even today a window may open connecting the Bushman's physical and spiritual worlds. !Nanni, another informant, told of a caution given to him by his grandfather: 'When we see an antelope, an antelope near that place where a person has died, we respect the antelope; for, the antelope is not a mere antelope. Its legs seem small, it is the person who has died, and is a spirit antelope.'[4]

I pondered some of these mysteries for a moment. If the Bushmen believe their ancestors are connected with living, spirit animals that roam the plains that might explain their forbearance in hunting, but is there any useable lesson that we in the West can glean from the Bushmen given that we hold such different beliefs?

A little further down the hill, I found a small pool of water tucked beneath an overhanging rock where it was fed by a natural spring and shielded from the front by some reeds. Under the low roof were feathers and droppings showing that it was a popular place for doves and other birds to drink: it smelt musty and I caught the acrid whiff of guano. It may have been a dream pool, the place where hunters met to divine which animal they should hunt; the place where shamans came to seek the rain-animal. Amongst the /Xam Bushmen in the south, this mythical rain-creature could be a large ox-like animal, a bull eland or even a cow hippopotamus. Here, perhaps it was that kudu-human creature.

According to //Kabbo, the shaman entered a trance and then sought the rain animal near a pool of water, being careful to approach from downwind.[5] He threw a thong over its head and either rode or walked it to the top of a mountain. There the animal was slaughtered, so that the blood flowed down onto the dry bush country below. This brought the soft 'she-rain' which sank gently into the ground wetting it deeply and thoroughly, 'cooling' the troubled earth; then the bushes flushed green, the bulbs and roots swelled and the springboks came galloping. I sat down to contemplate how the Bushman's spiritual beliefs about the rain-animal blended with their ecological knowledge about bulbs and roots which in turn heralded the coming of meat. And then something clicked into place, so obvious that it had been staring me in the face all along without my recognising it. The Bushman hunter combined, in one person, three key roles in society. He was a hunter, a naturalist, and a spiritual practitioner. He put dinner on the plate, knew about the environment and had a code of ethics. What better combination of skills for upholding the state of balance between a people and their environment?

I bounded down the hill like a springbok and strode back to camp. The veil separating me from the hunter-gatherer mind had, I felt, lifted just a fraction. Stu was sceptical. Being an arch pragmatist he was suspicious of unexplained phenomena and inner revelations. But he didn't argue about coffee or the suggestion that we break camp and get on the road.

6

LIONS OF GOD

Bedroll, doubling as a target

Back at the information centre, Stella was scowling like a parakeet with a nasty headache.

'Did you get a lift to camp last night?' I asked pretending not to notice the look.

'You're not allowed to camp here,' she informed me coldly. 'And thanks to you, I had to walk home last night.' Turning her back, she started fiddling with her Walkman. Not getting any joy, she whipped off the headphones and flung the set on the table before stomping over to the other girls. I felt badly for her. Idly I picked up the player and tried it out. It was dead as a dodo. I flipped open the battery compartment and noticed some corrosion where acid had leaked onto a connector. Carrying it over to Nomad, I squirted in some WD40, sanded the connector and wiped it clean with a paper towel. Then I popped in a new battery and switched on. Music flooded out of the earpieces. I held up the Walkman for Stella to see and gave a thumbs-up. She walked over suspiciously and put on the headphones.

Her face beamed with pleasure. 'Oh thank you,' she said. 'That's so cool.'

Stu asked what kind of music she liked and they were soon deep in conversation about esoteric African and British bands.

Having made our peace with Stella, we set off north to meet Flip Stander a friend of mine from Cambridge Uni who was making a long-term study of lions in the Etosha National Park. We had arranged to meet up at a bush airstrip somewhere in the southwest corner of the park. This area is undeveloped and off-limits to visitors, but Flip had secured an entry permit for us. We passed through the gate a couple of hours later entering a vast wilderness of flat desert scrub, and began searching about for the airstrip. Highly visible from the air, they can be surprisingly hard to find on the ground especially if there is no tower. At the first dead end, Stu was amused: 'You couldn't land a sparrow up here'. But his asides soon began to sound a bit fussed: 'I suppose you know what you're doing'. I concentrated on the map not wanting to get us lost this early in the safari. Eventually, more by luck than judgement, we stumbled on the right track, following it to a neatly graded airstrip that was dressed with a surface of dusty white limestone. 'Now that's navigation for you,' I remarked with a sideways glance at Stu. Halfway up the strip was a pole without a windsock and at the furthermost end was a dilapidated hangar. An old Chevy pick-up sat in the far corner with just enough space beside it for a single-engine aircraft. I parked Nomad outside and we walked over to take a closer look.

A tin roof protected the dirt floor from sun and rain, the open sides let in a cooling breeze, and strips of green mesh hanging from a wire kept out the larger animals. I recognised immediately that this was a real 'boy's camp'. Strewn about the hangar were fuel drums, rolls of canvas and wooden boxes; a mesh cage occupied one corner to secure lighter gear that was more likely to walk. Immediately outside was a three-sided shelter made of rough-cut poles half-eaten by termites and a stone fireplace. Branches from a dead thorn tree were stacked up in readiness for cooking supper or providing warmth on a cold night. Basic certainly, but this was a place where bush adventures were born; a base from which to fly into the coming dawn, lifted on broad white wings, to glimpse the hidden lives of lion and elephant and a thousand other mysteries. I felt the magic of it taking hold.

Stu perched on a fuel drum and rolled up a fag. 'You must have come across lions during your impala study,' he said casting his eye around the hangar.

'If you're on foot it can be pretty unnerving.' I poured myself a glass of orange squash and began telling Stu about one such occasion. I'd been walking through the woods on my weekly round of the research area, checking for animals wearing ID collars. A telescope and tripod were balanced on my shoulder and an old Webley service revolver swung awkwardly from my belt in its cheap leather holster. I'd bought it secondhand at a knockdown price a few weeks earlier. It came with five lead bullets, .455 inch calibre, heavy in the hand, and pitted with age. Too few to risk even a single practice shot. Approaching a long flat terrace next to the river with good visibility, I was anticipating some sightings of collared impala. I climbed an old termite mound at the edge, set down the telescope and scanned the terrace with my binoculars. It was a favourite haunt of impala but the place was empty. Just to be sure I let my gaze linger in the dark shadows under the trees where animals are easily overlooked. A low growl from close-up sent my stomach into my mouth. Looking down, I saw the lionesses – three of them. They had been lying in short grass on the edge of the clearing, basking in the midday heat. Two were now standing, staring at me; their tails raised and switching back and forth. They ran forward a few paces, still growling. I dropped my binoculars in shock, and fumbled for the revolver. The two turned abruptly and ran into thickets. The third lioness now rose to her feet, looking about for the cause of the disturbance. She spotted me and instantly charged, streaking across the grass, coming faster than any human sprinter. I had never experienced such naked menace. Shakily I raised the gun, holding it at arm's length, pointing the barrel at the yellow nightmare, knowing I must wait until she was almost upon me before firing. I squeezed the trigger, to cock the hammer, only the tiniest extra pressure was required to fire. At five metres distant, as I watched for the leap, the lioness veered in mid-stride and disappeared into tall grass. I sat down slowly, shaking with fright.

For months after that I had nightmares about lion attacks. It was always the same. The lions would appear from nowhere as I was walking in the bush, and immediately charge. I would raise the revolver and fire. The bullet would come out of the barrel slowly like a cork from a toy gun and drop uselessly to the ground.

'Just what I thought,' said Stu, 'bloody dangerous beasts.'

'It will be different today,' I assured him. 'Back then I was a greenhorn working at a research institute where most of the officers had even less bush experience than my own. Flip on the other hand is a top lion ecologist and a good mate.'

The sound of a light aircraft approaching broke into our conversation. Flip landed his two-seater Maule smoothly and taxied over to the hangar. He was looking lean, fit and every bit the professional field biologist that I remembered. Maybe the baseball hat was new, but not the piercing blue eyes, thick rufous beard or deep outdoors tan. The pockets of his khaki waistcoat bulged with essential gadgets: a sheath knife, Leatherman multi-tool, pens, notebook, tape measure, lighter, pipe, tobacco and an assortment of animal capture equipment. Completing the bush wardrobe were green shorts and suede desert boots with no socks.

'Martyn! You made it.'

'Hey Flip, that was a lousy landing!'

'Huh. Have I got some surprises for you guys. I've just located a dozen lions at the top end of the Dolomite ridge.' He pointed vaguely to the north. 'We need to get over there tonight.'

'I don't do lion bait,' said Stu, looking anxiously at the well-oiled rifle being unloaded from the aircraft.

With nothing much to do until nightfall, we sat about the hangar chatting over soft drinks. Flip told us about his study of the Etosha lions and his efforts to understand the bitter conflict raging between them and the neighbouring livestock farmers. He needed to know a whole host of things: the number of lions and lionesses in the park, what animals they preyed upon, their success in raising young, how far they travelled, how often they left the park, whether they bred with lions from elsewhere in the country, their mortality risks and life expectancy, and whether this population in Etosha, the most important in all of Namibia due to its size, would be able to survive with their current level of protection given the prevailing levels of shooting and poisoning in the surrounding areas. To obtain such a comprehensive picture, he was building up long-term records of individual lions and lionesses. Although he kept photographs showing natural markings, such as the whisker dots and facial scars, he found that the only way to keep tabs on lions that were moving about outside of the park, especially those that made sudden long-distance movements, was to track animals fitted with radio-collars from the air. He had already found out that males sometimes moved 200 miles without stopping; one of them had even walked 500 miles from Etosha, wandering far across southern Africa.

Picking up his jade-green bedroll, which had been doubling as a seat, Flip drew target rings on the side with a magic marker pen and stood it up outside the hangar. Next he fitted a Russian-made night-scope to his dart-rifle and sitting on a canvas chair began to sight it in; after a few rounds the tranquilliser darts were bouncing right off the bull's-eye.

'Don't look now but something is watching us,' said Stu.

'Monitor lizard,' said Flip glancing up at the top of the netting where a scaly reptile more than a metre in length was edging along with a precarious grip on the mesh.

'He's a great big Johnny,' said Stu.

'He's about to fall off,' I added.

'Come down you brainless reptile,' ordered Stu.

As we were chatting, a Land Cruiser pick-up arrived bringing Flip's capture team which comprised two rangers and an old Bushman tracker called Mafuta. They joined us in the hangar as we whiled the afternoon away. Shadows were beginning to lengthen when Flip finally announced that it was time go. Stu and I clambered into the front of the beat-up Chevy with Flip. We set off into the bush, the capture crew following behind. Everyone looked calm. I wondered if I did too: the prospect of close-up field biology with big cats was sending surges of excitement up and down my spine. We drove north, following the 40-mile long ridge of black dolomite that cuts across the flat Etosha landscape. It was deeply fissured with sinkholes extending far downward that could hold water throughout the dry season. At its furthest extension the ridge narrowed to a single point of rock, only 10 to 15 metres in height above the surrounding plains, and here there was a cave. Within the cave was a small Bushman painting of a giraffe in red ochre and, said Flip, 12 lions in polychrome, full-sized and breathing: four lionesses, four cubs, three young males – tall and lank – and a huge tawny-maned lion which had proved elusive and far too wary to be captured. Flip had picked up a faint radio signal from one of the lionesses as he flew over the top-end of the ridge that morning; circling low, he passed over the mouth of the cave and spotted the pride illuminated by the rising sun.

On our way to the cave we came upon a pale island of sand in the sea of green mopane bushes and tall grass. The pan was littered with dung piles from elephants and antelope, attracted perhaps by the natural salts. We pulled up on the edge and waited for the dust to settle. On the far side were two male gemsbok, standing close together on the bare ground; in the distance a mixed herd grazed in the tall grass. The nearest male edged sideways, tilting his neck as he went to keep his sabre-like horns ready to parry a surprise lunge. His partner remained indifferent to this slight posturing. They were magnificent. I knew what would happen next, what I didn't know was how I would react. Flip lifted his .308 rifle, ramming a high velocity cartridge into the chamber, and sighted in on the target. He needed bait if he was to capture lions. The two animals walked slowly forward, tied together by some invisible bond, then paused.

The front gemsbok turned sideways, stopped and scratched its flank with the tip of its unicorn's horn. His companion turned behind him. Their black and fawn markings stood out boldly from the white sands of Etosha. Flip fired. Both animals took off, kicking up twin trails of fine dust that hung in the air. After running 30 yards, one swerved and collapsed, disappearing in a large cloud of powdery calcite.

His body was lean and muscled, the front knees covered in hardened calluses where he had knelt to fight for dominance in male gemsbok society. He breathed once, air rasping in and out, his face a mask portraying nothing. The eyes dulled. A back leg kicked in spasm. Breath rasped one last time. I noticed a tick crawling out of the right ear – rats leaving the sinking ship. A smell of death pervaded. Flip's brief autopsy revealed that the animal was in good condition and that the bullet had hit the upper heart: the end could hardly have been quicker. The rest of the team arrived and pulled out a rope to tie the carcass to the back of the Land Cruiser. I had the same empty feeling in my stomach that I used to get on the train that took me to boarding school – a kind of resignation to the loss of something precious.

About 25 years earlier I had faced a similar predicament when attempting to capture male impala and fit them with ID collars. One afternoon I was crouched in a small canvas hide beside a pan, not so dissimilar to this one except for a small pool of water at one end. It was like a sauna in there and the sweat was running freely down my front. Wiping my forehead with a sopping T-shirt, I peered out of the slit across the muddy pool of water to the woods beyond. A male impala was approaching, stepping quietly along the narrow game trail, lyrate horns giving macho pride to its long Bambi face. I raised the rifle and waited, 20 more paces would bring him into range. The impala had taken a few hesitant steps and paused, looking anxiously about. There was no other source of water in the area. On it came, moving into range but obscured by a shrub growing near the water's edge. It stopped there, wary of what might be lying in ambush. I wiped my forehead again and attempted to dry my trigger hand on the wet T-shirt. The breeze at midday was erratic, mostly blowing towards me, but in the lulls a snatch of scent might easily waft backwards. The impala snorted, turned and took a step towards the woods exposing its right haunch. It was now or never. I fired. The silver dart streaked across the pond and hit. I felt a surge of jubilation.

Following on foot from a distance I saw the male slow to a walk; two minutes later it dropped in its tracks. I went back for my Land Rover and drove round to the recumbent animal, placing my jacket over its face to keep off the flies. Turning the animal over, my stomach sank. Only the end of the dart was visible: more than half the barrel had sunk into the buttock, pushing its way easily between the parallel layers of muscle. It had been a bad mistake to shoot from behind. I extracted the dart with difficulty, alarmed at the slow, rasping breath. I could hear bubbles and gurgles coming from deep in the windpipe. There must be fluid in the lungs. Forgetting about the ear tags, I dragged the front of the impala onto a mound and lifted the head and upper neck higher still, laying them on my backpack. Then I pulled off my shirt and suspended it from a bush to make a crude sunshade. It didn't seem to help, and there was no antidote to the drug which took about 45 minutes to wear off. Long before that, the breathing slowed to a whisper, and stopped. For some minutes I sat there, stunned. After awhile I got up and drove back to the office. For a long time afterwards, the conflict raged within me.

The conflict here in Etosha was different in that it involved killing one species in order to study another, but it boiled down to the same thing – how much can we justify in the name of science?

'Flip had to shoot that gemsbok,' I said to Stu, feeling my own need to talk about it.

'You have problems with that?'

'Yeah,' I admitted, 'it jars. I think Flip's work is great. But it still jars.'

'As far as I'm concerned, it's quite okay to shoot animals,' said Stu. 'You're just being sentimental. The gemsbok had no idea that harm was being done to him. It was quick, quiet and a bit exciting.'

Flip's capture team showed no outward sign of emotion, no sign of Stu's excitement, nor hint of my concern. It would be easy to assume that shooting an antelope was just part of a busy day's work for them, save that I noticed the youngest quickly patting the dead animal. A glance at Flip told me all I needed to know: there was regret written all over his face. Maybe it was just a fleeting trace of the inner conflict between rationality and emotionality, as Stu might argue, but Flip's expression and the quick pat by the young ranger made me feel happier.

There was no doubt in my mind that Flip cared about lions. In one way or another he had dedicated his life to them, slowly piecing together – through days of observation, nights of data analysis, and month after tedious month of project administration – a comprehensive understanding of their behaviour and ecology within the park, and their dangerous conflicts with farmers outside. The future of lions in Namibia owed much to this one selfless man. By synthesizing this hard-won knowledge, he had begun to piece together a viable conservation plan. Without this work, future generations would never witness the spectacle of a lion hunt or thrill to the sound of a pride roaring deep in the night. And Flip was being entirely selfless and open about his work, allowing Stu and myself, and our cameras and recorders, access to every detail, from shooting a gemsbok to drugging a lion. He did not hide what he was doing, because he believed deeply in its value. All the same, lions are large meat-eating predators. For Flip to do what he was doing, he needed to be a killer too: a hard fact to take, but a true one nevertheless.

Having attached the carcass securely, the capture team dragged it along the ground behind the Land Cruiser, laying a fresh scent trail for lions to follow, and then roped the partially dismembered gemsbok to a broken tree stump. We continued on our way, looking for a second animal to shoot. 'I select bait animals in proportion to the local population,' explained Flip. 'Sometimes it's an adult male, sometimes a female and sometimes a younger animal.' Coming across a small herd of zebra, we stopped so he could shoot a one-year old. He waited for the animals to stand quietly, and then shot once. Stu was fascinated by this new turn of events which was quite different from the slow hours spent pouring over rock etchings with me. 'Nice one,' he proclaimed as the zebra dropped to the ground.

The carcass was lifted into the back of the pick-up whilst Stu interviewed Flip about his research programme, capturing the conversation on a minidisc recorder. Although we'd shared an office together at university whilst Stu was writing up his PhD on burying beetles, I hadn't seen him at work as a journalist. He had a good technique, not too intrusive yet drawing out the vital information. It was a bit like fishing but with questions as the lure. The skill was in casting the question – in the right way, at the right moment – in order to hook a whopper, that quotable quote that had been swimming about in the depths.

On reaching the end of the dolomite ridge, the zebra carcass was lifted out and dragged for a few hundred metres before being tied to the base of a stunted tree not far from the entrance to the lions' cave. The capture team moved some distance away leaving the three of us corralled together in the front of Flip's Chevy, some 20 metres from the zebra, awaiting the lions. Stu continued with his interview for a few more minutes.

Shadows lengthened as the evening sun sank towards the horizon. Dusk crept across the plains. The stripes on the zebra blurred into a grey mass. Soon I could barely make out the broken tree next to the bait. Darkness descended. All was quiet in the cab. We waited, each lost in his own thoughts. 'Ah there he goes,' whispered Flip who had been scanning the area with powerful night binoculars, 'a young male, there, up on the ridge'. I raised my own binoculars in the direction indicated, seeing nothing at first, and then a pale shadow sauntering along the ridge heading away from us. The next second the night air was filled with a heart-rending scream. For a moment I was stunned. Turning to face Flip I saw he had been blowing through a reed to mimic the distress call of a hare. He stuffed the device back into one of his many pockets and scanned the ridge for signs of interest. I was beginning to feel a little out of my depth in this uncompromising world of predator and prey. Something was moving near the carcass. Flip risked a quick flash with his torch: a jackal.

At night jackals range across the wind, quartering the dark breeze for the scent of prey or the smell of death. Prey animals use the reverse tactic. Diä!kwain, one of the /Xam Bushmen who worked with Wilhelm Bleek and Lucy Lloyd in Cape Town recounted the story that his father had told him about the precautions taken by a porcupine returning to its burrow.[1] 'Father used to tell me that, when lying in wait for a porcupine, at the time at which the Milky Way turns back, I should know that it is the time at which the porcupine returns... Father said to me that I should not watch the wind, to windward, for the porcupine is not a thing which will return coming right out of the wind. For, it is used to return crossing the wind in a slanting direction, because it wants to smell; for its nostrils are those which tell it about it, whether harm is at this place. Father used to tell me, that I must not breathe strongly when lying in wait for a porcupine.' A colleague who works in Norway once told me how the ptarmigan stops breathing for minutes on end when an Arctic fox is near her nest, so that it will not smell her scent. There was a serious game of smell detection going on out there in the night. I decided to sit perfectly still and to breathe as lightly as possible.

A female lion walked boldly up to the carcass and started to feed. Flip clipped on the night sites and readied his capture rifle. Stu glanced nervously at his recorder. 'Don't run out on me now,' he begged. Other lionesses arrived and began to feed. In a few minutes the whole pride had gathered at the zebra, save for the cubs that were concealed nearby and the large, tawny-maned, pride male. The ripe smell issuing from the fresh carcass as it was rapidly dismembered must have been a strong temptation for the pride male, not to mention the grunting and snarling of lionesses fighting over hunks of meat, but he resisted. Flip whispered that the males leave the park more frequently than females, wandering far across the ranching country where they are shot at by farmers. It makes them wary. 'If he does approach the kill, he'll be careful. He'll use every bit of cover out there.' Just then one of the lionesses stopped feeding and stared straight at our vehicle, tail switching. She must have heard something. Flip was tense. This particular female was incredibly aggressive. On previous occasions she had charged his vehicle at the slightest pretext, once leaping right on top and biting at any moving object. It had been scary and dangerous. But tonight she was more interested in the carcass and turned back to feed. A few minutes later, Flip thought he glimpsed the male feeding on the zebra and decided to risk a quick shine of his torch. Instantly a large lion with huge mane reared up, tearing off a piece of zebra haunch in the process, turned and trotted behind cover. Once startled, he would not return.

Showing no sign of frustration Flip shifted his attention to the females who had ignored the male's sudden flight, remaining intent on demolishing the last of the zebra. Using the infrared scope to see into the night, he located one that had a faulty radio collar. She became the target but a young lion was just behind her making the shot too risky. Flip remained hunched over the rifle, waiting for an opportunity. Peering down the night scope, he looked just as formidable as the predator he was aiming at. Five long minutes later, the young male moved to one side. Flip fired. The dart struck the lioness on the shoulder – a perfect location as the drug would be injected straight into a large muscle causing no significant damage. 'Nice shot!' exclaimed Stu.

As we waited for the tranquillizer to take effect, the remaining lions continued to feed. When the last part of zebra flesh had gone, the pride moved off the carcass leaving one member lying down, head up but groggy. As we watched, she rolled over and fell unconscious. 'It's quite sexy the way she rolled over,' observed Stu. We waited quietly for 20 minutes to make sure she was fully under before approaching in the truck. It was a relief to get out of the cramped cab into the cool night air. Flip checked over the lioness, removing the dart from her shoulder with a tug, and then walked back to the Chevy reversing it a few yards further off to give the Land Cruiser clear access to the downed animal. With a word of caution, he walked round to the tailgate to sort out his capture equipment – leaving Stu and I alone with our torches. The great cat, a pale shadow in the starlight, lay stretched at our feet, breathing slowly and evenly; beside her a strip of zebra hide, the last remnant of the lions' feast. All around was the blackness of night. Without the vehicle, I suddenly felt exposed and sensed that Stu beside me was also feeling uneasy. This was new territory for him. Slowly I swung the narrow beam of my mini-Maglite making one complete circle. Eight pairs of eyes shone back, bright green and surprisingly large in the pale light of my torch. One of those pairs belonged to a lioness who would charge without fear if she sensed her sister was in danger. Neither of us moved.

'Bleedin' heck,' whispered Stu. 'Are you thinking what I'm thinking?'

'It's you they fancy,' I replied, trying to sound casual.

'They're not charging at us which is a bonus,' observed Stu.

I checked the night again. The lions had edged closer. Concern now turned to alarm. Stu was looking around anxiously for the Land Cruiser which was crawling slowly across the bush towards us. I kept watching those eyes. For once there was no humorous banter between us.

At last the Land Cruiser arrived and the moment of fear was forgotten. We moved the immobilised lioness to a safer location, about half a mile from the cave, where we could change the radio collar and take measurements without having to watch our backs, lest one of the sisterhood leapt unseen from the darkness. Here on the open sandy ground, we created a tiny workspace in the vast African night. Two pairs of headlights illuminated the stage whilst idling engines held back the silence. A smell of aromatic herbs hovered in the air. The crew was busy, their time limited. But every so often one would stop work to glance over his shoulder, checking for movement in the dark. Flip extracted a needle and several vacuum tubes from his box of capture equipment and took blood from a vein running along the inside thigh: it would add to his understanding of disease in the lion population and with luck DNA analysis would identify the parents of this lioness. Absentmindedly he stroked her pale thigh – an apology for this added insult. The old radio collar was removed. A new one tested and fitted. It squawked in a steady rhythm like a pulse beat. Someone smoked a cigarette, quickly and nervously. The lioness's mouth was opened, her pink tongue pulled to one side, and her teeth examined one by one for wear, decay or breakage. The length of the massive canines was measured with a vernier calliper to determine her age. Chest circumference, shoulder height and other body size dimensions were recorded. The young ranger crouched down next to the lioness and stroked her shoulder, gently, softly, as if caressing a lover. An ear tag was fitted. Diagrams and photographs from her first capture were compared with the living animal; a few notes were added and new photographs taken. Mafuta, the old tracker, glanced briefly into the night. Had he heard something? Stu put down his recording equipment to help the team check pulse, breathing rate and other vital signs. He too stroked the lioness, lightly brushing the heaving flanks. Each massive paw was inspected for thorns and cuts. Abruptly everyone was standing and talking, the work completed. There was more than a tinge of relief in their chatter. Flip lit up his pipe, and relaxed. The lioness lay quietly, potent in her sleeping. Acting as a tightly knit team, we carried her to the rear of the pick-up, placed her carefully inside and drove back to the dolomite ridge. There we lay her in a bed of herbs and grasses to recover. The young ranger patted her one last time.

Leaving the rangers with the sleeping lioness, Flip, Stu and I departed to check on the gemsbok bait. There was no sign of lions there, so we headed for camp where we chatted for a few minutes around the campfire, too tired to eat. I climbed into my sleeping bag, head spinning with images of the lioness. The capture team returned shortly afterwards, reporting that the lioness had now fully recovered. They were keen as Cape hunting dogs to continue lion watching and, after discussing the matter with Flip, left to keep watch at the gemsbok carcass. Sometime in the small hours the Land Cruiser returned once more, this time with news that a single male with a large mane had been seen near the second bait. Flip got up to try and dart him. Stu and I slept on.

Awakening early in the morning I noticed that the swelling on my ear from the bee sting had finally settled. I made some tea. Sure enough this woke Stu. We kicked Torran's football about the airstrip whilst waiting for the others. Eventually they arrived back having had a frustrating night. Flip reckoned that the lion hanging around the gemsbok carcass was the same one that had run from the zebra when he switched on his torch. It had remained wary throughout the rest of the night, refusing to approach the bait so long as his vehicle was present. Perhaps it was no ordinary lion? According to one !Kung hunter, the greatest of the shamans entered a violent trance when taking on feline form: they became 'real' lions that were nevertheless different from the normal 'lions of God.'[2] The Bushmen claimed that the shamanic lion could mix with a pride of normal lions without fear.[3] What was more the shamanic lions could go hunting, looking for people to kill, and when such a lion was shot with poisoned arrows, it did not die.[4]

It seemed that our chances of catching this particular lion were slim but Flip had one more trick up his sleeve – sleeping pills. Before leaving the gemsbok bait he had untied the rope securing the carcass to the tree stump, cut a hunk of meat almost free of the haunch and smeared it with green powder from the capsules. Seeing him drive off, he hoped the lion would gain confidence, grab the carcass and drag it away to a safe place for eating. The plan now was to wait for a few hours whilst the lion hopefully tucked into his doctored dinner.

I cooked up some *boerewors* for the team to raise their energy levels for the demands of the day to come. Soon afterwards Flip took Stu and I up for a recce flight with Stu perched in the back on Flip's bed roll now serving as a rear seat. We cruised slowly up the dolomite ridge, picking up signals from four lionesses, including the one captured last night. They all emanated from the cave. We made a broad circle and skimmed southwards across dry plains and stunted grey bushes. Animal paths, light and feathery in the scrub, sharpened into deep wrinkles that cut into the white calcareous skin of shallow pans. Our aircraft floated on its wide wings just above a meadow of waving grasses, slipping towards a single tall acacia tree. Beneath it a large bull elephant was resting. He turned, ears raised as with a whoop of joy we whooshed past. And then we were over the pan with the gemsbok bait. The carcass had been dragged into the bushes, just as Flip had hoped, and there beneath a scrubby mopane tree was a large tawny-maned lion. As the plane swooped past, he appeared unnaturally calm. A few minutes later, we touched down, taxied up to the hangar and transferred promptly into the Chevy.

Fifteen minutes of driving took us back to the pan where Mafuta showed us the marks left by the lion as it dragged the gemsbok away. Stu and I transferred into the open back of the Land Cruiser with the capture team. Our vehicle slowly followed the trail into the mopane scrub. Without warning, the lion stood up just 10 metres away and trotted briskly, if a little unsteadily, towards the next group of shrubs where he sank down out of sight. We stopped whilst Flip took a look at the remains of the gemsbok that had just been abandoned; half of the sedative had been eaten. I awarded one point to the field biologist – but the shamanic lion had yet to be captured. We waited a few more minutes then moved gingerly forward, lurching in and out of holes in the sand. Someone began to talk but was quickly told to be quiet. This was the showdown. Everyone was staring into the bushes trying to see the lion, all too aware that it could leap into the back and pull someone out in an instant. Meanwhile I was trying to change from a long telephoto to a close-up zoom lens without making a noise. The Land Cruiser dived into a hole and the heavy camera clunked against the side. Six pairs of eyes turned to stare at me. I squirmed uncomfortably but tightened my resolve and began to ready my camcorder. The sound of every little movement was magnified a hundred times. Reason told me that noise was not the problem here. It was my vigilance that the group was really demanding. Watch for that lion! It was a silent order. Stu hung onto the side, grimly staring into the scrub. Someone whispered urgently in Afrikaans. At 25 metres the lion, who must have been following our progress, rose and half turned, ready to run. The pick-up stopped and in the same instant the engine was cut. Flip had one possible shot at the turning lion, but it meant aiming under the leaf canopy of the short bushes whilst taking into account the arched trajectory of the dart. He fired. The dart passed through a narrow window of foliage hitting the lion squarely on the haunch. It was a perfect shot. Two–nil.

The lion walked off a short distance and lay down. We waited. Stu and a couple of others smoked a cigarette. Eventually we got out of the vehicle and approached slowly on foot. Flip went first recovering the dart and checking to make sure that the lion had received the full dose of tranquillizer. Close up, the animal looked if anything even more formidable. He was large, tawny-maned and in excellent condition despite a missing molar and worn incisors that indicated an age of about 12 years, usually well beyond the prime years of life. His legs were long and powerful with large footpads. This was a nomadic lion. With difficulty we dragged him a couple of metres into the shade of a small bush growing out of a knee-high termite mound. The Land Cruiser drove off towards the pan to fetch the Chevy which had much of the equipment for marking and taking measurements. Most of the team stood some way off behind a bush chatting quietly; they were pleased to have bested the lion.

Temporarily abandoned the lion slept quietly in the shade, its side heaving up and down with each breath. I walked over to gaze at him, aware as I did so that I was stepping into his space. He had such presence. As I raised my camera to take a close-up of the lion's head, his eyes met mine. For a moment I was rooted to the spot, spellbound by the menace in that yellow glare. I just had time to wonder if I could escape from lions a second time, when he sprang to his feet with a deep growl. I heard gasps from behind and the sound of running feet. There was no time to run, no time to think. With an effort I looked away from that gaze, and willed myself to flee. Turning hard I began to run; my movements were lethargic in comparison to the powerful acceleration of the lion, now turning swiftly behind me. I completed a tight semicircle, waiting for the inevitable; too shocked even to wonder how a deeply-sedated lion could awaken and give chase. An instant later, the lion lurched and collapsed. My surroundings swam back into focus and my heart rate, which would have done justice to a fleeing Springbok, began to calm down. The panic in the rest of our party gave way to relief, even hilarity at our close escape, but then edged quickly back to caution. We gathered together behind the small bush, keeping a close eye on the recumbent lion. Stu, journalistic training to the fore, was narrating the incident into his recorder. Flip approached the recumbent lion for the second time, moving one foot slowly and silently after the next, whilst signalling for Stu to be quiet. Silently, he administered more anaesthetic straight into a vein so as to obtain a faster and even deeper anaesthesia. We waited for a minute. Reassured that the lion was now truly under, the capture team got down to work. Flip applied eye ointment to protect the retina from ultraviolet radiation, and then dowsed the tawny hide in water, rubbing it thoroughly into the mane and coat to keep him cool. The rest of the team were busy preparing equipment: a new radio collar, brand irons, data sheets, collection bottles for blood samples and the other bits and pieces used for measuring and classifying.

The professional routine was re-established: the collar was quickly attached; TC was branded on the right shoulder and various measurements taken. Despite the speed of operations, the lion showed signs of waking up before we were finished. Everyone was edgy now. This lion obeyed none of the usual rules. The young ranger brushed bits of grass off the animal's side as we packed up and walked quickly over to the trucks. Barely had we done so, when he rose to his feet.

Stu was mulling over the morning's events on the drive back to camp. 'How long will Top Cat's collar last?' he asked.

'Top Cat?' queried Flip.

'TC… You know, Top Cat and his gang.'

'Oh yeah,' Flip smiled. 'The transmitters usually last a year, maybe two if we're lucky. The collars are pretty much permanent.'

I was reflecting too. In the past week I'd dreamt about a jackal as it sniffed me on the Skeleton Coast, been stung by a bee in the heart of a Bushman's cave, and been chased by a strange male lion that was hard to capture and quick to throw off the effects of tranquillizers. Coincidence no doubt, but then again if I were a Bushman I would have little reason to trust this inquisitive stranger travelling over my land without permission. And that lion… he was so powerful… he seemed to summon something else. I had ended up in a crazy dance with a magical creature.

The experience was making me think again about immobilising wild animals. Intelligent creatures like the lion surely cannot be unaffected by what they go through: they may be shocked by the feeling of powerlessness; they may even sense they have been abased in some way. I knew Stu would be amused by such whimsy but sometimes we need to think outside the glow cast by the fire of our own culture. In exercising our technological superiority we in the Western world take our probity for granted, seldom pausing to consider whether we may be usurping something that doesn't belong to us. Bushmen and lions, on the other hand, have a different kind of relationship; they appear to respect and tolerate one another.

Over coffee at the hangar, the conversation turned to Bushmen and their uncanny intuitions. I recounted an incident described by Laurens van der Post which seemed particularly mysterious. The gist of it was that he had been walking through the bush behind his Bushman tracker following the spoor of some animal. All of a sudden, the tracker swerved aside and went off in a different direction. There on the other side of a dense bush was a male impala. On being asked how he knew that the impala was present, the tracker replied that he'd felt the antelope's eyes on the back of his neck.

Flip was interested in the story having come across something similar himself. 'I know a tracker who has a set of scars under his arm: one for a lion, one for a kudu, and so on. When he feels the bottom one itching, he knows he is near a kudu, but if it is the third one up, he is close to a lion.'

'Do you think the trackers have some kind of expanded awareness?' I asked.

'I could not be sure about that,' Flip replied. 'Although I've read everything about Bushmen I can lay my hands on, I still can't figure them out.'

Stu was sceptical. 'Let's think about van der Post's tracker for a minute,' he urged. 'Suppose he was walking along through the bushes, aware without thinking about it that this was a favourite type of habitat for the impala male. Maybe he spots something – perhaps a bird alights on a nearby tree – and it registers as a possible indicator of an antelope. Or maybe he catches a whiff of impala. Quite spontaneously the feeling of an antelope staring at him is generated in his mind.'

'You could be right,' I nodded. 'Still, it shows how close the Bushman is to nature.'

Flip concurred. 'The survival of a Bushman hunter depends utterly on his knowledge of wild animals. We cannot compare with that.'

Refilling our mugs with coffee, Flip reminded Stu and me that it was time to get on the road if we wanted to make the next Etosha camp before nightfall. 'When you reach Botswana, I would head into the central Kalahari. You might just find Bushmen living in the old way. I'd come with you if I had the time.'

I was sorry to be leaving. My younger self might well have stayed on in Namibia, recognising a kindred spirit in Flip, and responding to the wild call of Africa. Perhaps I would have taken on a study of the desert elephants, and camped in the narrow canyons to learn their secrets. That passion for field biology still burned inside me, but it hadn't stopped the old-timer's mocking laughter. If I didn't push on now, I would never silence it.

7

NIGHT ON THE OKAVANGO

Okavango hippo – He watched our comings and goings

The verandah decking outside the bar of Drotsky Cabins was perched 10 metres above the muddy Okavango River. Standing on the edge of the decking, it felt as if I were riding on a paddle steamer with Huckleberry Finn. It had taken us several days to get there, driving eastwards across northern Namibia to an empty lawless corridor known as the Caprivi Strip. Then south across the border with Botswana and along a swampy corridor, affectionately called the 'panhandle', where the Okavango River cuts through dry bush before emptying into the 'pan' – an oasis of blue water channels, emerald reed beds and thickets of wild fig and date palm – from whence the overspill disappears into the endless sands of the Kalahari. Mrs Drotsky stood at the head of the wooden stairs looking as imperious as any riverboat captain keeping watch over their busy crew. She was overseeing a dozen tasks: booking a demanding party of guests into their rooms, keeping an eye on the sport-fishing being organised by her grown-up boys, sending a cot over to someone's cabin, re-stocking the bar fridge with beer, making arrangements with the cook for the increased number expected for dinner, and in-between times drawing a map of the Tsodilo Hills for us whilst checking we had the right kind of vehicle and gear to make the desert crossing. 'Leave early in the morning, before the sun is up,' she commanded.

'It's better to cross whilst the sand is cool.' Small, dark-haired and lively, she would have made a formidable skipper on the Mississippi River.

In front of the bar was an area of well-kept lawns and flowerbeds that must have been sorely tempting to the Okavango hippos, and beyond that was a sycamore fig tree leaning far out over the river. A troupe of vervet monkeys was busy picking fruit, chattering and screaming at the liberties brought on by such a bountiful crop. I strolled over to watch them. In midstream a hippo raised its head just high enough to lift ears, eyes and nostrils clear of the surface. Very quietly he watched our comings and goings. As a fishing skiff approached, he slipped beneath the surface with scarcely a ripple. On the far bank was an impenetrable wall of papyrus tall enough to hide an elephant.

It was twilight by the time I left the river and getting dark when I reached the campsite in the forest below the dining deck. Stu had set up his silver tent on a sandy spot near to the river and was halfway up a large albizia tree. A young vervet peered down at him from the upper branches, not quite sure if he was playmate or predator. Stu peered up at the monkey, wondering much the same thing I reckoned. I left them to their game and looked for a suitable camping spot. As it was hot and muggy I dispensed with the tent, simply suspending a mosquito net from an overhanging branch, and went in search of the communal shower. I found it down a narrow track in the centre of the forest. The water came in two temperatures: cold or scalding hot. I settled for cold and freshened up for dinner.

As night fell, Stu and I drove round to the bar to enjoy a chilled beer. On a unanimous vote against a tin of curried mixed vegetables in camp and in favour of a full riverboat dinner, we carried our beers onto the verandah deck where candles now flickered on a half dozen tables with views over the floodlit channel. A smartly dressed waiter came to take our orders. In the dark, we might have been dining on the deck of the *Delta Queen* herself. The waiter had just cleared away the plates from our hors d'oeuvre of shrimp on lettuce when a girl screamed, the shrill note carried on the still night air from the forest camp below. I hoped one of the overlanders camped next to us was just fooling about, but there had been nothing light-hearted in that scream. Then it came again and this time the fear was unmistakeable. A third scream quickly followed. There is something in a scream – a really dreadful scream – that turns you cold. It's the terror. And there is something else – the stricken appeal for help – that smacks in the pit of your stomach compelling you into action. Without thinking, I jumped to my feet and started for the campsite finding Eileen Drotsky, Stu and three or four guests running alongside. Scream now followed scream, each more desperate and terrifying than the last. Eileen shouted, 'Hang-on! We're coming!' Pulling a torch from my jean's pocket, I plunged into the darkness of the forest, following a footpath that led in the direction of the last scream. In a few seconds we were down in the camping area and running past a gully that led off towards the river. I heard a crash to the left and flashed my torch in that direction, catching a fleeting glimpse of a pale leopard hotly pursued by the Drotsky's Alsatian. Somewhere up ahead people were shouting and clapping hands loudly. The screaming stopped. I was dreading what we might find, remembering the appalling account of a tiger devouring a tourist in front of a group of helpless bird watchers in India. We ran on towards the central shower unit, spotting a waving light on the path just ahead. 'Are you alright?' someone shouted. Next moment we arrived to find a young woman in a bathrobe being comforted by her male companion. She was pale and shocked, but thankfully unhurt. Her companion told us that she had been on her way back from the shower when she walked straight into a hippo standing silently on the dark path, its massive bulk blocking the way back to her friends. Terrified, she instinctively began to scream. We took a minute or two to make sure the girl was unharmed, then turned to walk back.

Inevitably someone asked, 'Who received the biggest shock, the girl or the hippo?'

Stu replied, 'I dunno, I just thought we were going to die horribly.'

By the time we had reached the dining deck, it was established that the leopard must have been in the vicinity by coincidence, and was then flushed by the noise and commotion.

'There's an important lesson from tonight,' said Stu after we had sat down again at the dinner table.

'I don't suppose you're going to tell me?' I queried, making room for a little girl and her parents who were joining our table.

'In a crisis, scream. Ain't nothing like it for rallying support.'

'We're primitive underneath,' I agreed. 'Not as sophisticated as we like to think.'

The meal continued without further incident save that Stu, much to his satisfaction, was offered a second helping of custard and fruit salad by the little girl.

After dinner I ordered whisky on the rocks from a merry bewhiskered barman, offering him a drink at the same time. This he regretfully declined. It transpired that the barman was none other than our host, Mr Drotsky. He and Eileen had first set up their camp by the Okavango River some 25 years earlier, as a complementary business to farming. In those days it took them four days to travel to and from Maun, the provincial capital tucked in-between the Okavango Delta and the northern edge of the Kalahari Desert, so their provisioning trips were kept to a minimum. As a new tarmac road neared completion, their frontier isolation was replaced by daily connections with the outside world. Now their adventure in self-sufficiency had been supplanted by the excitement of commercial opportunity; I suspected Mr Drotsky was happier on the frontier.

At some point in the evening the conversation turned to the mysterious Tsodilo Hills. The name 'Tsodilo' is derived from the Setswana word, *Sorile*, meaning sheer and precipitous rocks. But to the Bushmen the hills evoked something else. Some called them 'the bracelet of the sunset', others the 'rock that whispers'. Most mysterious of all, the old Bushmen spoke of them as 'a place to enter' or 'a place where one goes inside'. There are caves in the hills with a long record of human habitation, but the Bushmen may have implied something even deeper. The !Kung believe that fearsome quantities of *n/um*, a supernatural power that can heal or destroy, emanate from Tsodilo 'issuing forth like pouring smoke' and that spirits haunt the surroundings. In 1955, Laurens van der Post led a small party to the hills in search of the 'authentic Bushman living there as he had once lived'. He forgot about the warnings of vengeful spirits and brushed up against a mystical presence that still haunted the sacred hills and which resented his lack of respect.[1] His cameras jammed and all kinds of problems beset them. Others who ignored the sanction against killing wildlife in the vicinity of the hills suffered strange accidents, at least one of which was fatal.

A heady cocktail of mystery and hearsay pervaded every conversation on Tsodilo, fortified if anything by the imperfect nature of the sources – speculations by early explorers, passing references in travellers' diaries, smatterings of archaeological data, and a few oblique commentaries in the folklore of the !Kung Bushmen. The chance to visit the mythical dwelling place of Bushmen spirits made me tingle with excitement. I wondered whether some strange power might still inhabit the hills. But whilst intrigued by the stories, I decided to keep my feet firmly planted on *terra firma* and to begin by noting whatever ungarnished facts came my way.

8

EMPTY HILLS

Combretum pod

The track to Tsodilo Hills leaves the main road some 21 kilometres south of Drotsky Cabins, and heads westward away from the lush panhandle into the dry Kalahari Desert. Turning onto the track early the next morning, we immediately sank into soft sand and needed low ratio, four-wheel drive to make progress. In patches, we sank in deeper still and Nomad floundered like a sea turtle making its way across a tropical beach. Where the going was firmer, mounds of sand heaped up by passing trucks set up a violent bouncing motion that called for a swift reduction in speed lest a torsion bar would snap. At slower speed, the rebound caused a sickening motion in the cab, woomm – woomm – woomm, which went on for hours. The sun rose before we had travelled far and the temperature inside Nomad soared. I was grumpy. Last night the mosquito net had flapped in my face, interrupting dreams of angry leopards and charging hippos. Stu wasn't much better. We lapsed into a sullen silence. Slowly Nomad advanced westward, the Kalahari bushland opening up in front, and closing off behind as we crossed the crests and troughs of ancient, rolling sand dunes. Some optical illusion gave the impression that we were driving uphill all the way.

So far I had gleaned only a few basic facts about Tsodilo. The three main hills, 'Male', 'Female' and 'Child' form a 10-kilometre line extending southeast to northwest. The highest, Male, rises little more than a thousand feet above the surrounding plain. Geologists describe the hills as outcrops of quartzite and micaceous schist and note that 150 miles of deep Kalahari sand separates them from the nearest rocky outcrop. They are as much an isolated archipelago as any cluster of oceanic islands and by way of confirmation there is an endemic species – a little brown gecko – that is found nowhere else. In amongst the hills is archaeological evidence of habitation by hunter-gatherers that stretches back over tens of thousands of years. More than 4,000 paintings, in outline and silhouette styles, are scattered over the hills on cave walls, shelters and rock panels.[1] The paintings are powerful but simple and, as archaeologists dryly note, without evidence of stylistic development over the years.

The site has one unique feature that sets it apart from other areas of African rock art. Here at the northwestern corner of the Kalahari Desert, the shrinking range of the surviving desert-dwelling Bushman meets the outermost bastion of the mountainous habitat utilised for paintings and engravings by earlier Palaeolithic peoples. This juxtaposition of living and lost hunter-gatherer cultures intrigued the early scientific explorers. Could there be a memory of the lost rock-art culture still lingering amongst the living Bushmen? If so it would be a discovery every bit as momentous as that of the Rosetta Stone. It might enable us to understand the real meaning behind the Bushman's enigmatic art; it would be a window into the soul of Stone Age man.

The first hill to rise above the near horizon of bushes and trees was Male, its grey-blue cone lifting high above the scrub as we approached the southern end of the desert archipelago. On its western side were great slabs of steel-blue rock that butted into the rolling dunes. Somewhere above this massive cliff was the most sacred site of all – a place where the first spirit knelt to pray after creating the world. The rocks were still molten and the indentations from His knees have remained to this day. It was hard not to feel humbled by this primordial entranceway. I wondered again whether these hills might hold a vestige of spiritual power from the past.

'What a flippin' shagheap!' announced Stu as Nomad bumped over the broken and splintered debris scattered around the base. 'Why doesn't someone build a decent road here.' Just then the neighbouring Female hill came into sight, lying lower than Male but with a wide central plateau surrounded by cliffs and gullies. In amongst these were the caves where Bushmen spirits dwelt. We turned between the consorting pair and came to rest on a bed of firm sand under a thorn tree outside the imposing entrance to White Elephant Cave. There was no breeze, not even a whisper in the thin crown of leaves to break the deep stillness of the place. It was blisteringly hot and the darkness of the cave beckoned. I got out and walked across the solar furnace to the dark haven of the cavern, sprawling across the cool stone floor. Stu was there ahead of me.

After a few minutes I began to take notice of the surroundings. On the walls, numerous paintings of animals and people were crudely outlined in white, perhaps daubed by finger. A large elephant trumpeted in rage, trunk pointing forward, ramrod straight; behind the fearsome face he was less impressive, being about the size and shape of a dachshund puppy. Nearby were various geometrical motifs and abstract squiggles. These white calcrete figures are thought to have been painted by pastoralists who arrived in these hills long after the Bushmen. Sure enough some of the white figures were painted over faded rust-red ones, but the red were never on top of white, confirming their more ancient lineage.

Above the main shelter was a warren of rockbound passages and smaller caves. Stu set off to explore, scrambling effortlessly up the rock face, picking one secure hold after another as if climbing on a favourite Scottish mountain. It occurred to me in my dopey state that he used the same technique in climbing as when debating some issue in the pub. With one point securely established he would lead off to another. Any suspect ideas were quickly rejected, especially dodgy spiritual ones which might fail under pressure and undermine his pitch. Sooner or later, one position following another, he reached higher ground that boasted a broader view. I, on the other hand, could be tempted by dodgy holds. They often failed, but occasionally one would hold opening up a hitherto hidden pathway. Discovery is something I relish.

Stu reached a narrow ledge, manoeuvred along it to a gap between the rocks and disappeared. A few minutes later he shouted down to say he had found another cave. He called out some directions that would take me up an easier route. I climbed up a pile of broken rocks, enjoying the stretch of limbs as I moved from one hold to the next, and joined Stu who was standing in a narrow passage between two huge boulders. He edged to one side to let me past. Inside the cave, my eyes were drawn to the faded ochre outlines of two eland, the most sacred of all animals, set above a flat 'sacrificial' stone. Surely this must have been a cave used by shamans. In the centre of the stone was a deep midden of scats – fox-sized, peppered with seeds, fur and pieces of grass, and piled up in a large smelly mound.

'Look what the spirits have left you,' murmured Stu, nodding at the large pile of shit.

'Sometimes you're not even funny,' I replied in a huffy tone.

'Well what kind of creature made this?' he asked.

'I think we're in the den of an African civet', I replied poking through the scats with my pocket-knife. 'They'll eat anything from hares to millipedes, including all of this stuff.'

'Oh yeah,' said Stu, checking about for signs of a large angry beast.

'It's like a big mongoose,' I spread my arms wide. 'You only see them at night so this one must be kipping somewhere else.'

Rock shelters in the oceanic sands of the Kalahari are as rare as empty apartments in San Francisco and so one like this with plenty of room would have attracted people over many millennia. Even rarer is a cave that provides an historical record of its occupation. The nearby White Paintings Rock Shelter furnishes just this unique combination. Working over several years, archaeologists excavated a deep pit at its entrance just beyond the overhanging roof. Digging down through seven metres of deposits, they sieved the contents of each 10-centimetre layer to create a time sequence of human occupation. Reaching the bottom was not easy: they had to remove several large boulders, truck in an extension ladder and, when this proved too short, cut out a spiral stairwell. Their valiant efforts uncovered a treasure trove of 20,000 bone fragments, representing 48 different species of mammal and fish, and an array of human artefacts, including beads, blades, flakes, scrapers, grindstones and lumps of kidney-red haematite – a mineralised form of iron used for painting. Half of me applauds their bold effort, the other half recoils at the destructive brutality of their methods. Either way, there is no denying the importance of their discoveries. Stone Age man had used the cave for at least 100,000 years, adapting to various environmental changes through this immense span of time.[2]

The collection of bone fragments was almost exclusively of wild animals, a single sheep's mandible being the only exception. Emphatically this was a settlement of hunters and gatherers. Bones of springhare, several antelopes, and zebra were all common; rhinos were also abundant. And curiously some of the animals that were present in the past, such as reedbuck, lechwe and the vlei rat, are absent today being confined to the Okavango Delta and neighbouring wetlands. The archaeologists also discovered remains of catfish, bream and cichlid fishes. I can imagine their surprise at these discoveries. Big fish and marsh-loving antelope don't live in the middle of parched deserts. But on asking local Bushmen, they were told that waters from the Okavango River and Delta used to flood back up the dry Ncamasere and Xaudum Valleys to within 17 kilometres of Tsodilo and, as the waters receded, the hunters impounded fish behind small dams. The discovery of bone harpoon points in the pit, pointed to a long tradition of fish spearing. There was even evidence of an ancient Lake Tsodilo that reached to within 350 metres of the rock shelter.

These are wonderful discoveries which show that Tsodilo is even more unique than we had realised; they provide further justification for its protection as a site of human heritage.[3] But they have come at a price. Until disturbed, each of the layers of sediment under White Paintings Rock Shelter harboured a memory of human history, the brushings of daily life buried one storey at a time over a thousand millennia. That is something immensely precious. This undisturbed basin of sediments, complete with its thin filling of bone pieces and worked stone fragments, was a slowly developing monument to humankind, almost unique in the world. It may not have been executed as a work of art but it can still be recognised as such, in the same way that an explorer is inspired by a lost city or a landscape artist by a pastoral scene. The beauty of these formations draws an involuntary gasp. Today our Tsodilo timeline has gone, scraped up layer by layer and sieved free of its heritage. Archaeological digs are destructive, more especially those in small and rare locations, and backfilling does little in mitigation. It poses us with a dilemma that is common to all the field-based sciences. What level of damage should we accept in our pursuit of new knowledge? Are not some archaeological sites so precious that their excavation should await development of less invasive techniques – a more sophisticated form of ground penetrating radar perhaps? And if so, should we grant them some form of recognition that would protect them from overly ardent professionals?

Leaving White Elephant Cave we climbed up the slopes of broken rock on the southern side of Female, exchanging the acacia and seringa trees of the plains for the monkey orange and plummy marula of the hills. At the top, I walked over to the western edge to stand above the high cliffs and enjoy the cool breeze coming up from the plains below. Tree-clad dunes rolled towards the base of the hills like a giant ocean swell with a mile between the crests. From beyond the far horizon where the plains melted into the sky, the pastoralists had come long ago with their great flocks of sheep and goats. By dating bone fragments, archaeologists determined that they arrived in AD 550 and abandoned the area some 500 or 600 years later.[4] In their villages on the plains they left behind sea shells, fragments of decorated pots, bones of domestic animals and objects made of copper and iron. Much was to change during their time at Tsodilo.

For many years, the two peoples coexisted: the hunter-gatherers in rock shelters on the hills and the pastoralists in their villages below, but the nature of the relations between these two nations, each with its own culture and traditions, is less certain. The single sheep's mandible at White Paintings Rock Shelter indicates no merging of lifestyles in the hills. But a mixture of stone and iron tools in the villages suggests a degree of integration on the plains. Perhaps the pastoralists brought Bushmen into their settlements as wives, or in a master-client relationship. Maybe they traded iron and copper ornaments for wild foods. The rock paintings provide few clues. There are no battle scenes, no reason to suppose that the two peoples met on other than friendly terms.

Climbing back down the southern side of Female, we entered a sandy arena surrounded by vertical rock walls. It was even hotter here. I wiped the sweat from my eyes with my shirt and looked about at the rock walls. Stu who was a little way ahead called to me. When I caught up to him he pointed out a striking group of animals painted on a huge slab of rock some 20 feet above the ground. The rock had been cleaved down the middle, leaving a vertical crack where the two sections abutted onto one another. Facing into this cleft were two black rhinoceroses, one with a baby at its feet, painted boldly in dark red, almost maroon. The adults were about a foot in length. Despite the heat and ever-present dehydration, I had to resist the urge to climb up and touch the heavy, full-bellied bodies with their little raised tails, short legs and powerful shoulders. The long tapering horns lined up to the cleft, seeming to point a way into the rock wall. The Ncae Bushmen who once lived here told how their ancestors had painted the rock pictures, 'God having guided their hands as they held the paint to form the pictures.'[5] Perhaps these rhinos were so inspired: the image on the rock coming from the mind of God and the artist only needing to mark its outline with pigment. And what was the significance of these two potent animals, pointing the way into the rock? Was this the 'place where one goes inside' – an entrance to the spirit world?

Back at Nomad, the air was still and deathly hot. The overarching acacias had flushed green in anticipation of rain but their thin leaves offered little relief from the daytime inferno of Tsodilo. I lowered Nomad's tailgate to make a makeshift table and pulled out a food box. Stu opened a tin of sardines for lunch and proffered them to me, 'This is what you need. Get some inside you before the spirits grab 'em.'

I focussed on the simple task of pouring out a couple of mugs of water from the 25-litre container. It tasted of plastic. I added a dollop of mixed orange and passion fruit juice but it barely improved matters. 'Here's what they are really after,' I muttered, handing over a mug to Stu, 'nectar of the gods.'

'This is bloody disgusting.'

'It's all the gods could spare.'

'Gods or no gods, I need a kip,' said Stu going off in search of a suitable cave.

He found one nearby, even darker and cooler than White Elephant Cave. What's more it contained a wide ledge at the back that looked ideal for an afternoon siesta. I followed him in, and lay spread-eagled on the ledge under a low roof. My stone bed was smooth, cool and surprisingly comfortable. I dosed fitfully, dropping in and out of a heat-induced stupor. Surfacing into wakefulness some time later I noticed a zebra in the far corner; she was about a foot long with neat black stripes. Two others fitted perfectly into rocky indentations above my head. Gazing about, I realised that the cave was full of zebra paintings that I had somehow overlooked. One was almost a yard long. What a magical cave! What was it Mr Drotsky had said? The longer you stayed in a cave, the more paintings you could see. I drifted back into sleep. On reawakening in the slightly cooler mid-afternoon, I mentioned the zebras to Stu who had been dozing on an adjacent ledge.

'Where?' he demanded.

Still lying flat on my back, I described the location of the first zebra. 'Far wall, just where the roof begins, look for two small indentations that are smooth as plates.'

'It's just shadows,' Stu claimed. 'It's the same with all the others.'

I woke more fully and looked about. Stu was right: there were no zebras. Had they been dreams then? If so my dreams were beginning to merge with reality. Perhaps it was just the trick of a tired mind. Yet afterwards Stu admitted that on first entering the cave he too had seen a zebra painting.

Later in the afternoon, we drove north along the western edge of Female towards a spot recommended for camping by the Drotskys. On the way, we passed a bright orange overlanders' truck pumping out the unmistakable sound of Pink Floyd from a pair of big speakers mounted on the back. In its own way their music is as seductive as the silence of the ancient hills – but like wine and whisky, neither can be enjoyed when mixed with the other. This was the only other vehicle to visit the hills during our three-day visit, but it was enough to make me wonder what would happen to the atmosphere of Tsodilo if the access road was ever tarmacked. Recently a local schoolteacher wrote his name and address over some rock paintings, presumably in complete ignorance of their age and significance. After seeing this graffiti scrawled over the panel of paintings named after her father, Laurens van der Post's daughter offered to pay for fencing and re-stocking the area with native game animals. Mr Drotsky was prepared to help. He considered the best way to look after Tsodilo was through a management concession granted to the private sector. The government had other ideas. It had opted for direct management and was already building a camp and museum near to Female. The low buildings with thatched roofs and daubed ochre walls were taking shape not far from the eland panel. They were tasteful, but any building in close proximity to these hills takes from their atmosphere. The Drotskys feared that junior museum staff posted here would have little interest in the place, and that the quality of the site could deteriorate quickly. On the other hand, government no doubt feared that private management would restrict access to a small number of wealthy clients. It was becoming a familiar dilemma – balancing the sensitivity and care of private ownership with the accessibility provided by national ownership.

Our campsite on the northwest side of Female was in a deep gully that Mr Drotsky said would provide protection from fierce nocturnal winds that whip through the gap between Male and Female. We pulled out the tents from the back of Nomad and began putting them up. Nothing stirred in the gully. As evening approached, the silence, if anything, thickened within our rocky cove. It was strange to be surrounded by African rocks and not hear the raucous calls of hyrax. Bones of the 'dassie' have been found in archaeological digs, showing that the hills were not always so silent but the animal was now locally extinct, as was the dainty klipspringer – another rock specialist.

Despite drinking over 10 tall glasses of water, I was still thirsty. Stu was in the same debilitated condition. We toyed with a supper of pilchards and hard bread, making better progress with the hot frothy beer. I retired early. It had been a long day and as my head touched the pillow – a jersey stuffed into a T-shirt – I was instantly asleep. Even in this sheltered campsite, the wind rose in the night reserving its full force for the small hours of the morning. The big red tent was blown wildly about until the flysheet began to detach itself, threatening to fly off into the night. I climbed out of my sleeping bag and set about securing the flapping guy ropes. According to the !Kung no person at Tsodilo should complain of hunger or thirst, or if plagued by wind, for the place is filled with spiritual potency. I brought the canvas under control and stood for a few minutes looking up at the sky. I didn't complain. The stars were living specks of iridescent blue in an inky black void. *N/um* emanated earthwards, rebounded, and headed skywards. Behind me, the looming cliffs stood hunched and firm against the desert tempest. It was all so grand and wonderful.

A muffled expletive from inside Stu's tent heralded his appearance a few minutes later. Blinking in the morning sunlight, and brushing desert sand out of a two-week beard, he whacked the living hell from his boots, just in case some unlucky scorpion had been seduced by the fustiness permeating his lower being.

'Blimey, what I wouldn't give for a mug of tea.'

'Have you seen my lighter?'

'Have you seen my pods?'

'Check the back of Nomad,' I suggested.

Stu disappeared inside re-emerging a minute later with his collection of seed cases, a splendid mix of winged, spiked, twisted and gnarled pods gathered from the acacia, wild seringa and combretum trees. He picked up the bag and began to shake a shush-shush rhythm, shuffling his feet on the sandy dance floor. 'There could be a song in here somewhere,' he remarked.

Stu had been missing his guitar but I hadn't realised that the composer within had been at work. I finally found my lighter, lit the gas burner and put on the kettle.

'What do you say we walk over to Child today?' I asked.

'Sounds good. Have we got any rusks left?'

I dug out the last bag and made the tea. Already the temperature was uncomfortably hot, and no matter how much I drank, it seemed impossible to satiate my thirst.

There was no vehicle track to Child, so we set off on foot, picking our way in between the thorn bushes, looking for signs of life but finding little evidence of either animals or hunters. Child was only a mile off but it felt more remote than either of its parents. Its sides were lined with broken boulders and thick scrub and there wasn't the hint of a footpath round the base. Stu walked on ahead looking for rock paintings whilst I lingered behind, endeavouring to tune into my surroundings. A minute later I heard a gasp. Walking quickly forward, I found Stu staring up at the rock wall.

'Fuck'n nora!' he exclaimed. 'You don't want to go into that one.'

'What one?'

'That crack in the rocks,' Stu replied pointing to a deep crevice about a metre tall and less than half that in width.

'Why not?'

'A bleeding great leopard just went in, that's why not.'

'You're kidding!' I exclaimed through cracked lips. 'They're not supposed to be here anymore.'

'Go on then,' said Stu, with a hint of malice. 'Have a peek. I'll just borrow your camera.'

'Maybe not.'

'I should think bloody not. It scared the jeezus out of me.'

I sat down and pulled off my daypack. 'Have some nectar,' I offered Stu a gallon can of fruit squash. He hoisted it up and gulped down a long drink. We both rested for a few minutes and then set off again. This time I found myself in the lead.

A bit further along I spotted a mahogany-red, cow-like figure set on a yellow rock panel on the hill above. I clambered over some broken boulders that were heaped at the base of the hill and scrambled up the rough scree slope, hoping that the loose rocks wouldn't give way under my feet. Near the top was a vertical slab. It looked a bit tricky until I spotted a couple of footholds on one side. Grabbing onto the roots of a bush, I hauled myself up to a wide platform, invisible from below. There were paintings at either end. The cow turned out to be the side view of a rhinoceros. Facing it on the opposite wall was the profile of another large animal, something like an eland bull but without the horns. The back of this animal was solid red, a symbol of potency; at its front a dorsal crest of hair extended up to a small pair of ears. Spiky hair in Bushman paintings is thought to signify an abundance of spiritual power similar to that generated in trance dancing. It is seen in several depictions of dying game animals. I wondered if this was the painting on Child much valued by the Ncae Bushmen, the original inhabitants of the hills, because it still 'worked' for them. Exactly what they meant by 'worked' is not recorded. Perhaps these animals were rain bulls that helped the shamans pull down rain from the heavens, or maybe they energised the platform with *n/um* enabling the hunters to find their quarry – an eland painting for a flesh-and-blood eland and a rhino painting for its living counterpart. In the Drakensberg Mountains of South Africa is a painting of a shaman directly superimposed on an eland which is thought to symbolise the spiritual connection between the two.[6] Other paintings, half human and half animal, with symbolic wounds suggest use of sympathetic magic to assist in the hunt.[7] Could some kind of telepathic connection have originated here between a hunter and some unknown game animal that had wandered into the Bushman's territory? I felt nothing stir within, no inner thrill of recognition, not even here in this remote platform on Child.

After a day of exploring, we walked back to camp in the gathering dusk and lit a fire to cook supper. I was even more dehydrated than before. There was dust in the food, in our hair, in our clothes, in our sleeping bags, in everything. There was no escape from the constant heat. It was exhausting. Stu chucked over a tin of beer and slumped onto a canvas stool. I pulled a jerry can out of Nomad as a makeshift seat. Popping open the warm beers, the talk turned to the central enigma of the silent hills.

'What do you make of this place?' I asked.

'Pretty much what you see – a bunch of rocks with some paint daubed on them.'

'And that's it?'

'I suppose you think it's all deeply spiritual and significant?'

I didn't want to trade insults but I was interested in what Stu really thought about the place. 'Why do you think the Bushmen left these hills?'

'Being greedy bastards, they probably over-hunted the game,' said Stu with a smirk.

'But they must have lived in some kind of balance first. I mean they were here for thousands of years.' I shifted on the jerry can which was digging into my bum.

'So everything went swimmingly, and then what? I suppose you're going to say the gods left them.'

'More likely a failure in ecology.'

'Well that's reassuring.'

'I reckon it began to change when the pastoralists arrived with their herds of livestock.' I explained how the hunter-gatherers would have been dependent on wild foods and that in a place like Tsodilo, which is effectively an island in the desert, they would have been careful not to over-harvest. But for the pastoralists it was different. They could safely hunt out local game animals as they had an abundant source of alternative food – their livestock.

Stu pulled out a folder of rolling tobacco. Despite the plastic covering, the baccy was dry and crumbly but his practised fingers soon manufactured a cigarette. He lit up and inhaled the hot smoke. 'You think these pastoralists wrought merry havoc on the local wildlife knowing they could tuck into roast goat once the venison ran out.'

'Pretty much,' I nodded. 'They left the poor sods up in these hills with no standby, other than the dassies that is.'

'Then they polished off the dassies because there was nothing left to eat?'

'Maybe they ate them and maybe they traded their woolly coats for meat. Either way, once the dassies were gone that was it. They walked off into the desert.'

'Carnage!'

'Did you know the dassie was the wife of their trickster God?[28] Imagine how it must have felt to be abandoned by your God.'

'Flippin' 'eck,' said Stu. 'Here we go.'

I went round to the back of Nomad and fetched two more beers. 'I've been wondering about the spirits that are supposed to haunt these hills.'

Stu shook his head sadly. 'If you get any premonitions, shake the pods,' he advised. 'It's wonderful how it clears the mind.'

'I've felt nothing menacing here, not even spooky.' I took a long swig of beer. The second one tasted much better. 'Well that's not quite true. I did feel something in zebra cave. It was like the memory of a time long ago, of something wonderful.' That feeling still lingered but it was hard to convey. 'And one other thing, there's a sense of desolation here. It's everywhere… a bit like the brooding emptiness of Culloden Moor.'

The mention of Culloden seemed to get through to Stu. He knew all about the massacre of Highland clansmen at the battle there in 1746. Rather than dismiss my speculation, he turned the conversation to near-death experiences and asked whether I thought there was evidence of self-evaluation at the end. But like me, he was exhausted by the constant heat and soon retired to his sleeping bag. Silence settled again over the empty hills and their hidden gallery of rock paintings. I settled down next to the fire.

For a while I lay in the sand by the embers: too tired to move, too restless to sleep. Why is Tsodilo so empty, I wondered? Could it be a harbinger of the great emptiness foreseen by the old-timer? The stars were again brilliant tonight, naked in the near absence of moisture. The Milky Way stretched far across heaven's dome. 'We who are fires, we must walk the sky; for we are heaven's things' is how one Bushman expressed his innermost feelings of connection to our universe. Adding about the shooting star, 'At the time when our heart falls down, that is the time when the star also falls down.'

Many stars have fallen since then, each small prayer diminishing the Bushman's galaxy, speeding its final eclipse.

9

The Filling Station

Etsha 6

ack on tarmac Nomad hummed down the panhandle highway just like
a family hatchback, as if the three days grinding through sand drifts
had never happened. If cars can have split personalities, Nomad had to
be a full-blown schizophrenic. We got on just great. Stu was fast asleep, making
the most of the smooth ride. At the sign to Etsha 6, we turned onto a small
track leading to a bush station on the edge of the delta with an all important
filling station. On arrival we found a white pick-up, loaded with empty cans and
drums, parked next to the only operational pump. Lounging in the back was a
cool-looking Tswana with curved sunglasses, close-cropped hair, black Cappa
tracksuit top, shiny pilot-style trousers and sneakers. I avoided the hard long
stare he gave me as we pulled in and waited for our turn.

At a guess, Mr Cool was filling the week's order for a small village further up
the delta – some of his containers for boat engines, others for motorbikes, maybe
one for a tractor and so on. I turned my attention to the pump attendant who
was flirting with the driver. She had a languid way of moving, accentuated by the
cropped top that clung to her lean belly and tight leather skirt. Framed by high
cheekbones and a shock of wild hair, her wide dark eyes knew full well the effect
they were having on Mr Cool. I didn't suppose my surreptitious gaze concealed
the effect she was having on me. A number of guys without vehicles were

standing nearby, a couple with empty cans; others just seemed to be hanging out. The attendant ignored these riff-raff. One of them had a container with a plastic bag stuffed in the top as a replacement for a screw cap; he had a sullen air about him. When he started to walk in our direction, it was a sure bet he intended to hustle some deal. I considered my next move. Nomad was full of gear, some of which could be damaged if petrol was spilt, or if it were shoved to one side. The guy didn't impress me. I resolved not to give him a lift, nor to make any pointless excuses. There was plenty of other traffic about. He could wait for the bus, or continue with whatever plan he had in mind before we pulled up.

'Where are you heading?' he asked staring me in the eye.

'South,' I replied, keeping a nice easy tone.

'I'm going to Gumare canoe camp with this,' he nodded at the petrol can. 'You can give me a lift to the turn-off.'

Well no subtleties there I thought, but that made it easier. 'No,' I replied.

There was a long pause as we both waited for me to continue with a weak excuse that could then be argued over. Nothing happened. Then the guy turned his head a fraction to look in the back of Nomad.

'Oh I see, you are too full,' he said.

'Yes,' I agreed. And that was that. I felt okay about it. He looked okay about it. We could both differentiate a needless hustle from a genuine request.

Meanwhile the pick-up had taken on board 250 litres and had one last can to fill: a large blue container sitting behind the cab and right in the middle where it was hard to reach from the sides. The attendant handed the petrol nozzle over to the Tswana who was still staring at me. Reluctantly he poked the nozzle into the empty can and then kept on staring, but at others now, and he continued to look cool and mean. Another pick-up pulled in behind, carrying two goats in the back, feet tethered so they couldn't jump out. One of them struggled and let out a hideous wailing cry, more like a human in distress than a goat's bleat. Everyone's attention was on the newcomers and it was a moment or two before it dawned simultaneously on me and the attendant that Mr Cool didn't know how to squeeze the trigger on the pump handle. He was just sitting there holding the nozzle, looking elsewhere and pretending all was well. With a scornful look, the attendant grabbed the nozzle from him. The incident was not missed by the others. Mr Cool had lost credibility and was beginning to look ever so slightly uncomfortable, but the final ignominy was yet to come. After paying for the petrol, not a simple task because of the multiple receipts, he climbed out of the pick-up and took up a shoving position at the rear. The driver shouted a command and Mr Cool began heaving with all his might, pushing the pick-up slowly off the forecourt onto the street where the engine fired once and finally caught. He jumped quickly into the back to take up his commanding position again, but by this time no-one was bothering to look. The attendant wedged herself in between Nomad and the pump at a kind of interesting angle, adjusted the tilt of her breast, and the amount of naked midriff showing, and looked around nonchalantly. For a moment her dark eyes met mine. Then she raised her left leg and laid the nozzle of the pump across her bare thigh so that the end fitted easily into the filler. In a slow sinuous movement, her long fingers eased round the pump handle, and squeezed.

'Fuck'n nora!' said Stu who had been watching with his mouth half open. 'She can fill me up any time.'

With the desert scrubland zipping past once more, I considered whether to keep heading south which would take us into the heartland of the Kalahari, or to turn left at the next junction towards Maun, which was on the way to Zimbabwe. It was the last day of October. Time was slipping by.

'The rains will be coming soon,' I announced suddenly.

'Does that matter?' asked Stu, pulling out his tobacco pouch and rolling a mini smoke.

'It's easy to get stuck if you're driving off-road.'

'Carnage…' he muttered, catching a glimpse of our impending fate.

'We better head north.'

Stu opened the road atlas and turned a few pages. 'That's Maun then?'

I sighed. 'I want to see Kalahari Bushmen.'

'That's not Maun then?'

'Maybe there's still time.'

'Well I'm happy to tag along, whatever harebrained scheme you come up with,' said Stu, taking a deep draw.

Not for the first time, I was grateful for his freewheeling approach to life. 'Alright,' I decided, 'we'll go looking for Bushmen.'

'That should be a piece of piss out here,' Stu remarked, gazing at the unending horizons of the Kalahari Desert.

'Let's head for Maun first. Hopefully we can pick up some leads there.'

'Yesterday it was the hottest place on the planet,' said Stu who was keeping up with the international news on his shortwave radio.

In spite of the heat, I was keen to visit Maun for another reason. It had been a long time since I'd heard from Isla and I couldn't help worrying about her. Two hours later, as we entered the range of the local cellphone network, I picked up a text message.

> Howdydoodie dad? I had a math test 2day - very hard. The boarding house goes 2 pizzahut tonight as it is halloween, makes a change from watching neighbours! love isla xoxox.

It was reassuring to know she was having some fun. I could just imagine her shepherding the youngsters to the outing. Isla stood up fiercely for the underdog at school and made a conscious effort to be friendly with the younger girls, who all knew her by name. The teachers adored her, except for the odd one she didn't get on with. I suspected she made their life hell. Isla had started there when she was seven and some of the teachers now took almost as much interest in her progress as did I. The school definitely had its plus points even if I couldn't persuade them to start a nature club. For most of the teachers nature was a nuisance, a deadly combination of pressed flowers and grubby children.

I missed Isla and Torran, but having this time to myself was doing me good. I hadn't realised how much I needed it. Life had become very busy back home with little time to breathe, little time to notice the changes or to work out where I was heading.

10

A Tale of Two Stories

Molapo hut

After two days asking around Maun we had learnt nothing useful about the whereabouts of mobile Bushmen. The conservation organisations couldn't help, the tour operators hadn't a clue and the only anthropologist was out of town. On our last evening Stu and I were invited to a meal at the camp of a safari operator who was reputed to know the back country better than any. The camp turned out to be a large dusty compound with colourful bell tents and tough overland trucks clustered under a scattering of hardy acacias. At one end was a patch of green grass that must have been watered daily and next to it a thatched bar. A long wooden table with bench seats was set for dinner on the lush lawn. The silver-haired chief sat at its head holding court over a group of overlanders, his air of easy authority occasionally sabotaged by cheeky schoolboy expressions. Picking up a Castle lager at the bar, I squeezed onto one of the benches. The chief was in full flow. Conversation sped from car mechanics to human evolution, to MP3 sound systems, to wildlife ecology, to African politics at a dizzying pace. Stu jumped in with glee enjoying the cut and thrust. He found common ground with the chief in his criticism of the Western conservation movement transfixed by its own self-image. I swatted at the mosquitoes which had developed a heady fascination for my ankles and wondered how to broach the subject of mobile

Bushmen. Back in Scotland I would have been enthralled by the fast-moving conversation; now that I had time to breathe slowly, my mental horizons ought to have been expanding but instead my world was shrinking. I just wanted to find a band of lost Bushmen. The moon riding high above our camp was a lucent crescent. I could imagine a little group looking up at it from their faraway corner of the Kalahari. A roll of clicks, pops and smacks roused me; to my surprise the chief had mastered a smattering of !Khung. He soon confirmed what I was beginning to suspect. The last of the mobile Bushman inhabited a huge area of the central and southwestern Kalahari but were shy of strangers due to accusations of overhunting and harassment by the game department. They were not going to be easy to find. Our best bet was to head for Ghanzi and ask around there.

The road from Maun to Ghanzi was in excellent condition. Having scooped a fortune from the country's diamond deposits, the government to its credit had invested in public works. Thanks to the diamonds we reached Ghanzi by early afternoon. The town centre looked surprisingly prosperous for such a small outpost: the streets were filled with shoppers, traders and scores of children in smart blue uniforms. There was a mixture of races in the throng: several Bantu tribes including Hereros with their wide 'Admiral Nelson' head costumes, a few Bushmen and the occasional European. We pulled up outside the Kalahari Arms Hotel and I dived quickly into its darkened interior. By luck I found the manager in the lobby and asked him if he knew the whereabouts of the First People of the Kalahari, an organisation of Bushmen that promotes their own cause. The proprietor looked a bit uncertain but directed me to a nearby backstreet. We found the street without difficulty and eventually located a rundown building at one end with empty rooms. A bystander suggested we try the coordinator's house which was out near the airport. We managed to find this too, only to learn that the coordinator was attending a meeting in Gaborone and would be away all week. When it came to finding desert Bushmen, Ghanzi was proving to be no more fruitful than Maun. We decided to stay the night at a nearby camp and continue our enquiries next day.

Thakadu Camp is a welcome oasis in the dry reaches of the western Kalahari. It provides a retreat for the occasional traveller and a few regulars who want to escape the noise and traffic of town. They can sit in the shade of leadwood trees with a glass of beer and a plate of home-cooked food and watch the wildlife coming and going at a small watering hole. The campsites are laid out to the southeast of the bar where the Kalahari stretches unbroken to the far horizon. The only feature distinguishing a campsite from the surrounding bush is a small dressing of creamy sand that makes an ideal surface for pitching a tent. Our camp was furthest away and shaded by a large leadwood with a pale grey trunk that was knotted and gnarled with age. It added a kind of knobbly noblesse to the common scrub surrounding it. After a plate of chips at the bar, we called it a day.

Poking my head out the tent early next morning, I breathed in draughts of crisp desert air whilst admiring the glow of caramel sky in the east that heralded a grand Kalahari sunrise. A vivid chorus of bird song had already commenced. The campfire was soon rekindled and by the time the vulture roosting above had begun to stir I'd already made tea. Stu roused himself, downed a cuppa and headed off for a shower. I went over to the bar for coffee and to continue the unrewarding hunt for mobile Bushmen. The camp's safari guide telephoned a friend at the nearby Bushman mission who recommended that we go back to Tsodilo taking one of their staff, 'Sixpence Sixpence'. This didn't appeal much. The Drotskys had warned us that the Tsodilo Bushmen were role-acting for tourists and had advised us to push on into the central Kalahari. Last night the manager of Thakadu Camp had suggested we drive to Ukwi Pan further to the south, set up camp there, and wait to see what happened. I walked over to one of the tables overlooking the waterhole to think it over whilst consoling myself with the knowledge that our difficulties were not unique. Early anthropological expeditions reported endless complications in finding mobile Bushmen. Nobody it seemed really knew where they were, and probably that was exactly how the Bushmen, assuming they still existed, wished it to be. We had one last card. Before I left UK, an anthropologist had given me the name of a Bushman friend who used to live for part of the year in Ghanzi. I only had a name, but maybe it would be enough.

In the afternoon we drove into town passing a sports arena (another diamond gift) and new service station, and headed out on the airport road. On impulse, I stopped at the first suburban house with well-trimmed lawns and asked a teenager who was hanging about in the yard if he knew Roy Sesana. Amazingly he did, and even agreed to take us to his house. Turning onto a rough dirt track we left the smart suburbs behind and entered the enveloping thorn scrub; after a short distance we crossed a railway line, arriving at a slummy area of broken-down tents and shacks. It looked something like an abandoned refugee camp. There were no trees or buildings, just a depressing vista of scrub, rubbish and shit. A couple of thin dogs were mooching about amongst some tin cans.

'Jeepers,' said Stu, 'nothing but carnage.'

I had to agree. 'Welcome to the Bushman's world in the 21st century.'

Following our guide's directions we drove past several hovels, entered a small compound with a ragged wire fence and pulled up, dust billowing all about. Facing us was a tiny metal hut standing under the full glare of the sun. Without so much as a window, it must have been like a furnace inside. A door with peeling paint hung half-open from one hinge. Crouched in the doorway peering out at us, was a Bushman with a big grin. I couldn't help but smile back.

He disappeared inside. Moments later he reappeared with two plastic chairs which he placed in the thin strip of shade next to the hut. We sat down to talk.

'Where are you from?' Roy asked looking steadily at me from wide crinkly eyes, filled with laughter and interest.

'From UK,' I replied, adding after a short pause 'I heard your story coming from afar, and have come to see you.' It was not quite the greeting recommended by Laurens van der Post, but it was the best I could do.

Roy smiled broadly and then turned to say something to a young woman hovering in the doorway behind. She came forward and introduced herself in excellent English as Roy Sesana's wife, Bulanda Thamae. With Bulanda acting as interpreter, I began to tell Roy about my journey from Cape Town. He listened closely and I found myself telling him all about my interest in the Bushmen's relationship with nature and how I believed their story might have unforeseen importance for the Western world. None of this seemed to surprise Roy. He said something to Bulanda in his own click language.

'Roy would like you to go to Molapo settlement in the central Kalahari,' said Bulanda. 'You can visit his brother and meet some of the G//ana and G/wi people.[1] They are living as mobile foragers for much of the year. But he is sorry that he cannot come with you. Some visitors from Survival International are coming here the day after tomorrow.' Without waiting for my response she turned back to Roy to discuss the matter further. 'Roy has asked me to accompany you with "Emergency", his oldest son from his first marriage. He says that you will want to ask many questions, and that I can interpret for you.'

As I thanked Bulanda and Roy, a baby cried from inside the hut. We were shortly introduced to Arthur, aged 11 months, and then to Markus, aged six, who had been playing outside with other children. Evidently we were going to have quite a carful. Just then a woman came running down the dirt road, arms waving and shrieking, as if possessed. She rushed up to Roy's compound, ripping off all her clothes on the way and started to roll about naked in the dust, over and over, legs akimbo, still shouting.

Roy was in stitches.

'She's pissed as a fart!' observed Stu.

Back at Thakadu Camp, I tried to reassure Stu. 'It will be quite different in the Kalahari, more like visiting an old encampment of Tsodilo rock artists.' Knowing that he had been enjoying *The Harmless People* by Elizabeth Marshall Thomas, I mentioned that her mother had recognised similarities between the scenes depicted in rock paintings in South Africa and the contemporary lives of the Kalahari Bushmen. The people she studied used the same bows and arrows, wore the same clothing, and carried bags just like those depicted in the paintings. They had similar dance formations. Even their postures looked the same, so much so that she had felt a direct link with our distant past.[2]

'Do these Bushmen in the Kalahari not paint at all?' asked Stu, obviously stirred by the prospect of meeting such people after all our discussions.

'No, it doesn't seem to be part of their culture. Of course the absence of rocks doesn't help.'

'True, unless they did really really small paintings…'

'Lorna Marshall said that their art today is expressed in music.'

'Desert songs rather than rock music then,' quipped Stu, once again in buoyant mood.

Next morning we picked up Bulanda and family early and set off for Molapo. The drive began innocently enough on a rough but manageable double track with well-compressed sand. We were entertained by continuous chatter from Bulanda who was in the back with baby Arthur on her lap. Whenever I asked a question, she answered with clarity and intelligence but sooner or later brought the conversation round to some incident of disadvantage: how Bushmen were being oppressed by government or cheated by local Bantu businessmen, how women were exploited by men and how she herself had been treated unfairly by employers and ill-used by tourists. Before long we turned onto a single ungraded track with an undulating surface of soft sand that restricted our speed to about 20 kilometres per hour. It was as bad as the road to Tsodilo. The same ridges of sand set up the same sickening motion: woomm – woomm – woomm. Nomad rebounded dangerously on her springs. I reduced speed further, conscious that the ride must be even more uncomfortable in the back. The sun rose higher stoking the temperature inside the cab; slowly we toiled through the stunted Kalahari bushland.

Bulanda prattled on, spicing long-winded accounts of injustice with several lurid tales of sexual exploitation in which imagination seemed to transcend reality, and always there was an undertone of victimisation. I reminded myself that she was raised in an urban setting, and that life could not have been easy given all the problems that beset an underclass. Stu was uncharacteristically quiet. Sandwiched in the back between baby Arthur on one side, and Markus on the other, with various bags and belongings competing for space, he had become a biddable source of tobacco for Bulanda who, like all Bushmen, loved to smoke. I felt for the guy. Soon, Arthur decided it was time to perform. We stopped to change his nappy; the dirty one was hung out the window to dry. I noticed that a hole had appeared in Nomad's rear seat where a burning cigarette had melted its way into the nylon fabric, but said nothing. A bottle of insipid water was passed around. In this uncomfortable way we rolled slowly along – hot, smoky, smelly and squashed tightly together. I kept searching for a place to stop and rest, but there were no trees tall enough to offer shade, and the only thing that kept the temperature half bearable in the car was our forward motion. Bulanda plonked Arthur on Stu's knee whilst lighting up one of his cigarettes. He (Arthur that is) started to wail. Glancing in the mirror, Stu looked desperate. Later he recalled it as being the most awful trip he had ever endured. In the front, Emergency and I had a slightly easier ride. My thoughts wavered between wondering what we would find in Molapo and worrying whether Nomad could cope with the harsh desert crossing. Every now and then we passed a big patch of tsama, the prolific desert melon and a vital source of water for Bushmen and desert animals alike.

After jolting along for a few more hours we arrived at the Xade ranger post, which marks the main entrance into the Central Kalahari Game Reserve.[3] Here at last were a couple of tall trees. Bulanda introduced us to the officer-in-charge who was standing by the gate in a smart uniform. Despite the heat he looked alert; in fact there was a distinctly astute air about him. Learning of our interest in wildlife he invited us over to some chairs in the shade of the largest tree. One after another we took long gulps of crystal water that gushed from a large brass tap next to the chairs. It was cool and sweet. It must have issued from a deep underground aquifer, a minor miracle in the Kalahari Desert.

'How do you expect the rangers and me to control the illegal cattle in the reserve,' the officer-in-charge demanded in a perfect Oxbridge accent, 'if the place is full of Bushman settlements where livestock are permitted?'

'Well,' I paused, wondering why a highly-educated officer should be posted at an entrance gate with barely one visitor per day to keep him occupied. I shrugged off the thought and gathered my wits as best I could. 'As I understand it the reserve was created to provide Bushmen with a choice of lifestyles.' Ridiculously I found that I had become more Oxbridge in my response.

'It was also created to protect wildlife and that is the primary responsibility of my department.'

'True enough,' I agreed, 'and if the Bushmen believe you are on their side, they will help you to catch the cattle rustlers.' No matter how dazed I felt by the midday temperature and the bizarre meeting place, I was keen to show that there is more than one way to look at wildlife problems. The officer-in-charge smiled broadly, clearly delighted to have found a sparring partner.

'Perhaps,' he said. 'But this is a game reserve, you know, and if they cannot hunt in a traditional way then how can we call them our friends?'

'From what I've heard, more animals are killed by outside poachers than by Bushmen.'[4]

The officer-in-charge peered at me closely, wondering whether to challenge my claim, but then changed tack. 'Answer me this, then,' he demanded. 'Why do the Bushmen not want to be settled outside of the reserve? They would have better access to health clinics and their children could go to school.'

'How can I answer that question,' I replied, 'when I am only a visitor here.'

The officer-in-charge smiled benignly and continued to press his point in the same suave style. 'But you would agree that it is in their interests to move?'

'There is no harm in trying to persuade people, or to educate them as to the facts of your case,' I replied, 'but it is not okay to force them to move somewhere against their will.'

'No one is forcing them,' the officer-in-charge responded quickly. 'But you must remember,' and his voice now deepened with authority, 'that government has jurisdiction over this reserve and can do exactly as it pleases.'

'Good government represents its people; it doesn't dictate to them,' I countered.

'Yes,' agreed the officer-in-charge, his voice back to its friendly engaging tone. 'And we have a good government.'

'Then, I feel sure it will not dictate to Bushmen. You will not force them out of their own reserve against their wishes.'

The officer-in-charge smiled thinly, no doubt unconvinced by my arguments. He went over to the office and returned with entry permits, waving us on towards Molapo with a stony expression. I was still riled by our conversation.

'You know Stu the wildlife department has some pretty underhand ways of getting these Bushmen to leave the reserve. A favourite trick is to sit down with the family and tell them that all the other families have decided to move, so they better sign up too.'

'Yeah,' said Stu. 'I can just imagine that.'

Bulanda had been sitting quietly smoking one of Stu's cigarettes. Now she sat up straight. 'That's right,' she said. 'They threatened us too. The man said, "You don't have to move, but then we can't help it if the soldiers come back and give you a hard time." So what choice did we really have?'

'I heard about one meeting,' I said, 'which brought together representatives from all the Bushmen in the reserve. An official put the case for moving the Bushmen out. At the end of his speech, the audience just sat there: they were sullen, but too polite to say anything.'

'I know about this meeting,' said Bulanda.

'Well, after a long silence, one ancient Bushman got up and made a joke. "We are nomadic people, are we not? We always move around. So why not move one more time, as the government wants." The meeting cracked up. Bushmen love a joke, and this one released all that tension. The official quickly seized this opportunity to say, "Great, then we have an agreement," and he pushed through the resolution.'

'What a cheap trick,' retorted Stu.

As we bounced slowly along the track, I thought about my conversation with the officer at the gate. Bushmen have occupied the Kalahari continuously for some 2,000 years[5] and those that remain have a better knowledge of its natural resources and their management than any modern conservationist. Rather than being 'persuaded' to live in urban centres adopting a lifestyle that diminishes their self-esteem, surely some could be permitted to live inside the reserve, acting as its conservators. Employing a few as junior rangers would not be sufficient as it would reinforce their subservient role in modern Botswana. Bushmen should have the right to use their land as they see fit, just as all the other tribal peoples do. They deserve the opportunity to manage wildlife in their own reserve in a way that emerges from their own self-expression.

By late afternoon conversation in Nomad was reduced to occasional croaks for water. Just when all hope of reaching Molapo had vanished, our track joined an ancient desert valley enabling us to pick up speed on its smooth compacted soil. A gemsbok lifted its head but fled as we slowed to look. A few minutes later, I noticed our track was heading towards a grove of trees that stood out boldly in the short grassland. Driving up, we found a hidden spring with half a dozen horses standing in a shallow pool of fresh water; a herd of springbok grazed on the far side. Markus stared at the antelope in excitement, placing his hands on his head, forefingers raised like horns; he bounced up and down on Bulanda's lap to imitate the way springbok leap. As we watched, a white Land Rover passed by at speed heading towards the entry gate. In the back was a large drum of dried meat.

'From a gemsbok,' said Bulanda. 'Molapo is near.'

Perhaps a little trade here for the officer-in-charge, I thought to myself.

We turned down an even smaller track and a mile later came across a scattering of round huts, thatched in loose yellow hay and varying in height from about six to eight foot. It was Molapo. Bulanda informed us that there were 500 people here when everyone was present and that by and large they maintained their traditional lifestyle, avoiding outside ways. Passing a herd of 20 goats, we came to a halt at the farthest edge of the settlement in front of a large hut belonging to Roy's first wife. Protocol dictated that Bulanda awaited her return before we set up camp. I took the opportunity to look around. Next to the main hut were two slightly smaller ones and an empty paddock made from rough sticks. A screen of thorn bushes was stacked around the main hut and the door was barricaded with large branches, presumably as a defence against lions, or maybe to prevent ravenous goats from eating the home. It reminded me of a painting in Isla and Torran's book of nursery rhymes that illustrates the tale of 'Three Little Pigs'. The main hut was like the house made of straw. Maybe it would be strong enough to keep out the big bad wolf but I doubted it would stop a hungry lion.

Molapo was definitely not a shanty town. There were no lumps of concrete or bits of broken glass, no rusty strands of wire or battered pieces of corrugated iron, nor was there any plastic, tins or other rubbish lying about. The grass huts simply blended into the desert sands. The next little grouping of huts was a good

200 metres away and barely noticeable. It gave the place a feeling of spaciousness that the inhabitants must surely enjoy. I was immediately charmed by Molapo. No wonder those who lived here were resisting government pressure to settle in urban ghettos. Who wants to exchange space and sovereignty for subservience and squalor? As we waited, someone galloped past on horseback.

Seeing that it would soon be dark we decided to find Molathwe Mokalake, the village headman. In fact spokesman would be a more apt title, for decisions in Bushman society invariably involve open discussion. We set off in the direction taken by the galloping horse. The headman's hut was somewhat smaller and scruffier than the others, just as might be expected in a society where envy is abhorred and people laugh at pretentiousness.[6] Molathwe came out to greet us as we pulled up, the big baggy wrinkles under his eyes stretching almost to his smile creases. Bulanda did the introductions and at the headman's invitation we sat down in a circle on the sand whilst he perched on a throne, an old 20-litre oil drum that provided a small, but not excessive, amount of status. Up there, he looked like a friendly old hawk. As Bulanda continued with her long introductions, he listened attentively, uttering 'Emmm' at each pause in a deep throaty voice. An occasional smile played across the corners of his mouth, 'Emmm' he said, 'Emmmm'. Whilst this was going on, I tried to find a comfortable sitting position. I've never been much good at yoga, lacking the patience for hours of slow practice, and so sitting in the lotus position wasn't an option. I tried leaning back on both arms, then kneeling with bottom on ankles, followed by slouching sideways on an elbow. Finally I grasped both knees to keep upright, put up with the discomfort, and took another look at Molathwe. He was wearing a red woolly hat with a gold ring in each ear; on his wrists were sky-blue bangles. Long brown trousers and a pair of old sandals completed the gypsy-like appearance. Eventually Bulanda turned to say that Molathwe was happy to meet us and especially pleased that we had come with Roy's wife and elder son, rather than showing up 'as a tourist simply to gaze at him'.

The headman's wife now appeared from inside the darkened hut and sat at the doorway. She was small and stooped and had a face creased with years. Her left eye was held shut – perhaps from an injury. She seemed quite at ease in our company and although her patterned shawl had seen better times, its cheerfulness matched the twinkle in her good eye.

We offered the headman a few small gifts that others had advised us to bring: a dozen rolls of local tobacco, several packets of sugar and a tub of salt. I included a scroll with detailed tracings from a famous South African rock painting. He accepted the bag graciously and, without looking inside, gave it to his wife who placed it within the darkened hut. The gifts would doubtless be handed around to others before long. One by one, other Bushmen arrived at our gathering. A white-bearded man with a big grin and laughter in his eyes walked up confidently and sat down near the doorway of the hut. He was introduced as the eldest son. A beautiful young woman approached from another direction, hips swaying to the rhythm of her walk. She sat down too, but a little to one side. Three or four more men arrived. Stu offered each of them a cigarette which was enthusiastically accepted only to be secreted away in a fold of clothing for later enjoyment, or sharing perhaps. Stu didn't seem offended. In fact there was a pleasant feeling of harmony in our little group.

When Bushmen hunters return to the camp carrying a kill, such as an eland or gemsbok, portions of meat are handed out to others in the band, sub-divided and passed on again, all according to a strict protocol which ensures that everyone has sufficient and all are united. When anthropologists suggested to the !Kung that they might eat meat *without* sharing it, the idea was so shocking that it made them 'shriek with an uneasy laughter'.[7] Imagine a world in which lending your car to a neighbour, or inviting them in for a meal, was as much a daily part of life as stopping at a red light. When giving, Bushmen consider the needs of the other person above the value of the gift.[8] Should that person have little tobacco, for instance, and need to share whatever he gets with others later on, then more is given. So Stu was doing the customary thing in handing out his cigarettes. For us in the West, it is more often the possession rather than the sharing of things that lends prestige. The needs of the recipient are usually ignored or perversely, should there be a strong demand, the price is hiked higher. Our pharmaceutical companies find it difficult to provide affordable drugs in Africa even when the poor are dying of need. The nearest many Westerners come to the Bushman's way of thinking is at Christmas, when family members and close friends give each other presents. In this festival, the politics of giving and sharing override the politics of possession. Part of the Christmas festival has been traced to the traditions of the reindeer peoples who inhabit the tundra and steppes of northeastern Siberia.[9] It seems only fitting that our yuletide traditions may be derived from the customs of nomadic herders and hunter-gatherers.

One of the men had something to say and began addressing his remarks to the horizon in a strong, quiet voice; a smile hovered on his lips. It transpired that there was anxiety about our accompanying them on a hunting expedition due to a recent incident involving the wildlife department.[10] The eldest son replied in an easy confident tone. I had the impression that he had sensed my disappointment.

Bushmen are practised at discerning the most subtle variation of mood. One anthropologist described how they could read cues as slight and fleeting as the momentary set of a man's neck muscles, from which they knew that he had struck a difficulty in his work, and would now require a period without distraction.[11] Social disharmony is dreaded, and stealing is feared above all

Above: A storm rising

Left: Ocean swell driving up against Cape Point

Below: On my first day on the road I came across this glorious Cape Protea

Hands wave and breasts swing as the women shuffle along to the throbbing,
pulsating rhythms that fill the shelter

Left: The hunter pursues his
diminutive quarry whilst
Mum looks on, helpless with a
broken limb

Below: A forest of ostrich heads
followed my every move

Above: Ostrich POW

Right: Feathered flowers in the desert scrub of Namaqualand

Below: Bushman cave in the Erongo Mountains

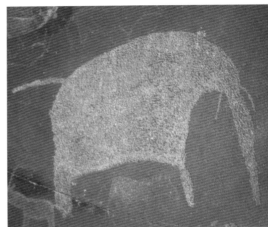

The big baggy elephant

The author in front of a panel of rock
engravings at Twyfelfontein

I came face to face with
a snarling leopard

Hidden dream pool

Mythic figure

Above: On three sides, the Kalahari stretches out to meet the sky in a far-off hazy union and on the fourth lies 'Female' and 'Child'

Pointing a way into the rock wall

Bleeding 'eck, it's a whale! Stuart Blackman on top form at the Tsodilo Hills

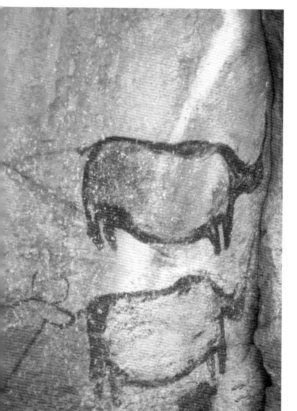

A lion that didn't play by the usual rules

Molapo women foraging in the Kalahari

Roots and tubers are staple foods

The root baby

Large burrow or den with scattered
tsama melons

Okavango elephant

Red hartebeest resting in Etosha

Peter Mundy in the Matopo Hills

Peeping out from a thicket near to the Okavango River
was a little pointed face above a fluffy rufous body

because it may lead to fighting which is easily lethal when poisoned arrows are close to hand. Differences are usually resolved in bouts of verbal sparring that can run on all night. All types of rhetorical device feature in these gloves-off encounters, including quotations of past speech, mutterings, loud complaints addressed to a bystander, and simultaneous talking. The need for total openness in discussion is backed by the belief that to hide something is a grave vice. As one old G/wi man put it: 'If you hide anything from people, it extinguishes the camp… Such a thing killed my grandfather and his people.'[12] Occasionally a song is composed to express disapproval about someone's behaviour and sung at night from the deepest shadows of the encampment.[13] This is said to be very effective. The most potent sanction however is group disapproval coupled with a mild form of ostracism.

Others present at our gathering now joined in the open forum and the conversation went back and forth until finally a plan was agreed. We would accompany a small group on a mixed foraging and hunting expedition the next morning, choosing a route that was not known to the wildlife officials. The group broke up with everybody happy.

Stu and I pitched our tents in a leafy grove some 60 metres from the hut of Roy's first wife. I started a fire and heated up meatballs and baked beans. Our only guest was one of the camp dogs, a charcoal-grey mongrel with long shaggy tail and pitifully exposed ribs. He lay quietly one metre behind Stu, waiting submissively until finally he was rewarded with some gravy on a slice of bread. We christened him 'Meatball'.

After supper Bulanda arrived with four other women and two men. Politely, they sat down at a little distance from our campfire, waiting to be invited over. By now Stu had run through his supply of packeted cigarettes but still had some reserves of finely cut tobacco. He began teaching everyone how to roll their own using delicate gummed papers. His audience mastered the trick quickly, tickled at this novel way of making a smoke. A few even lit up on the spot. Next the headman arrived choosing one of our camp-stools to sit on. With Bulanda's help, I asked how he would set about finding an animal to hunt. Molathwe seemed pleased to be asked such a straightforward question.

'Before we go hunting we consult with oracle bones, for if someone goes without consulting in this way, he will shoot and shoot and not kill a thing. Then he must realise that the hearts of the people in camp are not happy. So he will discuss this problem with the others; he may also pray to our ancestors. If he has prayed and still found nothing, he goes and digs up special roots and makes a potion. He says to the others, "I know you are still not happy with me". Then, everyone in the family bathes him in this potion. He also drinks it. We pour it over the bow, arrows and spear, and we pour the potion into the horses, and pray. Then he goes out with the horses and kills.'

'Are some of the animals that you hunt especially important?' I enquired.

'We respect all animals; but more than all the others, we respect the eland and the gemsbok.' Molathwe looked around at the women before continuing. 'The eland has nice meat, its skin can be used for blankets, and its fat has many uses. We put the fat on a baby to make it strong and healthy. If the baby becomes sick, we put fat in its ears, nose and mouth to make it better. When a woman menstruates, she uses fat to bathe. And if eland fat is poured into a fire, rain will come.'

'And when you hunt these special animals do you still use the bow and arrow?' I asked.

'We still use poisoned arrows,' Molathwe replied, 'and are not allowed to use guns. But even if there was no law against the gun, we would prefer to use our own method. Guns make too much noise. The animals run away; they become scared of guns. But with the bow and arrow they remain close.'

'If eland and gemsbok are highly prized, and your poisoned arrows are efficient weapons, do you not kill so many animals that their numbers decline?' I asked thinking of the accusations levelled by the officer at Xade Ranger Post.

Molathwe looked into the fire as if searching for something. 'Bushmen were created with animals, so we do not hunt them frequently. We know that certain animals must have their young at a particular time of the year. We do not hunt them in that season. We also gather roots in the right season, and we move from place to place before exhausting what is there.'

Not only did the G//ana Bushmen understand wildlife ecology, it governed their lives. I was beginning to appreciate how much there was to learn at Molapo.

On the spur of the moment, I asked Molathwe if he would tell us a story. At first he prevaricated. Then he asked for 50 Pula. Finally, seeing that everyone was eagerly watching him, he hunched down closer to the fire, stared into the flames again, and began. His voice had grown soft but respectful, in recognition of the high regard for stories in their culture.

'There was a place where the people had plenty of fine things, and one woman in particular had a big family and kept many goods. One day she collected a tsama melon whilst she was out walking. She carried it home and, taking out the seeds, she roasted them on the fire. One popped out of the fire and turned into a human. Then suddenly a large black beast came and devoured all of the woman's family and all her possessions, including that human who had been a tsama seed. The woman said "Oh! What can I do?" Then the great beast vomited out the human that had been a tsama seed, and went away.'

At this point, one of the old ladies who had been sitting near to the headman, flopped onto her front, putting her hands under her chin and began listening intently to the story. All the others were listening too. Taking my cue, I abandoned attempts to maintain a yoga sitting asana and with a sigh of contentment lay flat on my back.

'The woman said to the human that had been a tsama melon seed, "Go and find that great beast so that I may ask for my family back". And the human that had been a tsama melon seed, went looking, and came back with a hare and put it in some special trousers made of gemsbok hide, and gave it to the woman.[14] She said, "Oh no! This is not what I want. I want the great big beast that swallowed my family." And so the human that had been a tsama seed, went off, and in a little while came back with a steenbok, and put it in the gemsbok trousers. But the woman said, "No! This is not what I want either. I told you before that I want the great big beast that swallowed my family." So the human that had been a melon seed went off to look again, and this time came back with a duiker. But the woman said, "No! This is not what I want. I want the big, big beast that swallowed my family." So off went the human that had been a tsama seed. And when he came back he put a springbok in the trousers. The woman said, "No! You must not bring me these small animals. What I want is the big animal that ate my family." So the human that had been a tsama seed went off, and brought back a kudu and put it in the trousers. But still the woman was not pleased. "This is not what I want. I told you I want the great big animal that ate my family." So the human that had been a tsama seed went off and brought back a hartebeest and put it in the trousers. But the woman berated him again, saying, "This is not what I want. It is the great big black beast that I want." So the human that had been a seed went off again and this time he brought back an eland and put it in the trousers. The woman said, "You are not listening to me. What I want is the great big black beast that ate my family." So off went the human that had been a tsama seed and this time he brought back a giraffe. On seeing the giraffe, the woman was happy for a few moments but then she realised that this was not the right animal. "The beast that ate my family is big and very black too," she said. So the human that had been a melon seed went off and this time he came back with an elephant, and put it in the trousers. When the woman saw the elephant, she thought, "Oh! Is this the animal that ate my family?" And at first she was happy, but later she realised that this was not the right animal either, and she sent the human off to look again.'

'Now the human that had been a tsama seed was out walking in the bush, wondering where to find this big black beast that the woman wanted, when he came across some trees under which there was some deep black shade. It was so dark in the shade that he could not even see what was there. "I wonder if the beast that the woman wants is here in the shade," he thought to himself. So he took out the bones that he used to consult the spirits, and with their help he found that the great black beast was lying there in the shade. He plucked it from the shade and carried it home to the woman in the magic trousers. Then the beast vomited up the woman's family and all her possessions, and went away. The woman was happy at last. She was so happy to have her family back that she gave half of all her things to the human that had been a tsama seed.'

The night had grown cold, and our little band was now gathered tightly around the tiny fire. It was easy to see how important the campfire must be for the Bushmen. It brought everyone together. It was their café, pub, dance floor and committee room all rolled into one, but more intimate than any of these. How many times had this story of the tsama seed been told around a campfire in the heart of the Kalahari? The wisdom of generations must be held within these fables which serve as a kind of policy to guide the Bushman's actions. I had an uncomfortable feeling that in telling the story on this occasion, Molathwe has given me a lecture on the dangers of material greed in Western society. If so, it was a most gentle remonstration.

Stu suggested that we return the evening's 'flow' with a story of our own. I was ill-prepared, but sat up again and asked Molathwe if he would like to hear a British joke. He said he would be very pleased to hear one. So with Bulanda translating and Stu miming the various animals, I told them the story of the wide-mouthed frog, spinning it out and adapting it to the fauna of the Kalahari Desert.

'There was a frog who had a great big wide mouth. He was a happy frog but very curious.' There was some confusion in the translation at this point, but eventually everyone was satisfied, and I continued. 'One day he was hopping along a game trail in the Kalahari when he met a hare. "Hello!" he says. "I am the w-i-d-e mouthed frog," and he showed off his big fat grin.' Stu's animated impersonation of the frog was greeted with giggles from the children. '"I eat flies! Who are you and what do you eat?" "I am a hare," came the reply, "and I nibble on the wild flowers." "Oh how interesting!" says the frog, and he hops on down the path. Soon enough, he meets an eagle sitting on its nest. "Hello!" he says. "I am the w-i-d-e mouthed frog," and again he shows off his big fat grin. "I eat flies! Who are you, and what do you eat?" "I am an eagle," is the reply, "and I eat hares." "Oh, how very interesting!" says the frog, and he hops on down the path.' By now the Bushmen, children and elders alike, appeared totally absorbed in the tale. 'The next animal he meets is an aardvark. "Hello!" he says. "I am the w-i-d-e mouthed frog," and once again he shows off his big fat grin. "I eat flies! Who are you, and what do you eat?" "I am an antbear," is the reply, "and I eat termites." "Oh how interesting!" says the frog, and he hops on down the path. The next animal he meets is a hippopotamus.' There is general laughter at Bulanda's translation and I realised this wasn't the most inspired example of a desert animal – but it was too late to go back. '"Hello!" he says. "I am the w-i-d-e mouthed frog," and he shows off his big fat grin. "I eat flies! Who are you, and what do you eat?" "I am a hippopotamus," is the reply, "and I love to crop the grass next to my pool." "Oh my, how interesting!" says the frog, and he hops on down the path. The very next animal the frog comes across is a snake. "Hello!" he says. "I am the w-i-d-e mouthed frog," and again he shows off his big fat grin. "I eat flies! Who are you, and what do you eat?" "Sssss – I am a snake," is the reply, "and I eat w-i-d-e mouthed frogs." "Oooh!" says the frog, pursing his lips into a narrow 'o', "I've not seen any of those around here!"'

There were hoots of laughter from the audience, especially at Stu's frog performance. I suspected they were mostly being polite, but Stu told me later that our joke entirely changed the atmosphere, 'Afterwards it was more like a party to which we were all invited.' And I remembered that amongst the Bushmen, each person's story is respected for its own truth.[15]

11

RING OF BRIGHT PEOPLE

Making gooey liquid from a tsama melon

Awaking in the heart of the Kalahari within a ring of bright people in a sea of sand and scrub was surreal. From my hidden tent, I could hear sounds of village life stirring: the occasional bleat from a nearby flock of goats, a cock crowing in the direction of the headman's camp, children calling to each other outside the hut of Roy's first wife, and the distant braying of a donkey. It occurred to me that camping in Molapo, with all the elders gathered together, was like staying on the campus of a great Bushman university. Hopefully I would learn a bit more from the professors today. Rousing myself, I rekindled the fire and filled up the kettle from our precious supply of spring water. Meatball uncurled himself and came over to watch. Breakfast was basic – 'Weet-Bix' and UHT milk – but tasted fine; Meatball enjoyed a plate of milk too. Stu uncurled himself next and lent a hand with unpacking Nomad to provide room for our foraging party.

Before long Bulanda arrived with half a dozen Bushmen including some of those who visited yesterday. The men brought long thin rods for hooking out nocturnal mammals that hid deep in burrows during the day. Their preferred quarry was the springhare, a kangaroo-like rodent with large appealing eyes and soft bushy tail that bounds over the desert sands at night in search of roots and bulbs. Another favoured prey was the bat-eared fox, a gentle creature with a thick furry coat, pointed face and enormous cupped ears that can detect underground insects. The women brought their stout digging sticks and skin bags. We tied the thin rods along the side of Nomad and helped the women to climb in the back, laughing and chatting with a flurry of clicks and clucks. Most of the party were wearing Western-style clothes but one of the women, with a particularly wide smile, wore a kaross of softened antelope skin. I found it difficult to estimate their age: none were young. Perhaps the younger generation had moved to the urban ghettos on the fringes of the Kalahari. Unless Roy and the other elders brought about a resurgence of pride and purpose in the traditional Bushman customs, there would soon be no one to keep the old ways alive.

With the men directing we picked out a small footpath and, all aboard feeling rather pleased with themselves, slipped out of camp the back way. It was thrilling to be part of a Bushman expedition. We drove across hummocky ground with scattered shrubs for four or five miles, avoiding the many dips and hollows, before stopping in the shade of a small tree. Eager to be off, the women disgorged from the back of Nomad, spread out and began to search for roots. Within a minute there was a call from one of them. She had found a thin dry vine bent flat on the sand in amongst some thorn bushes. It was so insignificant I would never have noticed it, but to the G//ana 'the people of the well' it was a prize. 'Ga!' They called. There was much excited chatter and laughter. Rapid hand movements indicated the likely lie of the underground parts. Two, then three women began to dig into the hard sand; deftly wielding their digging-sticks they exposed the thin paired stalk as it descended underground. It reminded me of a group of medical students nimbly exposing a white nerve from the mass of surrounding tissue. Within minutes the three of them had scooped out a two-foot hole to reveal the upper part of a large brown tuber. At the sight of it, the woman with the kaross began to dig even more vigorously, squatting in front of the hole and scooping out great handfuls of sand that flew over her back, showering the rest of us. The men laughed in anticipation. Soon the 'Ga' was fully exposed, like a giant toad deep in its hole. Two women reached down, grasped it, and tugged. They kept heaving away until a root broke and the tuber shot out. Lifting it up in triumph, the women smacked it briskly with their palms to knock away the loose sand. One of them, Roy Sesana's first wife, seized the tuber, turned it over and bit with great relish into the white flesh where the root had broken off. 'Haiii!' shouted one of the men intoxicated by the sight. Another woman took the 'Ga', holding it in the air like a baby. It was about the size of a baby. It even had a baby's bottom. On one side there were two rounded sections that came together in just the right shape. The woman with the kaross grabbed it now, and she smacked it again while the men roared 'Ga!' in encouragement. I could feel the energy surging about our little group: primordial and potent yet somehow also playful and filled with joy. Turning it right side up, the woman placed it back in the hole, carefully covering it over with sand. Bulanda explained that in the coming rains it would double, and they would return to harvest part and replant the rest.

The G/wi memorise the location of many individual plants so that they can find food in different seasons, or at times of particular need. They are especially careful not to overharvest the large tubers. If the supply becomes scarce they refuse to gather more even if coming across a tempting specimen.[1] The close identification of Bushmen women with wild plants is delightfully illustrated in the caution given to Dia!kwain by his mother: 'Therefore, mother and the others said to us about it, that we ought not to go to the flowers which we see standing in the water, even if we see their beauty. For, they are the girls whom the Rain has taken away, they resemble flowers; for they are the water's wives, and we look at them, leaving them alone.'[2] The women have the same kind of respect for animals. If they come across a nest of ostrich eggs for example, they only take a small number, perhaps two or three from a nest of 10 or 15.[3]

Our four women now continued their search, crossing a meadow of tall dry grass, hands clinging lightly to their digging sticks, slung horizontally across the back of their shoulders. Several false holes were started and abandoned before more tubers were found, smaller ones, something like large white radishes. These were gathered up and stuffed inside skin bags together with some plants that looked like spring onions. There was a constant animated chatter amongst the group. Foraging in this meadow was the Stone Age equivalent of shopping in a supermarket. Only the women here did not store the food in their homes. Why should they when they viewed the entire Kalahari as a living food store.

It was hot and tiring work and after a couple of hours we gathered in the shade of a thorn tree, sitting down in a small circle. Not long ago death from dehydration was an ever-present threat for the Bushmen at this time of year and, according to the experts, a good supply of tsama melons was critical for their survival. Someone had gathered a dozen or more from roundabout. I chose a plump greeny-yellow one, about the size of a small cantaloupe and sliced off the top with my Swiss army knife. The woman with the kaross pulped the flesh for me using the rounded end of her digging stick to make a gooey liquid. As she worked away, bangles made from ostrich eggshell rattled on her wrists. She handed the melon back to me with a warm smile. I smiled in return but with one eye on the goo, which didn't look very appetising. I stuck a finger into the melon and scooped some slime into my mouth. It wasn't sweet or juicy, but nor was it sour or dry. It had a pleasant nondescript marrow type of flavour. It hardly seemed moist enough to keep up with my dehydration but, hoping that the experts knew what they were talking about, I set about relieving my thirst without the pleasure of drinking.

In a month or so it would be the season of little rains, when Bushmen feared starvation even more than dehydration. They might have to shift camp frequently, perhaps walking for two days or more to find supplies of tubers and game animals. Their lifestyle could be held up as a model for the 'sustainable utilisation of natural resources', but I think it is better viewed as a model for 'sustainable participation in a natural ecosystem'. Ingested seeds, for instance, are passed within faeces and deposited on the camp's periphery where they are worked into the ground by dung beetles providing ideal conditions for germination.[4] Through this unintended cultivation of edible plants, the Bushmen have helped to shape the flora of the Kalahari just as surely as forest elephants still shape the forests of central Africa through their patterned dispersal of seeds, and tapirs shape the distribution of palms in the Amazon. Maybe we in the West might learn something here: that sense of participation in an ecosystem which conveys the notion of inter-dependency. We might realise that respecting nature is simply another way of respecting ourselves and find the strength to reject our utilitarian approach to nature.

In lean years Bushmen dispersed into smaller bands which might migrate long distances to avert a crisis. Ultimately the resource base was limited however and the people had to be sensitive to symptoms of overpopulation. Under such marginal conditions, the women found it necessary to space out their families as they needed to feed each infant from the breast for three or four years. Most of them had three or fewer children in their lifetime.[5] In times of extreme deprivation, a woman might become so emaciated that she had no option but to sacrifice her newborn child, snuffing out the life before her infant had taken its first breath. According to Elizabeth Marshall Thomas, the women abstained from intercourse for long periods rather than suffer the pain of killing a child.[6] Men too took responsibility by abstaining from intercourse.[7] In addition to infanticide, the women might resort to abortion if conditions turned particularly harsh.[8] Bulanda said that a woman who was unfortunate enough to have twins was only able to keep one – even under relatively favourable conditions. All this painful responsibility was a humbling revelation to me. But out of the pattern of their subsistence, with all its care to avoid overhunting and over-harvesting, and out of the painful planning of their families, was born something very unique in human terms: a balanced relationship with nature. It was a cultural achievement of great significance and something far removed from the way we in the West are living today.

Back on the veldt, the guys began testing likely-looking springhare burrows with their flexible four-metre probes, thrusting them down a tunnel to their full length, and jigging them about. I looked on uneasily hoping the burrows were deep. Tunnel systems up to 45 metres in length have been recorded with over a dozen exits. That should provide sufficient shelter for springhares; on the other hand the guys looked determined. I was beginning to work out their strategy. Burrows with recent tracks at the entrance or with darker sand that was moister, and must therefore have been recently excavated, were the most likely ones to be occupied. In that case the probe was inserted. If the sand was white, the burrow was ignored.

With all these hunters living close at hand, with so much skill, it was hard to imagine any animals surviving. Perhaps hunting was controlled by taboos. In the 1960s anthropologists found that tortoises were only eaten by infants or very old Bushmen and that similar restrictions applied to springhares and steenbok. Even the large antelopes were protected, not so much by taboo but by a special relationship with the Bushman's god. In the case of the southern /Xam Bushmen, the great trickster deity, /Kaggen, loved eland above all other animals.[9] The depth of this love is revealed in a conversation between J. M. Orpen, the Chief Magistrate of St John's Territory, and Qing, his Bushman guide, which took place in the early 1870s in the midst of the Maloti Mountains of modern-day Lesotho. Orpen began to question Qing about some rock paintings they had examined on an evening when both were 'happy and at ease smoking over the campfires'. Qing mentioned the great god /Kaggen who made all things. Orpen asked, 'Where is /Kaggen?' And Qing answered, 'We don't know but the elands do. Have you not hunted and heard his cry, when the elands suddenly start and run to his call? Where he is, elands are in droves like cattle.' In this way the magistrate found out about the Bushman god, how he created the eland and how he dwelt amongst them, protecting them because of his love for them.

The hunters of the /Xam Bushmen believed that /Kaggen might cease to love them if they killed an eland.[10] What is more, they knew that /Kaggen could be present beside them unseen. If the elands were wild and hard to stalk, it was a sign that he was present protecting them. His presence might even be felt 'with the heart'.[11] In seeking to kill the creator's favourite antelope, the hunter set himself a perilous task. The way round this was to seek permission for the hunt before it commenced. Yet /Kaggen might still come to the aid of an eland after it had been shot by attempting to break the spiritual link that connected the hunter to his quarry. He might buzz or hiss in the hunter's ear or bite his eyes. In order to counter such distractions and hold firmly to the link with his quarry, the hunter abided by an elaborate set of rituals whilst waiting for the arrow poison to take effect. A similar set of customs applied to hartebeest and other large antelope. Thus, the god of the southern Bushmen brought an ethical dimension to their hunting: his presence helped limit excessive killing.

Here in the central Kalahari, the G/wi Bushmen also believed in an all-powerful being. They called him N!adima.[12] The G/wi god created the universe and all the plants and animals therein, and as all of his creatures had a common status with Man, they were in turn respected by the Bushmen. That is why the G/wi strongly disapprove of 'greedy hunting' in which someone shoots more than is required for their immediate needs.[13] The G/wi told the anthropologist, George Silberbauer, that all forms of life must live within certain limits of tolerance lest they cause affront to N!adima. 'Everything must grow. It must bear its young. It must live. But not so that anything becomes too numerous in one place and takes everything'. They evidently included themselves in this obligation.

Further north, the folklore of the !Kung Bushman centres on the exploits of their trickster god, Kaoxa, whose crowded adventures bear some similarity to those of /Kaggen. The mythologies of these three Bushmen nations, whilst distinctive, share certain core values, including reverence for the great game animals and respect for all of God's creation. They keep the earth 'cool' and underpin the balance sought by Bushmen in their dealings with nature.

We moved into new terrain where the ground was pock-marked with the holes of a small burrowing rodent. As I stumbled along behind the hunters, the sand periodically gave way beneath my feet. It was disconcerting. I fancied it was the rodents' defence against Bushmen. We combed the ground ever more rapidly, testing one fresh-looking burrow after another. From time to time the hunters stopped probing and attended to the still rod, feeling for any slight movement. If the hunters did detect an animal, they would attempt to hook it with a barb at the end of the probe. At one time this was made from a steenbok's horn but these days it was sharpened metal. At best it would be a messy end for the springhare. As they worked, the hunters talked quietly to one another. Armed with his minidisc recorder, Stu kept up with the leaders fascinated by their technique.

When hunting, Bushmen communicate solely by clicks and hand gestures to avoid spooking their prey; it has been suggested that the first language of humankind arose out of such preverbal clicks and gestures.[14] Van der Post recounts an occasion in which his companion, a Bushman, commanded him to listen to the cries made by the stars as they hunted in the heavens, calling out 'Tssa!' and 'Tssk!', sounds still used widely in Africa to set dogs after game.[15] A few clicks have spread to neighbouring Bantu languages such as that spoken by the Zulus but otherwise, and despite their ancient origins, they are heard in no other tongue on earth. Some have likened their language to bird song but not, I would judge, from any melodic quality, perhaps from its rhythm and cadence. I found that listening to Bushmen chatting was soothing.

After a couple more hours the afternoon's hunt was declared unsuccessful. Personally I was relieved. The last thing I wanted to see was an injured springhare or fox pulled from its burrow and cudgelled with a stick. Back at camp, Stu took me up on my wimpish attitude.

'You eat meat,' he pointed out, 'why shouldn't the Bushmen?'

'I am more than happy for Bushmen to eat meat.' I explained how much I respected their customs which forbid waste and needless killing. 'As for me,' I finished lamely, 'I eat meat sparingly and I think about it.'

'So you don't mind clubbing springhares then, provided you think about it?'

I had to laugh. Stu has an uncanny knack of revealing people's inconsistencies. 'It's like the Bushman story of Pishiboro and the elephant wife,' I explained. 'But I still think of the elephant as wife, not meat. It's the same with springhares. I like them. I think they're amazing. They have big eyes and baggy coats and I love the way they hop along at night.'

'People have their own ideas about what is and is not okay,' said Stu. 'In China, it's okay to eat dogs, in Britain it's not. In India it's not okay to eat cows – they are holy – but in Britain it is. Bushmen find it okay to club springhares.'

'If you kill without real need,' I replied, 'something closes off inside you, a connection is broken.'

'And if you don't kill,' said Stu, ever the pragmatist, 'something else closes off and that's your stomach.'

Meatball enjoyed a piece of bread soaked in the oil from a sardine tin. Happily, he was oblivious to our ideological altercation.

Later in the afternoon, Bulanda arrived at our camp with Molathwe's sister and Roy Sesana's first wife. They sat down next to the dormant campfire and waited for us. I walked over and plonked myself down beside them, beginning some polite conversation whilst Stu burrowed in his bag for the last of his fine cut tobacco. This he cheerfully offered around much to everyone's delight. It was a noble sacrifice. We were busy chatting about this morning's foraging trip when the headman arrived. He picked up the camp-stool as before and brought it over to the group. I wondered whether he used the stool because he thought outsiders expected that of him, or because he enjoyed the status. During a lull in the conversation, Molathwe's sister asked us if we would like to come to a dance tonight. I began to demur. Stu and I had talked about this kind of thing; we didn't want to be tiresome visitors that needed entertainment. But something in her expression combined with an unmistakable look of anticipation in the others, reassured me. 'We would love to come,' I finished. An excited interchange ensued. Then Bulanda informed us that they would hold a gemsbok dance at our camp later in the evening.

Several explanations have been offered as to why the Bushmen named this dance after gemsbok – the boldly marked, southern oryx. It may derive from the striking courtship circling of gemsbok in which the bull follows the cow round and round, as she tries to circle behind him. In another explanation, a Bushman informant is quoted as saying that 'a gemsbuck cow is very vicious when she has a small calf. She does not let lion, tiger (striped hyaena) or the wild dogs come near to it. We want to explain this beautiful love of gemsbuck to the young ones.

Then they, too, will care well for their small children'.[16] My own bet is that the name derives from rarely witnessed displays, called 'oryx tournaments'. These are described in the closely related Beisa oryx of eastern Africa but not so far in gemsbok. In the oryx, the tournaments usually occur at dawn or during a rain shower – times when n/um is at its strongest. The young animals then sprint into a high-stepping, showy 'floating' pace with chin raised high and head swinging from side to side.[17]

As soon as our visitors had left, I cleared up the camp and set about lighting a fire in preparation for our gemsbok dance whilst Stu frantically prepared a meal of curried vegetables in the last of the fading light. Barely had Meatball licked the last tin clean when people began to arrive, stepping out of the gathering night into the circle of firelight. Bulanda and the four women from our expedition turned up first, dropping down together on one side of the campfire. Their gaiety and easy confidence was picked up by others who now arrived from all directions. They had brought some children too who stayed close to the women; their large round eyes illuminated in the firelight as they peered about at newcomers, both young and old. The men crowded around the fire on the opposite side from the women whilst a couple of teenage boys hung back at the edge of the camp near to some tall bushes, looking a little nervous and awkward. There was a buzz of conversation.

I looked out into the darkness, wondering what might be there; sometimes, wild animals will draw close to stare in at Bushmen dancers. Amongst the / Xam, the great god himself may stand as an eland beyond the glow of a fire.[18] It is then that the shaman's spirit leaves, departing from his upper back and travelling out into the night. He must be careful for dangerous spirits can hover at the edge of the dance looking for people to kill, particularly the sick and elderly. A struggle may ensue between the trancing shaman who tries to save the sick person's life and those loving relatives already dead who want the sick one for themselves. In their efforts to cure the sick, shamans draw thorns out of the body and shout insults at the spirits, even throwing burning brands into the night. The most powerful will undertake a terrible trance journey, travelling to the home of their god where, at great personal risk, they argue, reason and cajole him into surrendering the soul of the sick person.

The great shamans of the past performed many feats: drawing wild game onto nearby pastures, capturing rain beasts and leading them over the band's territory to bring soft rain; transforming into lions to defend their people from other spirit-lions,[19] or joining in battle with the shamans of invading tribes. On completing a spiritual journey, they descended once more to the corporeal world. One contemporary shaman explained, 'You return to where everyone is… and you come and come and come and you finally enter your body again'.[20] The shamans brought back profound knowledge from their journeys, which enhanced their understanding of the Bushman community and its relationship with the cosmos.

One of the women started a soft wailing song that wavered about high G before dropping to D. I recognised the scale used worldwide for haunting folk melodies. Immediately a couple of others began clapping in time. The clapping was explosive: palms being driven hard together so as to trap a pocket of air, making a fuller sound even than castanets. The timing was precise, one woman setting the main rhythm with others providing embellishments that cascaded about the fundamental beat. After some false starts followed by laughter, the women got into a groove, and a couple of young men responded, rising to their feet and stamping out an answering rhythm. A few others rushed off excitedly, returning with strings of silk cocoons that they began winding around their ankles, perhaps 200 per leg. Each cocoon contained a number of tiny ostrich shell fragments that must have taken hours to prepare. Once attached, the ankle-bandoliers produced a soft 'shuck, shuck' that augmented the heavy stamping. The dancers formed a snake, which moved in a slow circle round the women.

Four of the younger children were huddled together outside the ring of dancers, watching them intently. Further out still the embarrassed teenagers were becoming emboldened by the rising power of the women's singing and clapping. They moved in to join the dancers; only one held back. The heavy tread of the male dancers came together into a single coordinated beat that was transmitted through the ground, felt as much as heard, a visceral signal to which the women responded. Energy flowed back and forth. N/um began to rise. I could feel the potency and wondered at it. Different songs heat up different kinds of spiritual energy. There is n/um for healing, n/um that enables a shaman to fuse his spirit with that of an animal, and another that empowers him to converse with God. All are strong. All are dangerous. They arise from an ancient stratum of Bushman culture.[21]

Smoke from the fire mingled with smoke from the glowing Bushmen's pipes, gathering in a haze around the gleaming, animated faces deeply creased with the dual imprint of cares and laughter. A whisper of night air turned and came towards me, carrying a cloud of richly-scented smoke: the tangy smell of smouldering firewood, the acrid aroma of rough tobacco burning in tubular Bushmen pipes, and the unmistakable sweet spicy scent of the Bushmen themselves. All of a sudden I was no longer an observer, but part of a small group sharing the intimacy of a campfire somewhere, way, far away, in the desert sands of the Kalahari. A half moon hung above; beyond, the bright stars were hunting.

A woman began her lament. In the flickering firelight I recognised Roy Sesana's first wife. Her voice was deep and commanding. It urged me to follow, to stay close. I let myself go and was drawn into an even more distant place, where I sensed my ancestry in a time so long in the past that it was forgotten. She was answered by eight or nine women, echoing the refrain, comforting the lone voice. All the time the explosive rhythmic hand claps, and shuck-shushing of stamping feet, added to her song, creating an irresistible tension. More men were rising to their feet now and joining the circle of dancers. An elderly man appeared from beyond the firelight and danced into the ring with great finesse and agility, remembering his youth. He added his voice to the refrain, deeper and hoarser than the women's, but still soft and musical and a cogent reply to the first woman's call. Soon all of us men were up, stamping our feet, bodies leaning forward, arms held slightly back and to the side, like the wings of a hawk. Stu was somewhere down the line of dancers. The women clapped. I stomped my feet in reply. Following the snake we weaved around the fire past the shadows flickering in the trees, and past the seated, keening women. Power flowed from their inner circle. The men stamped harder. The energy was intoxicating. Without warning a man stumbled into the fire but was quickly helped out by two companions. He lay quietly on the sand. Filled with *n/um* he had entered a trance state known as !kia.

The mood began to change. We came closer together, more here and now, sharing in the rhythms of the dance, glad to have returned safely from our lonely journeys into the past. The men lightened their heavy tramp, shuffling the sand with their bare feet; the women sang more happily, clapping on the men. One of the women rose up and began to dance in a light capering step to one side of the men, coming slowly clockwise against the moving snake. She blocked one of the hunters, smiling and laughing, and tantalizing him with her bobbing movements. Hands floated on either side of his face, and then gently caressed the top of his head. An instant later, she turned and disappeared. Is that how a young woman shows her affection to a Bushman hunter? Carefully choosing just that moment when her small band is most united, she stands and dances, boldly and freely, declaring her love for all to see.

The evening was now at its peak with about 30 Bushmen in our camp giving up to the gemsbok dance. I sat down by the fire for a few minutes to take it all in. In a pause between two songs, the lead woman lent over towards me, earnestly saying something in her click language. Bulanda called to me. 'She is offering a prayer for your safe journey home. During the last dance, she asked her ancestors to protect us from lions. She asked them to see that we travelled safely.' I looked back at the woman wishing that there were words to thank her. Healing and blessing are two of the great benefactions of the gemsbok dance.

The women were sitting closely together during a lull in the dancing, shoulder to shoulder, knee touching knee. An argument that had flared yesterday between two of them had been settled, and this morning's coolness between Molathwe and his wife had been replaced with warmth. All misdemeanours were forgiven, all differences forgotten. In the harmony brought by the gemsbok dance, not even the arrival of danger could dent our mood. Bulanda suddenly called to me in alarm, 'Oh! What was that? Something is moving.' I looked down to see a glistening gem slide quickly and silently across the pale moonlit sand, passing a foot length from my toes before scuttling beneath a small piece of cardboard. There was menace in its passing. Sitting up quickly, I flicked on my torch and gingerly lifted up the piece of cardboard. There, with its claws open and sting raised, was an amber scorpion. Someone tried to scare it away towards the dark rim beyond the firelight, but it turned and ran rapidly towards the seated throng. One of the men gathered it up and quickly flicked it into the fire. The chatter and laughter continued unabated. Firelight flickered on happy faces. Occasionally a woman strolled over to a clump of trees, some 10 metres from the dance circle and peed into the shadows from a standing position. When the men went, they moved further off, crouching down first. Even in this mundane part of daily life, Bushmen avoid any show of domination.

Spontaneously the women began to clap again. A pulse of energy surged about the campfire. A new song began. The beat was insistent. Men rose to dance. Voices gained in strength. The snake swelled. The pace gathered. The dance grew frenetic. N/um rose… Out in the desert scrub under a pale half-moon, surely the lions would hear our song.

Later in the evening, I noticed that the old man who danced with such agility was tiring. On the spur of the moment, I fetched a can of beer from Nomad and offered it to him, guessing it might help him to revive. In my book alcoholism, whether in a Bushman ghetto or Scottish housing estate, is a symptom not the cause of despair, and my companions in their desert home were secure in their traditional lifestyle. The old man didn't respond. Thinking he had misunderstood the gesture, I held the can out further hoping he would see that it was definitely meant for him. One of the other men called out. Immediately the old man bowed, bringing his hands together, opening two palms in the universal gesture of appeal. I was taken aback. Noticing my confusion, Molathwe gently took the can and placed it in the old man's hand. Only then did I realise that this wonderful old dancer was completely blind. How he could have pranced around the fire and the seated women in a stranger's camp, I had no idea. He snapped off the ring pull, located the opening carefully with his mouth, threw back his head all the way so that the can was tipped completely upside down, and sucked out the entire contents at speed! He surely loved the n/um of alcohol.

Reinvigorated, the old dancer now returned to the snake. The pace of dancing rose again, reaching an even more fervent pitch than before. The night advanced in waves of energy; until someone decided to go home. In minutes everyone was rising to leave. I hardly had time to register before finding myself standing alone at the campfire with Stu. All that remained of the great gemsbok healing dance was a circular depression pounded into the sand by our feet, and a few glowing embers in the fire. The camp was dark, empty and deserted. A cool night breeze stirred the ashes.

'Flippin' 'eck!' said Stu. 'Did somebody shout "time"?'

12

EASY TO GET

Springhare

The sun had risen above the horizon by the time I awoke. For a minute or two I lay in my sleeping bag listening to the sounds of Molapo coming to life, remembering our evening together. Just as I was getting to know these people, we had to leave. It was a pity, but I had promised Bulanda that I would get her home today. After a while I got up, crawled out the big red tent, stretched, and looked in the back of Nomad for something to eat. I decided on tinned peaches and sweetened condensed milk: another of those combos that work in the bush but taste sickly sweet at home. As I rummaged about, I was thankful for the propriety of Bushmen, none of whom had come to watch or ask the usual questions that beset the traveller in Africa: 'Where are you from?', 'What is your name?', 'Where are you going?' Meatball uncurled, scratched himself, and came over to watch, staring curiously with his big appealing eyes. I patted him. Funny how quickly a dog can grow on you.

Stu emerged from his silver tent grinning with delight at an emerald green beetle with a bright orange belly that was crawling over his hand. 'It's a little miracle of evolution!' he declared, placing it out of harm's way on a leaf. Then he rolled up a cigarette from coarse pipe tobacco – the only kind left to him – and lit up, barely grimacing at the harsh smoke. He was adapting to the Kalahari too.

We packed up the tents and stored our gear in the back of Nomad. As a going away treat we gave Meatball the other half of the tin of sticky milk. He licked it up slowly and carefully, enjoying every drop. According to Elizabeth Marshall Thomas, the usual diet of Bushman dogs is human excrement. I tried not to think about it.

Driving out of Molapo having collected Bulanda and family, and said our goodbyes, I thought again of all that there was to learn from the Bushmen and wished that I could stay.

'I wish I could stay,' I repeated out loud.

'I thought you wanted to get north before the rains come,' Stu reminded me.

'I could learn so much from these Bushmen... how they live each day, what they think of life in the towns, how they manage their economy, whether they still stay in balance with nature.'

'Didn't you see the meat store yesterday?' Stu asked.

'I saw a tree platform when we were driving out with the guys.'

'That's where they hid the meat that caused all the fuss with the wildlife department.'

Roy had not wanted to talk about the incident in Ghanzi, and I hadn't raised the matter in Molapo. Stu's comment made me think again. We had seen horses at the nearby spring on the way into the settlement and there was the matter of that Land Rover with meat in the back. What was going on here?

'Do you think they shot some gemsbok from horseback?' I asked.

'Dunno,' replied Stu, 'seems a lot easier than using poisoned arrows.'

'I don't get it,' I said. 'Is this indiscriminate slaughter of wild animals by Bushmen or another example of government harassment?'[1]

'Maybe one drives the other,' said Stu, who was hard on the heels of his own Bushman story.

Bulanda asked for some water for baby Arthur. She didn't want to talk about the current problems.

Anthropologists who lived with isolated bands of Bushmen in the 1950s and 60s were impressed with their frugal lifestyles. The hunters rarely killed more than one large game animal at a time, and every part of that animal was used. If it was a gemsbok, all the meat was cooked and eaten, even down to the brain and the muscles of the cheek. The only part thrown out was the area immediately surrounding the wound made by a poisoned arrow. The hide was dried for a day, scraped clean, smeared with a mixture of fat, marrow and brains, and cured; then it was cut and trimmed to make a kaross that could serve as blanket and cloak. The skins of smaller antelope were used to make loincloths for men and skirts for women or they made bags that ranged in size from the hunter's shoulder pack to tiny one-inch by two-inch sachets. The thicker skin of the giraffe was ideal for making the soles of sandals which were worn, hairy side up, when the sand was hot. Sinew, taken from the back muscle of eland or gemsbok, was used to make bowstrings whilst finer pieces were spun together to make thread for sewing leatherwork. The bladders of springhares were cleaned, dried and used as water-containers. Ribs of giraffe were made into sweat scrapers. The scapula served as a chopper. The foreleg of an ostrich or the horn core of a gemsbok were made into bone arrowheads if no iron was available. Liquor was squeezed from the rumen cud of antelope, filtered through grass, and drunk. Even the amniotic fluid of a gravid female antelope was drunk.[2] It was about as waste-free a society as you can get.

There are detailed accounts of these Bushmen and their lifestyle and beliefs, from several unrelated anthropological studies: each portrays a society intentionally living within the bounds set by its environment. Yet there are also reports of Bushmen trading in skins, ivory, ostrich feathers, eggshell beads, salt and copper in both the 19th and early 20th centuries. Would these groups not have hunted additional animals to supply this trade? Over a period of two decades in the second half of the 19th century, Bushmen hunters killed several hundred elephant per year[3]: clearly this was for trade. The !Kung recall the period with great affection, remembering that they were provided with guns and ate enormous amounts of meat. They expressed no regret at the diminution of elephants, which they regarded as pests.[4] How does one square these conflicting accounts?

The director of a famous UK conservation organisation once remarked that if you armed a 'noble savage' with a Kalashnikov automatic rifle, you would end up with 'overkill'. He cited the bison traps of North America as an example of early mass-killing technology. According to him, we are harmless without weapons and mass killers with weapons. But is it really that simple? A friend of mine once advised me, 'You will never solve a problem if you don't go back to the beginning'. In the case of hunting and overkill, the beginning of the problem takes us back a long way – to a period when human hunters and game animals had yet to come into contact.

What was the world like for the Early Race of Bushmen before the world was 'spoilt'? A hint of that innocent past still lingers on amongst the wildlife inhabiting deep oceanic islands. Many of these islands were settled for the first time only in the last century and a small number remain uninhabited to this day. The tameness of the island birds and reptiles is legendary; it would have made them easy to get when humans did finally arrive. *Easy to get*. It seems such a trivial observation but it may be an important part of the problem underlying our destructive relationship with nature. The dodos on Mauritius, and the tortoises on islands in the Mascarene and Galapagos groups, were quickly exterminated by European sailors who used these harbours as convenient sources of fresh meat when voyaging in the Indian and Pacific oceans. The flightless dodos, chubby as turkeys in the right season, were readily captured with sticks, nets and muskets, whilst the giant tortoises could be picked up by a handful of beefy crew and carried alive to waiting boats.

Easy to get on islands, but what about our wily mainland animals? Deer are timid and geese take flight: they don't sit around waiting to be clubbed. But it wasn't always like that. To this day there exist one or two gardens of Eden deep within our continents where humans have yet to make their presence felt. They are literally the remotest places on Earth. A couple of years ago, a group of ecologists reached an out of the way corner of the great central African rain forest never previously visited. Their objective was to investigate a natural clearing in the forest, known as a 'bai', that was first noticed on a satellite image. It took four days to hike in from the nearest track, but thanks to GPS navigation they found it. The bai was full of wild animals, none of which recognised humans. They were able to walk right up to a group of wild gorillas.

'At first, they paid us no attention whatsoever,' one of the ecologists told me.[5] 'Only when I got to within 15 feet of them, did they turn to look – just curious as to whom I was. The buffalo also ignored us. So did the sitatunga – it was wonderful to see them in the open, all shaggy and striped. When I sat down, the monkeys came right up to look at me.'

I was amazed at her experience having grown used to alarm calls, backsides and galloping hooves. 'Were all the animals fearless?' I asked.

'Only the elephants were timid. But they wander for miles through those forests and we guessed they had come across people elsewhere.'

As she related her adventure, I imagined a Stone Age hunter, armed with a spear or throwing stick, coming across a bai like that. He would surely have been delighted to find so many naive animals, ones that were *easy to get.*

One of the stories of /Kaggen, the god of the southern Bushmen, may even preserve the memory of a time when a mobile Bushmen band moved into a region where animals had never encountered hunters before. 'Whilst /Kaggen was still making the eland and all the other animals and things in the world, he went on a journey to his nephew to get arrow-poison, and he was away three days. While he was away his son came upon the eland and killed it with a spear whilst it was sleeping. When /Kaggen returned, he was very angry and called to his son. "Now begin to try to understand the mischief you have done, for you have spoilt the elands when I was making them fit for use." Then, /Kaggen made many new elands, but they were wild, and he told his son, "Go and hunt them and try to kill one, that is now your work, for it was you who spoilt them."

His son ran and did his best, but he came back panting and footsore and worn out; and he hunted again next day, and was unable to kill any. They were able to run away because /Kaggen was in their bones.'[6]

Some 22,000 years ago the first humans entered Alaska to stand unknowingly before two continents filled with naive animals.[7] It did not take them long to spread across North and South America to reach the farthest corner of Tierra del Fuego, a distance of 11,000 miles. The pioneers on this epic journey must surely have feasted on naive animals all the way, enjoying en route the most enormous free lunch in human history. Some scientists believe that humans were so efficient at killing that they caused the extinction of large mammals during this early migratory phase. Their argument has become known as the 'Pleistocene Overkill' hypothesis.[8] Following the pioneering phase, Native Americans settled in different regions across the two continents, developing a wide diversity of societies. Some may have lived in balance with the large mammals, others hunted so effectively that they reduced the numbers of their favoured prey,[9] and yet others such as the Anasazi of the southwest of North America and the Mayans of Central America used up their vital resources prior to collapsing as societies. It is not understood why.

Why should some hunter-gatherer societies live within the regeneration capacity of their land over long periods but not others?[10] Perhaps some cultures revered the spirit of game animals, like the Bushmen, and struck a balance between hunger and the need to please their gods. The Algonquian-speaking tribes in eastern Canada had an elaborate mythology in which their game animals were safeguarded by powerful spirit keepers who took the appearance of giant animals, such as beavers or bears, generally whiter than the rest of their animal tribe. The hunters propitiated these keepers by respecting the game. Trust broke down when the arrival of Europeans precipitated a series of epidemics. Outbreak following outbreak of deadly infectious disease was a catastrophe beyond the power of the healers; it was taken as a sign that the keepers of the game had forsaken the people. Angrily the Algonquian tribes discarded their sacred agreement with the keepers opening the way, perhaps, to an excessive exploitation of beavers and other fur-bearing animals that followed soon after.[11] Spiritual collapse may have triggered the episode of overkill.

A more prosaic explanation is that the Algonquian overkill was triggered by the advent of new hunting technology. When new weaponry comes along it alters the balance between humans and prey, giving a distinct advantage to humans. Arrows kill animals from a greater distance than spears, so prey that had been too nervous to be speared is brought down easily by an archer. It is again *easy to get*. Once more it is tempting to hunt extravagantly; once more there is the potential for over-exploitation. At Abu Hureyra in Syria, archaeologists found evidence of a switch from an 80 per cent dependency on gazelles to an

80 per cent dependency on sheep and goats during the period 8,500 to 8,000 BP, which is when walled 'kites' were first used for gazelle drives. It looks as if the new 'kite' technology led to an over-exploitation of gazelles and the subsequent shift in diet.[12]

We have become so used to guns that we forget how radically they improve hunting success when they first become available. To enter a familiar hunting ground, armed for the first time with a gun, must be even 'better' than entering a virgin hunting ground with a spear or throwing stick. The animals are exceedingly *easy to get*. In time of course, the prey animals increase their wariness and extend their flight distance, but there are limits to these countermoves.

Some years ago, I was camped in the treeless steppes of eastern Mongolia with an American student who was studying the migrations of gazelle for his PhD. We were sleeping in small tents that were pegged down tightly against the wind, which drove across the plains without hindrance. A million gazelle inhabited these steppes but they had disappeared into the vastness without trace and, despite driving all day long, none had been found. We decided to investigate a pond lying some distance to the east amidst gently rolling hills, reckoning that some of the herd might have gone there to drink. Early in the morning we drove across the grasslands navigating by compass. Leaving the vehicle some way off, we approached the pool on foot. I was relishing the feel of walking in the wilderness again with nothing to carry but binoculars and a pocket notebook; all my senses were alert. Reaching the top of some surrounding hills, I saw a herd of gazelles running up the far rise, more than a mile and a half away. They were fleeing at top speed and didn't stop running until they had crested the hill and disappeared from sight. I scanned all about, looking for signs of wolves or poachers. It was a minute or two before I twigged that the gazelles had been running from me.

I had seen something similar many years earlier on the open savannahs of northern Tanzania. A herd of 60 or more elephant started to run whilst so far off that I had mistaken them at first for buffalo. They were all teenagers. The matriarchs had been shot for their ivory and the very youngest animals had been lost, perhaps unable to keep up. The remainder – the teenagers – were moving about in a tightly bunched group alert to the slightest sign of people. They had learnt that humans meant death.

The gazelles and elephants were being exploited intensively by hunters using vehicles and automatic weapons. This kind of pressure is deadly and very hard to counter. The steppe conservation project that I worked with in Mongolia was well-funded and had taken many positive steps. It had established new protected areas, written management plans, promoted monitoring and ecological research, and made efforts to involve local herders, but the killing continued. We recommended stronger law enforcement with increased surveillance by rangers, and called for aerial surveys to monitor the number of gazelles and the incidence of poaching. Out in Mongolia I was still looking for technical solutions. I never imagined that the root problem in gazelle conservation might be a collapse in spiritual values.

Bulanda nudged Stu who had fallen asleep. 'Cigarette?' she asked.

Stu looked seriously pissed off, but handed her his last packet of pipe tobacco.

'Bulanda,' he said, 'now you have more tobacco than me.'

She responded with a short laugh, 'It is good that we share so freely.'

I settled for a swig of water. It was getting hot inside Nomad and it was going to be a long day of driving. Fortunately, baby Arthur was sleeping.

About an hour out of Mulapo, Stu spotted a khama's hartebeest running from the car – a solitary bull with a thick circle of horns above its long face. 'Look, it's a Sikh antelope,' he called out. At about a hundred metres the hartebeest turned to stare. If ever there was a noble game animal, this was he. Out of range of arrow; in range of rifle.

In recent times, some Native American peoples have redeveloped sustainable forms of hunting and trapping. They still have guns but they've opted for restraint and long-term benefits. Looking in from the outside, it would appear that they have regained control of their land, their economy and their society following a period of massive social disruption that extended over several centuries. Could the capacity to reverse direction, to move from overkill to sustainable hunting, explain the contradictory evidence in Bushman society? From time to time they too have gained access to more advanced forms of hunting technology, and this may have precipitated periods of disruption in which they killed game animals with impunity. Later, when trade routes closed and traditional values were reasserted, they resumed careful management of their environment. If my hunch is right, then the return route to sustainable hunting would be easier in societies that retain a spiritual connection with nature.

Where do Bushmen stand today in this cycle of overkill and sustainability? The large Bushman settlements situated on the fringes of the Kalahari put pressure on the local wildlife. Starting in the 1970s, people of the Xade settlement began to mount expeditions on donkeys and horses, hunting over much greater areas of the Kalahari than previously. They used iron-tipped spears and guns rather than bows and arrows and ended up killing many more of the larger game animals.[13] They no longer used every bit of the dead animals, nor divided the meat so as to strengthen and affirm kinship and other ties within the band.[14] They were finding it *easy to get* another animal.

The wildlife department not unreasonably became concerned about the over-hunting of large animals in these areas. It is a difficult subject to broach, but my guess is that Roy Sesana is also concerned. He and others like him want to reinvigorate the Bushman's traditional use of the Kalahari, which was careful, frugal and sustainable. But in order to do that they need the Botswana government to recognise their claim to the land and its resources, in the same way that Australian, Brazilian, Canadian, South African, US and other governments around the world are now recognising the land rights of their indigenous hunter-gatherer peoples. This is something the Botswana government has consistently refused to do.

We continued crawling north across the central Kalahari, not meeting another car all day. On reaching the edge of the reserve, we turned westwards to follow the boundary fence. Two metres high and comprising 11 strands that are cross-linked with vertical runners to produce a narrow mesh, it is one of the most formidable barriers in Africa. Surely it is impassable to any large animal just as the veterinary service intended. As if in demonstration, an ostrich ran in front of us for about two kilometres, seeking a way into the reserve only to be forced back into the ranching lands. Near Kuke corner we turned northwards again, following an undulating track that passed several herds of fat cattle. Soon we reached the small frontier town of Rakops. The dusty streets were empty without so much as a single tree to deflect the blinding heat of the midday sun. I found a dilapidated petrol station and filled up Nomad's empty tank with a manually operated pump. Bulanda was anxious to get news of five members of Roy's extended family that were rumoured to have been killed by a lightning strike. We drove into the centre of town looking for Bushmen, finding some outside a tin-roofed beer hall with cream painted walls covered in gaudy cartoon figures. A drunken group were hanging about on the open verandah. They reassured Bulanda that the news was not as bad as she had feared. One Bushman was in hospital, the others were fine. Word on the street put the blame on a Bantu witch doctor.

After the tranquillity of Molapo, the urban squalor of Rakops came as a shock. In today's bruising encounter with the outside world, the Bushman's customs and traditions are threatened as never before. Anthropologists who have worked with Bushmen in their new urban surroundings say that the continuation of the trance dance tradition is the key to their future.[15] Not only does it increase harmony within the Bushman community in times of social stress, but it enables the Shaman to track down intuitive solutions to their new problems. This is surely true, but I wonder if it is enough. Suffering amongst Bushmen in the past has arisen not so much from a failure in their own beliefs and traditions as from a failure in their means of subsistence. When the weapons of powerful incomers have decimated their game animals, or when great herds of livestock have entered their lands and laid their wild pasture to waste, that is when the Bushmen have suffered most. A letter from a magistrate of Namaqualand to the Cape Parliament confirms the devastation being visited upon Bushmen along the Orange River in 1863: '... in consequence of the colonists having guns and horses, and their being expert hunters (the pursuit of game being their daily occupation), the wild game of the country had become so scarce, and almost inaccessible to the Bushmen, whose weapon is the bow and arrow, having a comparatively short range. That ostrich eggs, honey, grass-seed, and roots had all become exceedingly scarce, the ostriches being destroyed by hunters, the seeds and roots in consequence of the intrusion of colonists' flocks. From these various causes, the Bushman's subsistence failed him, and in many cases they died of hunger ...'[16] History suggests that more than anything else, Bushmen require title to their land.

We pushed on late into the night, dropping Bulanda and family at their mean little shack in Ghanzi before setting up our tents under the vulture tree at Thakadu Camp.

13

UNDER THE VULTURE TREE

Stu kipping

At first light I crawled out of my tent to enjoy the cool morning air. The great Kalahari embraced me as it lay, hushed by the night, awaiting the curtain to lift on another day. In the east, the thorn bushes were etched black in the fire of coming dawn, above them tops of leadwood trees were silhouetted against a lemon wash, and higher still grey clouds drifted in a sky of eggshell blue catching the first rays of morning in their shining halos. The whole empyreal stage held its breath in anticipation. A hidden bird trilled an opening note of welcome, then another, and then one to another in a thrilling duet; soon birds were calling on all sides, each adding its distinctive melody to the Kalahari chorus. I breathed in deeply. It was to be a day of rest. I would do some writing; Stu had even talked of washing. The vulture stirred itself at the thought.

In the afternoon, I prepared to drive to Ghanzi to meet Roy Sesana. Stu had no desire to accompany me, having entirely fallen out with Bulanda.

'Just when I was kippin', that evil bitch-cow from hell jabbed me in the ribs and demanded a bloody fag. No, I'm going to stay here and chill.'

I had primed myself with a few questions, realising it might be my last chance to discuss wildlife issues with a Bushman hunter. Over at the metal shack, Bulanda and Roy greeted me warmly and we sat down on the plastic chairs in the thin strip of shade. Roy was wearing a skullcap made from the facial skin and horns of a steenbok and below it a headband of soft brown leather decorated with ostrich eggshell beads. I gave him two tins of aromatic pipe tobacco from Scotland. He opened them, smelt and savoured each, and smiled broadly.

I was curious as to how mobile Bushmen coped with a prolonged drought. Did they hunker down and hang on for rain, or did they move to a favourite range? Bulanda took on the role of translator.

'In a drought we follow the track of the rain,' said Roy. 'For before the drought there was surely a lot of rain somewhere and that is the place where we go. We look for the place with good roots, rich from earlier rains.'

It hadn't occurred to me that the Bushmen might keep a mental map of rainstorms and the condition of local roots. Once again I'd underestimated their ecological skills. 'How far can you travel when following the rain?' I asked.

'We cannot trespass into the neighbour's land,' he answered firmly, 'for the boundaries are given to us by God.'

I wondered whether there were still mobile bands that somehow kept away from authorities. 'Can you can still live in this way today – moving from place to place?'

'Our difficulty today is with the government's policy.' Roy turned to discuss something with Bulanda. I thought they were deciding whether to tell me something, but then I gathered that Roy wanted to be sure I understood his answer. 'They interfere with our traditional ways. They force us to follow a settlement policy even when many want to live in our own way. I am trying to address this problem through my work with the First People.' Roy shook his head in frustration as he talked.

'Do you think that government will listen?'

'We have some few supporters who are listening'. Roy described a new management plan for the Central Kalahari Game Reserve produced by some enlightened staff in the Department of Wildlife and National Parks with the participation of Roy and several other Bushman representatives. It acknowledged for the first time that these reserves have been the home of Bushman and BaKgalagadi peoples for many centuries. In terms of an agreement worked out between the department and lawyers, those living in the reserves would have rights for traditional hunting, residence and resource utilisation. 'But,' Roy continued. 'Many others in government want us removed.' They have big plans for tourism. They are hunting for diamonds. We are in their way.'

I really felt for Roy. Just one little guy without any education, brought up in a culture unused to handling wealth, influence and patronage, trying to take on the big barons who were intent on grabbing resources and control of the last patch of free country in Botswana. To them, the Bushmen were irritating flies that needed swatting.

Moving on from the realpolitik, I asked Roy for his views on wildlife management. 'On the way to Rakops yesterday, we saw the veterinary fence on the northeastern side of the reserve. About 20 years ago, some friends of mine used to live not far from there at a camp in Deception Pan.[2]

'We call Deception Pan *Xanare,*' said Roy. 'I know this man very well.'

My friends had seen wildebeest dying in thousands along the fence, and in the wastelands around Lake Xau, as they tried to reach the Boteti River in the dry season. I described the scene to Roy and the government's argument that they must keep the fences because they confer disease-free status on the cattle which is vital for the economy.

'I have seen the problems caused by these fences,' said Roy. 'Once there was a big veldt fire up that way, coming from outside the reserve with smoke and flames leaping high, driving animals before it. The antelope tried to get through the fence into the reserve. They tried to escape the fire but couldn't. They died at the fence.' Roy's fists were clenched and his whole body moved from side to side as he recalled this incident. 'I have heard of a new plan,' he continued more calmly. 'It involves two fences and will keep cattle out of the Kalahari whilst allowing wild animals to enter. We need something like that.'

It was growing dark. Bulanda went into the shack to light a candle. She came back out with Arthur who was hungry for his next feed. Soon I would need to leave. 'People are saying that there is no place for wild animals in Africa unless they pay for themselves. Even President Mugabe is reported as saying "*If we can't use them, lose them.*" Would you accept this?'

'Maybe the people who say this thing are crazy,' said Roy emphatically. 'It is not true.'

He seemed so disdainful of this way of thinking that I wondered whether he held to the spiritual world of the Bushmen at their first contact with the West, sharing perhaps their belief in an early time when people mingled with animals. 'Do you think animals have a right to live?' I asked, 'just as people do?'

Roy smiled, no doubt amused by my peculiar questions. 'Everyone knows that the government here protects animals because they can provide an income from wildlife tourism, not because they have rights. On my side, I regard wild animals as a very important part of Bushman life and culture. I do not want the wild animals to be finished. I want to protect our culture.' He paused for a moment, before adding, 'We live with the wild animals.'

I drove slowly back to Thakadu camp, thinking about Roy and the small band at Molapo, and wondering what kind of threat they posed to the dominant culture to warrant their endless persecution. Perhaps it was the opposite – the lack of threat from a harmless people – that kept triggering the greed of others? A wind got up that night and I slept fitfully. At four o'clock I was wide-awake and decided to go for a walk. Outside a warm breeze brushed against my skin and the soft sand rubbed between my toes. A glowing moon, now three-quarters full, hung low on the horizon. The Bushmen used to pray to the moon, sitting on the ground holding out their hands, palms upward.[3] Turning, I noticed my dark shadow cast 30 feet across the pale desert floor… strange how shadows under moonlight can be more striking than their bolder cousins under the sun. The legs of this shadow extended for two-thirds of its height, elevating the body and head, giving it the same exaggerated proportions as some Bushman figures painted on rocks. Perhaps moon shadows inspired the artists.

An answer to my question of how Bushman societies had lived in balance with nature was beginning to take shape. In their mobile bands, the Bushman's environmental consciousness was shaped by three great imperatives: the hunt for food, the hunt for knowledge and the hunt for God. The three had fused within the heart of the shaman-hunter. Their lives were filled with the hunting and tracking of great game animals, observing the seasonal rhythms of nature, sharing meat and skins with those in need, telling stories of the ancestors, dancing with kin and trancing with spirits. Here, one dimension of reality blended easily with the next. And from that union, with all the inevitability of an emergent property, there had arisen a pattern for sustainable living. Far more than ours, the Bushman's life in the Kalahari was embedded within the fabric of nature. Perhaps it was their willingness to commune with her at the deepest level, and to accept her ultimate authority over their lives, that ensured both survived. Could there be a lesson in sustainable living for the West here?

Meanwhile amongst the urban Bushmen living on the fringes of the central Kalahari, two of their three great imperatives have been knocked away. They can no longer hunt for game animals and they have had to surrender the hunt for knowledge. Only the hunt for God remains, carrying with it the despairing hope of healing and renewal.

14

FATE OF FIFTY THOUSAND

Okavango elephant

Over tea with the vulture next morning, I realised that I was no longer preoccupied with Bushmen. It was not that I'd lost interest, more that my inner wondering had been stilled by all I had seen and heard. It felt as if they were now waiting to see what I would make of their story. It would take time to sink in and meanwhile I needed to move on with my journey. That raised the question of where to go next. It was not hard to find an answer. They had made their presence felt just a few days earlier when we were camped on the outskirts of Maun. We had pitched our tents at the edge of a flooded channel on the southern fringes of the Okavango Delta with a grand view across the rippling waterway to the woods beyond. I knew that the channel marked the southern edge of the elephant's distribution in Africa. From there northwards they roamed freely throughout the delta and the adjoining woodlands of the Chobe National Park, and eastwards over waterless country to the Hwange National Park in Zimbabwe. Friends had driven for a hundred kilometres along the Linyanti River and Savuti Channel without ever losing sight of elephants. It was their territory. Although we hadn't seen any, it was easy to imagine them drinking from the channel or idling on the grassy knoll where I'd set my tent. They had even infiltrated town, adding a buzz of excitement to every conversation.

Wild elephants are more than just the largest land animals on Earth. They conjure up our past like powerful magicians. The deep rumble from a distant valley, the grey shadow slipping through the woods, the mottled imprint in the sand the size of a dinner plate, each awakens the memory of an earlier time, in a long-forgotten homeland where the evening sky ignites the setting sun and a crackling fire shoots living sparks into the starry heavens. Their majesty, their mystery, opens a window into the timeless soul. Allied to our romance with elephants is a darker side. The placid bull that rests in the shade of a wild fig tree during the heat of the afternoon may be filled with hungry purpose at night, smashing down fences, laying waste to fields of maize and striking terror into the hearts of small-time farmers whose last moments won't warrant column space in the national press. Elephants are possessed by a third djin: they are the gallant bearers of ivory, that creamy smooth enamel beloved by carvers for its warmth, strength and elasticity. Its allure has incited a ruthless trade in tusks which, on more than one occasion, has brought these majestic creatures to their knees.

No other animal embodies such contrast, no other poses such difficulty, and no other discharges so much human passion. That is why elephants are the touchstone species of wild Africa. If we cannot accommodate them, we have failed as conservationists.

Long after the vulture had taken wing, flapping across the plains to find a thermal that would lift her high above Thakadu Camp, Stu and I took a leisurely breakfast at the bar, packed up Nomad and headed down the road. We were making for Gaborone where I had an appointment the next morning. Paved with diamonds, the highway south of Ghanzi ran flawlessly across the veldt. There was hardly any traffic, just a watery mirage on the tar up ahead and the odd thorn bush on either side. Stu was quiet at first, savouring his fresh supply of rolling tobacco, and reflecting perhaps on life without Bulanda. We stopped once for petrol at a modern filling station and picked up a couple of mauve cans of ice-cold granadilla. In the late afternoon we arrived at the Mokolodi Nature Reserve on the south side of Gaborone and pitched our tents in a shady coppice. This was as near to a city as we wanted to get.

Next morning I was up early to prepare for my meeting. In the grey light of dawn I walked barefoot along a small path leading to an outdoor shower, trying to avoid the scattering of thorns that had fallen from a tree above. I'd stoked up a fire under the water barrel half an hour earlier. Now I turned on the tap in anticipation of a hot soak. Nothing happened. Cursing the unknown plumber, I gave the barrel a few hefty whacks. When this failed I gave up, grabbed a bucket from the back of Nomad and splashed myself with cold water. I shouted at Stu to get up whilst donning my semi-smart black jeans and one pressed shirt. Dispensing with breakfast to save time, we jumped into Nomad and headed for

Gaborone. My appointment was with a UK government advisor who would hopefully be able to fill me in on the details of some upcoming conservation projects. Stu was keen to do some shopping. I dropped him at the bank, and then searched about for the ministry building. It proved to be a high-rise office block close to the House of Chiefs. Eventually I found the advisor's tiny office tucked away in the basement.

He seemed a pleasant fellow, dressed in collar and tie, more used to dealing with matters of governance than nature conservation. He confirmed that the wildlife department lacked properly trained wardens, and that even routine decisions on day to day matters in the parks were being taken in Gaborone, causing lengthy delays. He briefed me on the new measures that were being planned and on a forthcoming conservation project. Before leaving, I asked if there were any other wildlife matters that the government might need a hand with in the future.

'Something will have to be done about the elephants in Chobe,' he blurted out. 'We need to cull them.'

I looked at the advisor in dismay wondering where he had got such an idea. There had been no mention of it in Maun. It was probably just gossip in the expat community, perhaps someone complaining about damage to the riverside woodlands. Just to be sure I paused to explain some of the difficulties with elephant management.

'The latest estimate puts the number of elephants in northern Botswana at between 120, and 130,000,' I began. 'As a rough rule of thumb, ecologists reckon that you need to remove half of an abundant herbivore population to bring about a recovery in the vegetation. That would mean an initial cull of 50 or 60,000 elephants.' The advisor was listening but wearing a taut expression that gave little away. 'It would be difficult to manage a slaughter of that scale. It would certainly attract worldwide condemnation. What's more, it would need to be followed by further culls of perhaps 2 or 3,000 animals each year in order to prevent the population building up again.' To my surprise, the advisor remained completely impassive. Hoping that I wouldn't torpedo any chance of future work with the government, I drove home the message. 'Besides that, many ecologists doubt the necessity of culling at all.' The advisor shrugged dismissively and turned back to the papers on his desk. I picked up my canvas briefcase and stormed out the drab office. I knew of only one person who could have swayed an entire government department to adopt such a strong-arm policy.

Standing in the windy taxi rank at Brussels Airport, dressed in an old Harris Tweed jacket, with a tie picked out by my sister-in-law, I remember feeling absurdly out of place. I was surrounded by businessmen in square-shouldered raincoats and unsmiling women in power dress, part of a different world that I didn't understand. Eventually my taxi came and I directed the driver to the labyrinthine headquarters of the European Commission. Africa felt a million miles from those grey city streets, but when it came to wildlife conservation I knew the real action was here. It had finally dawned on me that field biology, even at its most innovative, could not halt the steady erosion of wild places. In fact the pace of change was quickening. Whilst fiddling with my binoculars and notebook, all around the old forests, the richest habitat of all, were burning. I had decided to get involved in conservation and whenever possible to work on location to see for myself what did and didn't work.

Up on the 12th floor the offices looked drab and uniform. Unlike the university corridors I was accustomed to, there were no posters of exotic animals, or charismatic scientists, or rock artists or DNA molecules. No paintings. No calendars. In fact nothing to indicate any passion. In room 1249, the desk officer was fluent in four languages, and chain-smoking unfiltered Gauloise. In between an almost continuous stream of interruptions from the telephone, a secretary and various colleagues, I asked him about the commission's environmental work in Africa. At one point three colleagues burst in together and spoke rapidly in a combination of French and Italian before rushing out again. It had something to do with a major shake-up going on in the commission. They seemed to occur every year or two. Maybe the passion in these corridors was reserved for survival.

'Have a look at this,' the desk officer rasped, passing over a typed document whilst still on the phone. 'Let me know what you think.'

There were 10 pages of recycled paper stapled carelessly together; the print was smudged and skewed. I glanced at the top page. It called for the review of a project in Botswana that was upgrading the management of the northern wildlife areas. The reviewers would visit the project on site, report on progress, or the lack of it, and make recommendations for the final two years of funding. The drab office faded from view to be replaced by dusty plains, riparian forests and hippo-filled lagoons. Looking through the document I found only one possible snag: the manager of the project was a foremost scholar of African wildlife with a reputation for intolerance.

'It's right up my street,' I replied. 'I'll let you have our proposal.'

Putting the document in my briefcase, I headed for the door. The desk officer nodded goodbye, still on the telephone.

Realising it would be a tricky assignment, I had asked three highly regarded consultants to accompany me: an economist with a razor-sharp mind offset by a boyish sense of humour; an institutional expert who was an ace at smoothing out dysfunctional development projects, easy in manner but with the tenacity of a terrier; and an information technology expert who was principal troubleshooter for a company in Silicon Valley, and was also my younger brother. The first few days were spent at the Department of Wildlife and National Parks in Gaborone but then the team had moved to the project headquarters in Maun. There we met the project manager in his temporary caravan office. He was a big fellow with a commanding presence and a wave of chestnut hair across his forehead.

Initially, discussions with the project manager were strictly along formal lines but I'd hoped that once we were away from the office we could relax a bit and talk shop. On our first visit to the nearby parks, I raised several knotty topics in African ecology. He was interested enough but on each occasion our conversation was sullied by a fundamental disagreement on wildlife management. I tried to avoid confrontation, recognising that there was a job of work to be done, but a simmering tension began to build.

Early one afternoon we set off in convoy for a tented camp on the edge of the Okavango Delta, arriving just in time for the evening's game drive. We followed a dirt track that ran alongside one of the flooded channels, winding around broken limbs and pieces of dead wood that lay scattered along the banks. Pointing to a cluster of fallen trees, the project manager observed, 'You get this kind of thing all over. We have a real problem with elephant damage here.'

Not wanting the others to be swayed by rhetoric, I decided to challenge this anthropomorphism. 'Not damage,' I said, 'it's just habitat modification.'

The rest of the team thought this highly amusing and it became a bit of a game. From then on whenever anyone spotted a broken tree, the cry would go up, 'Oh look! More habitat modification.' The project manager didn't join in the fun. Sooner or later I knew we were in for a showdown; it turned out to be sooner.

After showering in our luxury tents, the group met for dinner, joining the proprietor at a long wooden table laid with ornate cutlery and crystal. A cool breeze wafted up from the nearby channel carrying the sweet musty smell of elephant into the open dining room. The disharmony was obvious and the talk was stilted. The soup course had barely finished when matters came to a head.

Contemplating me over his glass of South African Pinotage, a bit like a Kalahari lion eying up a dainty springbok lamb that some kind Bushman had tied to a tree, the project manager declared smoothly, 'You know, don't you, that sport hunting is the best hope for protecting wildlife in northern Botswana?'

I realised at once that this deceptively bland statement was just the opening shot in a salvo, intended to undercut my philosophy and undermine my credibility in front of the review team. I had dared to challenge the king of beasts; now I was to be given a public lesson in manners.

The project manager had made a strong opening move, one that was supported by a growing number of wildlife specialists in Botswana, particularly those working in the safari business. In return for exclusive rights to a large chunk of northern Botswana, and for the opportunity to shoot a quota of wild animals each year, the hunters paid a hefty fee to government, maintained the tracks and camps, and kept poachers off their property. I decided to play for time and get a better feel for how the attack would build.

'It seems to me that these parks,' a sweep of my arm took in the surrounding Moremi and Chobe protected areas 'and the revenue from tourism are already doing a pretty good job. In any case,' and here I mounted a small diversionary foray, 'is it right that Bushmen who once lived in the hunting concessions should now be treated as poachers?'

Ignoring the dig about Bushmen, the project manager chose to emphasise the economic strength of the case for hunting, well aware that the economist was listening closely.

'The money from parks and reserves barely pays for the cost of their management. So the extra revenue provided by sport hunting is crucial. Without it the whole of northern Botswana would soon be overrun by cattle and goats.'

'Tourism is growing rapidly,' I replied, 'and in any case do you not think there is more to a wild animal than the price on its head?'

The project manager snorted. He was not going to have any of this namby-pamby talk.

'Look, wildlife is disappearing rapidly in this country and being sentimental about it won't help. The Batswana don't much care about it. It's not part of their cultural heritage. So bringing in fat-cat clients who will pay to shoot trophies is the only way to save it.'

I wavered for a moment. Within its own economic framework, the logic was strong. In a way I admired its single-mindedness and the consideration it gave to people's livelihoods and income, but I distrusted the narrow frame of the argument. The difficulty was in how to reveal its narrowness without appearing over-sentimental.

'If we follow your argument to its logical conclusion, then eventually you will want to shoot animals inside the parks.'

'Why not,' the project manager replied without a blink. 'It will provide money to pay for better anti-poaching patrols and it will relieve the damage being done to the trees.'

The gloves were on the table now. I noticed the proprietor was getting fidgety, probably unaware of the real nature of this exchange. My brother, sitting at the far end of the table, was silently willing me on. The rest of the review team were quiet, listening intently; they couldn't help but be impressed by the project manager's gravitas. I needed to say something, but what? Maybe the debate could be raised to a higher level.

'When you live in a national park amongst the wild animals that you are studying,' I began, hoping to loosen the project manager's vicelike grip on economics by introducing a scientific interest, 'you find a world full of marvels that is much richer than could be imagined by the client who arrives for a short visit and a triumphant kill. Look at what we have learnt about the lives of wild elephants: the individual recognition of hundreds of animals living in their vicinity, their close family bonds, their long memories, their awareness of even those that have died, and their altruism for those in distress.' I found it hard to conceal the passion in my voice as I came to the nub of the matter. 'The last places in Africa, where you can find undisturbed elephants living freely within the bounds of nature, are inside a few national parks such as this one. Is this undisturbed world of nature such a trivial luxury to you that you would seek to destroy these places by turning them into yet more hunting concessions?'

The project manager picked out the line of my serve immediately and smashed his reply back across the net.

'I wouldn't destroy the park; I would protect it with hunting.' A fleeting smile of triumph crossed the otherwise impassive face.

Although reeling from the relentless strikes I was not yet beaten. 'It has taken 5,000,000 years of hominid evolution to understand that we have a duty to preserve wild creatures not just for hunting but for their own inherent value.'

'It has taken 5,000,000 years of hominid evolution to reach a point where we manage wildlife rationally for its valuable products,' came the swift retort. 'Answer me this: which is better, a few animals shot by safari clients using powerful rifles under the watchful eye of a professional hunter or a whole population of animals snared and shot for bush meat in the space of a few years?'

As the project manager's ruthless logic tightened its squeeze, I cast about desperately for some way to break free of the lock, a way by which the others could understand the poverty lying at the heart of economics.

'Do you know what President Kruger said about the Kruger National Park as he put his signature to the paper that brought it into being?' I paused for a few seconds looking around at their faces. '"It shall be a nation's dream, an animal's sanctuary."' I finished the quotation slowly, letting it fall softly over the dinner table.

Outside a light breeze was rippling the waters of the Okavango, but inside the tension was palpable. The local waiters, all of whom spoke excellent English, edged closer to the table to listen in. I thought I had him floored, but the project manager was no more impressed by the president's eloquence than by my own sentiments.

'That was in an age when the pressures on land were far less severe. There is no place for such *luxuries…*' he embellished the word, glancing at the others with a satisfied smirk '…in modern Africa. Wildlife in Botswana will have to pay if it is going to stay.'

I recognised the battle cry of the 'consumptive-use' conservationists and tried to deflect the attack.

'Tourism is a perfectly acceptable way of generating revenue from parks.' Too late, I saw the trap I had laid myself. The project manager spotted it, and pounced.

'And what about outside the parks?' he asked, a rising note of victory in his voice.

Despite the liberal tots of excellent Cape brandy being plied by our host, my mind was racing.

Paradoxical though it might seem, I knew that the sport hunter loved his quarry for the intensity of feeling it draws forth from his heart: pride, appreciation of beauty, and a sense of belonging in the primordial drama that unites predator with prey. Bushmen describe their hunting as 'walking with God'. So I could empathise with the sport hunter's passion even if I could never admire his sport, unless he could show some pressing need to take the life of another creature. And of course that would no longer be sport. That difference, apparently so slight, was the nub of the thing. For Bushmen, hunting is born of necessity and the animals they hunt are their brothers and sisters from the time of the Early Race; for the sport hunter a sense of mastery over nature predominates.

In northern Botswana, the conservation elite was promoting sport-hunting as part of a business strategy in which the Western demand, *hunting in return for money given*, was translated into a local supply, *animals for money received*. It was a commercial transaction with as little inherent warmth as the trade in engine oil, or lamp shades, or any other commodity. Of course, many professional hunters study the habits of wild animals closely, take pride in conserving the populations on their concessions, and ensure that the carcasses shot by their clients are properly butchered and that the meat is not wasted. The project manager was right; they took much better care of their wildlife than most of the local ranchers. Nevertheless, I disliked their corporate attitude and the sense of dominion over nature and didn't want to see such sentiments transferred into the management of our wonderful national parks.

By this time it was late in the evening and I doubted whether such abstract notions would stand up against the down-to-earth clout of the project manager's thesis. I decided to settle for a truce.

'I can see your logic on safari hunting outside of parks, although it isn't for me. On the other hand, I don't accept your logic within the parks. Can we not agree at least to separate the management policy in parks from that in hunting areas?'[1]

I was feeling quite beneficent at this point and hoping for some reciprocation, but the project manager merely snorted to show his contempt for any form of compromise. In truth, I had little interest either. At this point the party began to break up. Some plans were made for the next morning, followed by an exchange of gruff goodnights. Our review team walked slowly back to the tents, pitched in a row along the river channel. We were quiet, listening to the sounds of the night, and thinking about what had been said.

Turning to me, the economist remarked, 'You were never going to change your stance, no matter what the project manager said, were you?'

'I don't want to seem pig-headed,' I replied.

'No,' the economist said, 'on the contrary, I like the constancy of your values.'

I thought about this remark before falling asleep, wondering why the views that the project manager and I brought to the dinner table had been so little changed by the evening's debate. We shared similar interests, education, career and African experience, and had talked over the technical details of wildlife management for two weeks, yet we had found no common ground that evening. As scientists, we had been trained to evaluate new facts and discard ill-fitting ideas, yet those skills had failed to narrow the gap. In the small hours of the night, I finally saw through the enigma. The project manager had argued from the standpoint of economics and I from that of ethics. Inevitably the logical constructs that we employed in the debate supported these different value systems. In the words of Francis Bacon, we worshipped different idols. The one thing that the debate had highlighted was the poverty of our shared environmental philosophy: it was quite unable to bridge differences in value, even though it is these which incite the most fundamental disagreements in society.

Outside the entrance to the ministry, I stamped my feet angrily on the paving stone to shake off the dust of that monumental indifference to harmless people and sentient animals, and then strode across the main thoroughfare in the direction of the President's Hotel. A few minutes later I came to a pedestrian square filled with carvings and leather goods laid out in small rectangles each under the watchful supervision of a street merchant. I hurried past being in no mood to buy and entered the hotel's dark interior. Upstairs and across the dining room I found a balcony which caught a slight breeze and chose a table overlooking the square. I ordered a sparkling granadilla with lots of ice from a hovering waiter, and slowly relaxed. The street merchants weren't having much joy. It was already baking hot and they had no shade to offer the tourists. After a while I pulled out my cellphone and made a series of expensive calls – one to a colleague in Scotland to keep him abreast of news on conservation projects in

Botswana, one to my accountant who somehow kept the financial wolves at bay, and several within Botswana in an attempt to track down a local company that might join in a bid for conservation work.

That done, I looked again at the latest text message from Isla:

> Hi dad hope ur doin well, 4 my art project ive decided 2 make a theatre stage. im doin ok thanx. . . I miss u loads, lots of love isla xoxoxoxoxoxoxoxoxox

All thoughts of elephant culling evaporated as I contemplated this message. She would be combining two of her passions, acting and art, into one assignment. I smiled, remembering her first acting lesson. It had been in the living room of our rented home, a few miles from the dreaming spires of Cambridge. I had stood in one corner and she in the opposite one, reading out a story whilst projecting her voice so that I could hear it easily. She had signed up for acting classes as soon as we moved to Edinburgh and was now a member of the Lyceum Youth Theatre. I knew she would put her heart and soul into this project, creating a magic world on a tiny floodlit stage. I keyed in a reply:

> Hello my tsama melon, leaving Gaborone 2morrow 4 Bulawayo. Kalahari Bushman r wonderful. Your stage project is brilliant idea. Miss u lots, love Dad oxoxox

Whilst I was doing this, Stu arrived with some shopping, sweating but carefree in his baggy shorts and Namibian T-shirt, followed a few minutes later by a colleague of mine, Philip, looking harassed in creased slacks and collared shirt. He was a British conservationist who had been working with the wildlife department for four years. I was hoping he could tell us the real intentions of government regarding the resettlement of Kalahari Bushmen. We gathered platefuls of salad and vegetables at the self-service bar, ordered iced drinks and sat down under a ceiling fan. Phil's brow was more creased than I remembered and his eyes were tired. I wondered what life was like for expats here. I knew he would be wary of talking openly on contentious issues. But to my delight he pulled out a detailed map of the Central Kalahari and spread it out on the table. He hesitated for a moment, frowning, and then pointed to a network of 'community use zones' which had been drawn up in consultation with Bushmen. I noticed a large area around the Molapo settlement was marked off as one zone. If this plan were to be approved, it would provide Bushmen with official recognition of their traditional Kalahari lands. It would grant them a real homeland. Although Phil made light of the work, I recognised its importance and could imagine the effort invested in compiling the map. Beyond that was the patience needed to wait for the precise moment – a combination of the right person in the right place at the right time – to best sell the idea in the higher echelons of government. It was a real art. And of course there was always the knowledge that his efforts could easily be undermined by a word from a powerful opponent.

Phil had time for a quick coffee before leaving for his office. I mentioned my unease at the casual comment about elephant culling in the ministry. He gave me the address of a publicly available web site, suggesting that I take a look, and departed.

Sitting in the internet café an hour later, I could hardly believe what I was seeing. It was a government announcement, newly posted, inviting companies to tender for a project concerned with elephant management. It stated that the policy objective of the Government of Botswana was to reduce the northern elephant population from 120,000 to 55,000 animals by culling and cropping. As the import of this sunk in, I slumped back in horror, flinching at the weight of the intention. The operation they had in mind would require a small army of helicopters, planes, trucks, handlers and meat processing facilities. I felt my anger rising. This was industrial management. It was no way to treat wild animals.

15

MIRRORS IN THE HILLS

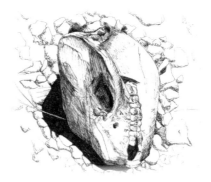

Dassie skull

Leaving the tall office blocks of Gaborone behind us with all their city hassles, a hungover Stu and I turned onto the single lane highway that snakes northwards 500 kilometres to the border crossing with Zimbabwe at Plumtree. The cool beers last night had slipped down a treat. Stu had recovered some of the bonhomie which had been missing since his nightmare journey with Bulanda, and I'd dreamt up a love story about a travelling bum and his artistic girlfriend in Edinburgh. This morning we were paying for the evening's excesses and the mood was subdued. It was not long before we reached a checkpoint where armed guards controlled the passage of travellers through a gap in a formidable fence that straddled the wilderness on each side. These steel shrouds bar the migration of game animals across the Kalahari as surely as the iron curtain once blocked free movement of people across Europe. Every vehicle was being ordered to stop before it was cleared to pass. As we pulled up, a veterinary guard stared at us suspiciously, automatic rifle at the ready, whilst another peered into the back of Nomad. The atmosphere was tense – a million miles from James Herriot and the animal doctors portrayed on British television.

'Forget your police states,' I whispered. 'All hail to the vet republic.'

'What are these stroppy bastards looking for?' asked Stu.

'Goats?' I suggested. 'Maybe meat or anything that might carry disease. These fences separate cattle country from wildlife. They ensure that Botswana's beef qualifies for disease-free status and can be exported to Europe.'

'I thought we had a beef mountain back home,' said Stu, flummoxed by the absurdity of exporting beef from a protein-deficient continent.

'Even so, we import this stuff at a fixed price and then flog it at a loss to the Russians. It's known as the European Commission's beef subsidy to Botswana.'

'Sounds harmless, if stupid,' said Stu lighting a roll-up and sharing in my relief at being waived on by the guard.

'Not that harmless.' I retorted, telling him about the impacts of the fence. My friends who set up camp in Deception Pan had flown over the Kalahari in a light aircraft on a daily basis. They had seen how the fences funnelled wildebeest herds into the last available water point, creating intense conflict with local pastoralists. One herd of emaciated animals had stumbled right past their camp looking for water.[1]

'What happened?' asked Stu gazing out at the endless Kalahari scrub.

'They drove over to the lake only to find that it was dry. A jeep was driving up and down the lake bed, its back stuffed with people shooting at the wildebeest with automatic rifles. There was a mass die-off that year.[2] Thousands of carcasses were strewn along the fences and up and down the lake shore.'

'Bleedin' carnage!' said Stu. 'Were there no survivors?'

'The last great migration was in 1983. Then the population collapsed from around 250,000 to 15,000. The survivors stay down south with just enough water to keep them going.'

'Didn't anyone realise that would happen?' asked Stu.

'The government were advised against fences[3] but like most governments they dodge advice they don't like.'

'But isn't it illegal for the EC to bankroll a disaster like that?'

'You would think so,' I replied recalling that my friends had mentioned that both the European Union and the Botswana Government had disregarded Article 35 of the Lome IV Convention which states that the parties agree to avoid harming the environment as a result of any programme or operation. 'But they seem to get round legislation they don't like.'

'So why doesn't someone do something?'

'It's very tough to do anything. The beef barons of Botswana are untouchable and the unelected moguls of the European Commission – the ones who wield serious power – keep out of sight. They are shielded by a smokescreen of committees.'

Stu was silent for a minute and then changed tack.

'You can't just turn the country into a great big Pleistocene game park. All those cattle must boost the economy.'

'They boost the economy of the cattle barons. It's the defenceless poor and the wildlife that pay the price.'

'By defenceless poor, you mean the Bushmen? But aren't they employed to look after the cattle?'

'Maybe.'

'For all you know, they are happy as Larry about the fences and fat cows, right?'

Stu had a point. Over a long period, Bushmen had helped Bantu people with cattle herding and surely benefited from the employment. 'Roy Sesana told me about animals trapped against a fence by a veldt fire. In describing their death he hunched forward, lifted his hands and wrung them violently backwards and forwards in opposite directions, and all the while his face was contorted in pain.'

'Bloody nora!' exclaimed Stu. And then after a slight pause: 'He must have been upset at losing all that meat.'

'Sure.'

'You sound a bit cynical,' said Stu flicking his stub out the window. 'Didn't the EC finance your review of their conservation project?'

'Their main business is commercial development,' I replied, ignoring the cheap shot.

'So you think the future of wildlife is bleak then?'

'I give the EC full credit for its conservation work, but bringing back the migration is not something they've even thought about.'

'Does that mean yes?'

'If one day I come back and find herds of black wildebeest trekking across the Kalahari,' I grinned at the thought of all that noise and commotion, 'I'll happily eat my floppy hat.'

A bank of clouds threw a dark cloak over the last of the evening light as we arrived at the outskirts of Bulawayo, not the best of conditions for finding a friend you haven't heard from in 20 years. Back then Peter and I had been based at a government research station in the remote bush working on our doctoral studies in animal ecology. And that's where I'd first run into the conflicts lying at the heart of wildlife management. It was a bruising encounter with a government authority that had little tolerance for outsiders. Now I wanted to trace that younger guy's journey and see if I couldn't make more sense of it. Catching up with Peter would be a good starting point; if I could just find him.

The only clue to his current whereabouts were some vague directions from a British ornithologist. 'Drive south from the centre of town until you reach a big hotel, then take the next road on the left and you'll find his house second on the right.' With directions like that you just know something will go wrong. Sure enough it was not long before we were befuddled. Taking a wild guess I knocked on the door of a house with a 4×4 in the drive. Luck came to our aid in the form of a charming Irishman who was not in the least phased by the sight of two scruffy strangers on his front doorstep. With the help of a local telephone directory and street map, he located Peter Mundy's address and drew us a sketch map. It was only five minutes away.

Verity, Peter's lovely wife, grasped the situation in an instant and pointed to the study urging me to go in and surprise him. And there he was, lounging in an easy chair pouring over the writings of some early naturalist in southern Africa. He looked every bit the long-haired, wild Cockney intellectual that I remembered. For a moment he looked blankly at me through his reading specs.

'Well I never, Martyn, how long has it been?'

'I'd put it at 22 years, Pete.'

'Blimey, is that right. I hardly recognised you without that bushy red beard,' and then turning to his wife who had just come in, 'Verity, this 'ere fellow used to lead them girls a *merry* dance back in the days when I was doing my vulture thing,' and turning back again, 'How are you man?'

'Don't believe a word he tells you.' I said to Verity. 'I'm top flight, just happened to be passing on my way up to Sengwa.'

'Huh, what do you want to go there for? You won't even *recognise* the place.'

'It's the elephants and the woods,' I replied enjoying the high of seeing Pete again. 'I want to smell the imbalance.'

'You always were a *crazy* bastard.'

I introduced Peter to Stu who had been chatting to Verity in the kitchen.

'On the road with this geezer?' enquired Peter. 'You better have a beer.'

We sat down amongst the books and carvings and cracked open some tins. Pete and I began to reminisce, catching up on old friends, recalling some of the wilder personalities we had known. Soon we were taking stock of the women and children in our lives. His two youngsters turned out to be the same age as Isla and Torran. After a couple more beers, Peter began telling Stu about his life in the 1960s when he played saxophone in a top British rock band. To his friends' amazement Peter had joined the wildlife department on finishing his vulture study despite its uniform and paramilitary style of management. Unlike most of his fellow park officers, he had elected to stay on in government after independence accepting the drastic drop in salary. He kept himself out of the limelight by living in the country's second city, Bulawayo. From there he headed up the national office for bird conservation and, in his spare time, studied black eagles in the nearby Matopo Hills. He had been tempted by several job offers, but even though it meant turning his back on financial security, he declined them all, as the price asked in each case was giving up the fieldwork that he loved.

I awoke in a real bed revelling in the luxury. It was 7.30 and I was starving. Outside the sun was already high in the sky. Stu had elected to camp on the lawn and by the time I had pulled on some clothes and made my way outside he had already helped himself to a 'Nomad's breakfast' of stale bread and fruit juice. Stu accepted people as they were, which made him great company, but he needed personal space. He'd been edgy since the Kalahari. I hoped he wouldn't exit from the safari like a scalded cat. I left him to do his own thing and scouted about for the Mundy family, finding Peter already hard at work in the study. We carried a table into the garden and placed it in the shade of a large Kenyan coffee tree and, for a touch of style, spread a white linen table cloth, setting three places for breakfast. Verity returned from dropping the children at school and cooked up sausages, eggs, toast and marmalade which Peter and I devoured. Later over freshly brewed coffee, our conversation turned to wildlife management.

'There is a *gulf* between East Africa and us lot in southern Africa,' said Peter who had a way of dramatising key words in a sentence. It added a whole new dimension to the conversation. 'We want to trade our *tusks*, see, and plough profits back into wildlife protection. The Kenyans want to ban trade because they reckon it will *stimulate* poaching.'

'The Kenyans are surrounded by countries in which bandits can operate freely,' I ventured, 'they come across the border to poach elephants, especially the Somalis, so it's not as easy to control poaching as it is down here.'

'Yeah. But the real problem is that the East Africans have no monitoring of elephants on which to *fix* CITES decisions about management, whilst in southern Africa we do.'

'They have some good counts of elephants in Tsavo National Park,' I remarked whilst pouring myself another cup of coffee – an excellent Arabica brew from Chipinge – and reflecting for a moment on the joy of debating wildlife over breakfast on an African lawn. It's not just talk; you're on the edge of action.

'It's not only counting,' responded Peter, 'it's the whole *science* of monitoring. If you don't *shoot* the elephants, you don't have to make any decisions about anything. If you do shoot them, you need to know how many there are, what their seasonal movements are, how many can be safely included in a *quota*, what sex and ages can be shot, and so it goes on. You end up with aerial census capability, *aging criteria*, herd classifications, computer models of the population and models that predict the state of the vegetation. You get science.'

'There is plenty of science in East Africa,' I countered. 'It's just different. In the Serengeti, scientists have measured how energy flows from plants to herbivores to predators and scavengers and so on. They know how it is affected by rainstorms and wild fires, and herds of grazing antelope. They've got a handle on the productivity of the entire ecosystem.' I paused to think about some of the other projects. 'The work on predators is phenomenal. The studies on lions and hyaenas, and cheetahs, and even mongooses, have been going on for 30 years or more. They've worked out all the social strategies being used to increase survival and reproduction.'

'Huh. It's a difference in *heritage*, then' said Peter. 'Don't the East Africans study populations?'

'It is different,' I agreed. 'In East Africa the focus is on long-term studies of individual animals. They know entire lineages of lions and elephants. It's almost like anthropology. In southern Africa the science is based on populations, and you get your data from counts or shot samples. You know all about the ages and sexes and numbers of animals in an area. It means you can predict births and deaths and model populations as they expand or contract.'

Stu had been listening in to the last part of the conversation, having succumbed to the aroma of freshly brewed coffee. He butted in now.

'All those arcane details of animal behaviour will do us a fat lot of good. Don't the East Africans realise that the crucial issues are economic? The farmer isn't interested in the breeding success of a mongoose, he wants compensation for damaged crops.'

'Their work is important,' I insisted. 'It expands our awareness of nature. We know now that the lives of wild animals are full of subtlety, emotion and interconnection. That knowledge changes things. You can't just treat them as meat on hooves.'

'You are using science to push your point of view onto the hapless farmer,' said Stu. 'He doesn't want cute behaviour. He wants meat.'

'Are we going to sit here *all day*?' said Peter, glancing at his watch. 'I thought we were going to the Matopo Hills.'

If rocks can be organic then surely the worn rounded hills of Matopo, awash with multicoloured lichens and adorned with feathery shrubs, are only sleeping. They are the antithesis of the icy, knife-edged puritans of the Alps. Under the midday sun they reminded me of half-submerged hippos lazing in a weed-covered pool. In places, great slabs of skin had sloughed off their backs leaving jumbled heaps of debris at their feet. We were standing at a high spot where black eagles perched to dismember their prey before carrying pieces to the nest.

Under the eyrie, acid from their droppings had etched away darker lichens to reveal the pewter-grey granite beneath. At my foot was the skull of a rock hyrax lodged beneath an everlasting bush that clung tenaciously to the edge of a vertical cliff. It was about the size of a large hare's. Peter was wearing his parks uniform, green floppy hat perched at a cheeky angle over his long sun-bleached hair. He was telling us about the records he kept on the Matopo eagles, going back 20-odd years.

'This dassie would have weighed four to four and a half kilos. That's more than the eagle itself,' he said, rounding off the morning's lesson on eagle biology.

'Do you have any idea how many dassies are in these hills?' I asked, wondering whether the hyraxes might have provided a basic food for the hunter-gatherers that used to inhabit them.

'It comes to 80,000 or something like that.'[4]

'That would keep a few Bushmen alive,' I said, prodding the skull idly with my desert boot.

'Oh yeah I see what you mean – this is your *Tsodilo Hills* hypothesis,' said Peter. 'Well I'll tell you something. The gestation of these dassies is a full *seven and a half months* – that's not much different from people – and like us they only have one young in a year...'

'...which makes them really vulnerable to over-hunting,' I finished his sentence.

'Exactly. Not that they eat much dassie meat around here, but the *skins* are valuable. See? They cure them; sew a bunch together to make a blanket, or a *kaross* as the Afrikaaners call them. I've seen a kaross with 80 skins going for 1,000 American dollars. And for a local that's what, well thousands and thousands. He'd be a flippin' billionaire.'

Peter led the way back to the vehicle and drove on to a picnic site next to a small lake. Two black eagles circled overhead, soaring and swooping, before making a final gliding descent to their nest high up on the opposite kopje. They had staked a claim to the best territory in the Matopo Hills, the one that over the years had fledged more young than any other.

A large sow warthog trotted towards our table casting a hungry eye on our sandwiches.

'Here comes Tina Turner,' observed Peter. 'Who's been feeding you? You *predator*.'

'She's so funny,' said Stu. 'Where are your babies then?'

'Only a male warthog would *want* you, that's for sure!' said Peter watching her grubbing about.

Another warthog arrived.

'Are the locals here interested in wild animals?' asked Stu.

'Definitely,' replied Peter. 'My Ndebele friends are even named after totem animals. One of them is called *Ndhovu* which means elephant, another is "crocodile". Mostly though they come at wildlife from a utilitarian point of view.'

'That's exactly it,' said Stu. 'They have their own point of view. We shouldn't be projecting our interests onto their culture.'

'Many urban Africans haven't even seen wild animals,' I said. 'Take them into a national park, and they're amazed.'

'There shouldn't be any parks,' responded Stu. 'They don't interest the locals. What they want is hunting reserves.'

'What do you think, Peter?' I asked. 'You've worked in rural Africa all your life. Do you think the locals are interested in the behaviour of wild animals?'

Peter was perched on the table and idly swinging his foot against a litter bin. 'We've got several young scouts in the office who are really keen. One is in a class of his own. He's incredibly motivated. His whole thing is *understanding* birds. He's just as fluent with their names in Latin as in Shona.'

'It makes no difference who you are then?' I asked.

'Once you've *unlocked* a person's head… it makes no difference at all.'

'Once you've filled their bellies, you mean,' said Stu.

'We have a little junior wildlife magazine called *Bush Beat*,' said Peter. 'These African kids write in with the most amazing poems – one was about an elephant, about how the animal moves around and what it means, and it's so beautiful. *Poetry!* You tell me they aren't interested. Bleedin' eyewash!'

It was time to take a look at one of the Matopos caves. Half an hour later, we arrived at a deep hollow in the base of a cliff, its entrance almost invisible behind a screen of tall shrubs. Within the chamber the walls on all sides were covered in paintings of animals and people, most of them rendered in deep red ochre but there were also several shades of brown. On the right hand side was a line of 30 or more naked men, marching steadfastly towards the interior. They were tall with small buttocks, tasselled genitals and squared shoulders. Some carried long quivers over their shoulders and bows that were quite different from those of contemporary Bushmen. One or two had long rods that might have been spears. Perhaps they were warriors.

'Look at those tall skinny military types *mincing* along,' said Peter. 'They are carrying something over their shoulders.'

'It could be an invading army,' I suggested.

'The Matabele arrived in 1836,' said Peter, 'but these people look more like hunters.'

'There are a couple more lines marching in from the left,' observed Stu. 'They're smaller looking.'

Few of this second group were carrying bows although some were carrying fly whisks or other odd objects. On the back wall of the cave was a strange scene.

It looked like half a dozen arctic-style sleeping bags, each containing two people, or four in one case. To the right of the bags was a flight of crescent shapes, like new moons resting on their backs.

'I wonder if this is some kind of burial,' I mused.

'These are vultures,' Peter announced suddenly, pointing to the crescent shapes. 'You can even tell which way the birds are flying; that would fit in with a burial scene.'

'Those ones are coming in from the right,' said Stu indicating the first line of tall warriors, 'and these ones are coming in from the left, and look there is a bit of a carnage scene here in the middle.'

'So the mayhem is there,' agreed Peter, 'and the dead bodies are here…'

'It could be a whole battle scene,' said Stu.

'*Bold* hypothesis, *Sah*.'

I took a look at the carnage area that Stu had indicated. A line of four warriors was facing a single adversary. Although the paintings were faded making interpretation difficult, the nearest of the four warriors apparently had his right arm drawn back ready to launch a long arrow-like spear, straight towards his enemy.

'Is that one surrendering?' asked Peter. 'Huh! You could have a bleedin' field day trying to work this out, couldn't you? And this is only one cave in a *thousand*.'

We were so engrossed in the hidden meaning of the rock art that we failed to notice the heavy clouds building up outside.

'You know, it must be quite something to be in one of these caves when the thunder and lightning is going on all around,' said Peter quietly.

'You could start seeing things,' I agreed.

'The resident leopard might come home,' said Stu peering outside.

'What's that coming out the rock?' exclaimed Peter in mock alarm, causing Stu and I to start and laugh uneasily.

We left the cave with its mysteries and drove quickly over to a small museum. To our surprise we found a depiction of the burial scene, as sketched by Cran Cooke, a former curator of National Monuments.[5] We gathered round.

'It doesn't look quite the same,' I said, noticing that his vultures had rounded heads on their wing tips, which turned them into funny little people.

'I don't remember those heads,' said Stu.

Peter read out the inscription: "A dormitory scene of sleeping figures wrapped in skins or blankets." What is he on about?'

'It just goes to show, people see what they have in mind already,' I observed.

'It's difficult for an artist to make a strictly *factual* recording,' agreed Peter. 'Maybe that's what we were taught in biology. Do you remember peering down a microscope and drawing all that *cell* stuff?'

During the drive home we chatted on. The scene in the cave grew in our minds from a light skirmish between different hunting parties to a glorious portrayal of the last stand of the Matopo Bushmen, possessing all the drama and historical prominence of the Bayeux tapestry. Back at Peter's house, I pulled out my camcorder and looked over the images of the Bushman battle. I froze a frame of the burial scene and studied it carefully. There they were: faint but distinct circles on the tips of the vulture wings. Almost every bird had one, just as Cran Cooke's illustration had shown. The glorious battle scene crumbled into dust. Even with all our biological training, the three of us had been caught in the selfsame trap – seeing only what we believed in. Our epic battle had been born on the breath of an idea, carried aloft on a chain of coincidence, and sustained against buffeting by ignoring bits that didn't quite fit. I offered a silent apology to Mr Cooke, although I remained dissatisfied with his sleeping party.

'Guess what guys,' I said to the others whilst showing them the image, 'Mr Cooke got it right.'

'Well I'll be damned,' said Peter. 'It just shows how easy it is to *follow* one's own idea.'

'There's a good lesson in that,' said Stu.

'It happens all the time in science,' I added.

'How's that?' asked Stu.

'We think of scientific truth as the absolute answer, but it's really only a mirror. We only get answers to the questions we ask.'

'And silence to the questions we don't ask,' said Peter.

'We just follow our ideas, and they pretty much reflect the culture we're in.'

'You think that different cultures have different questions?' asked Stu.

'Yes I do.'

'And that you are blind to their special way of thinking?'

'Pretty much.'

'Then why do you want to hoist your truth on them?'

Stu can hold onto the same line of questioning for weeks, so I shouldn't have been surprised by his return to our morning's conversation, but it stopped me for a moment.

'I don't force my ideas on anyone,' I eventually replied.

'Does that mean you would get rid of the parks if the locals rejected your way of thinking; if they wanted to eat animals instead?'

'It comes down to *how* you do it,' said Peter. 'If you show them fellas the animals in their natural habitat, and it *grabs* their imagination, they'll want to keep the parks. It's their choice alright.'

I left the two of them to argue it out, and found a quiet place where I could run through the video sequence again. There was no doubt about it, the crescent shapes still looked like vultures, even if they had little heads attached to their wings. Half animal, half human. Hmmh. That made them therianthropes. And now a new idea. They must be spirits. A quick count revealed the same number of vulture-human spirits as heads in arctic sleeping bags. The battle scene erupted back into life. We were off again.

The night was sultry and the chilled beers – locally brewed Lions and Castles – slipped down easily. We were sitting under some tall jacarandas in the garden of Peter and Verity's local watering hole. White peacocks were perched on the outspreading limbs, mewing eerie cries up and down the deserted street, whilst the mauve blossoms filled the air with a heady scent. Verity was delighted by our stories of the cave paintings. She told me about her wish to undertake an initiation one day with a Native American group in the States where four days of solitude are followed by one night staying awake. A barn owl took flight from one of the eaves of the hotel flapping on silent wings to the canopy of a nearby tree.

'I am called out every year on *account* of these fellas,' said Peter.

'Don't people like them?' asked Stu who found it peculiar when people didn't like grubs and beetles, let alone beautiful owls.

'They don't like them nesting in the roof. They complain about them scratching about and making a mess,' explained Peter. 'So what I do is catch the young owls and block off the hole into the roof that the parents are using. That way I *disrupt* their breeding cycle. Then I carry the young ones back to my garden where I let my resident pair of barn owls adopt the orphans.'

'Your owls take on somebody else's chicks?' I asked in surprise. Birds are not supposed to be altruistic like that.

'Last year they fledged 18 orphans,' confirmed Peter.

'What's the point?' asked Stu. I mean doesn't that just cause massive problems in the next year?'

'The adult birds give up on their former nest sites,' said Peter. 'That keeps the *citizens* happy, least those who don't want owls in their gardens, whilst most of the young owls that we rear, disperse and keep the population going.'

It was one of the most heart-warming techniques of pest control that I'd ever come across. I didn't know if it was the beers, or the white peacocks mewing overhead, or the way Peter told the story, or quite what it was, but for some reason it struck me as absurdly important. Those owls... they were scratching away at something.

16

FORGOTTEN RESEARCH STATION

The way in

As the last mark of civilisation, it was a joy to leave the tiny outpost of Gokwe behind and follow the narrow trail that wound its way along ancient elephant paths into the untamed Zambezi Valley. In 1974, a single rutted track linked the shop at one end of the village to the police post at the other. Bumping along, you passed an agricultural office, a post office, the district commissioner's office, a hunting club and a few breezeblock residences whose flame trees and bougainvilleas added exotic red and crimson splashes to the native green woodlands. As we entered Gokwe today I was amazed at how the dusty administrative backwater had metamorphosed into a bustling modern town of concrete and glass. Peter Mundy had warned me about the pace of change. He had radioed through to the Sengwa research station first thing to tell them we were coming. Then, waving us off, had made me promise not to leave it another 20 years before coming back.

'You know Stu, I had my first experience of rural Africa in Gokwe. In those days the village store was a humble shack with a rusty tin roof and dirt floor. I remember how dark it was. There was no window or electricity and you could barely make out the shelves. My nearest point of comparison was a wee village shop in the highlands of Scotland.'

'So what did you ask for – a bottle of "Irn-bru"?'

'A Scotch egg and an apple!' I laughed at the memory. 'Then I realised just how little there was for sale – a few foot-long blocks of laundry soap, some bars of Lux toilet soap, toothpaste, a half dozen sacks of mealie meal and some tins of dried milk. There were a few chipped bottles of Coke in a wooden crate.'

'Did you buy anything?'

'I couldn't decide whether to give the shopkeeper some custom or leave what was there for those who needed it.'

'Bollocks! The guy was running a shop, wasn't he?' said Stu.

Reaching the other end of town, we located the large police barracks. I went in to ask for directions, heeding Peter's warning about the confusing network of farm tracks that had sprung up between Gokwe and Sengwa. In the duty office a smartly dressed constable gave me instructions on the new route to Sengwa Gorge – a well-known landmark where the river squeezes through an ultra narrow gap as it enters the Sengwa Wildlife Research Area.

'Take the Charama road from the centre of town, then the second turn to Mateta 1 business centre, keep going to Mateta 2 business centre, then take a right turn to Choto, and from there proceed to Wronga Wronga School. After that, the road goes straight to Sengwa Gorge. You should have no problems.'

It sounded straightforward but even before we dropped off the tar at the edge of Gokwe, I was having forebodings. 'Take a right turn to Choto' sounded simple enough in the police station, but there wouldn't be any signposts on the road and we would need to examine every farm track heading north.

At first, fortune smiled on us. We gave a lift to an old man returning to his home in 'Mateta 1'. He agreed that the countryside had changed completely. He had arrived in Gokwe District in 1954 as a small farmer. In those days the whole area had been filled with kudu, bushpigs and lions. Today there was nothing; just the occasional elephant coming through on its way to the upper reaches of the Lutope River, creating alarm amongst the farmers. Right enough, as we drove along the empty road I could see that the woods had been entirely converted to farmland. Soon we arrived at Matete 1 which comprised two bottle stores and a general store. It didn't look much like a 'business centre'. Perhaps the police were using shorthand for 'business of drinking centre'. We thanked the old man who pointed out the track to 'Matete 2'. At the next general store, a teenager gave us directions to Choto School. So far so good. At intervals we asked people on the road for more directions. They seemed to navigate by schools. In fact the larger part of the population on this stretch of road was comprised of neatly dressed children walking home from school.

After a long interval we arrived at the next 'business of drinking centre' which looked like it might be Choto. The only people to be seen were slouching outside the main liquor store at the crossroads. I instinctively turned right to face north, reckoning we must be pretty much due south of Sengwa. It was late afternoon and the guys were leaning against the fence or slumped in wooden chairs under a makeshift verandah. I parked Nomad and walked over to the first fellow whose head was lolling to one side, pupils dilated, wondering as I neared if he would prove friendly, belligerent or insensible.

'Can you tell me which road goes to Wronga Wronga School?' I asked. He pointed me back to the road we had been following. I thanked him and with some reluctance turned Nomad back onto the road heading west. It was evening when we reached the next 'drinking centre' with only half an hour of daylight remaining. At least this time I was able to choose a sober, elderly-looking man in a smart jacket sitting quietly on the stoop. I asked him if he could show me the way to Wronga Wronga School. When I saw that the name meant nothing to him, my foreboding grew. Peter had mentioned that he had tried twice to find Sengwa recently, and failed each time. I decided to keep that to myself. But Stu sensed the problem.

'Are we going Wronga?' he yelled to me.

After consulting with others on the stoop, he pointed down the road. 'Go to the next centre. It's three kilometres. From there you turn to the north.' There was something in the way he looked at me which said, 'I really don't have a clue, but I don't want you to know that'. After 11 kilometres, we arrived at the next centre. It was deserted. We pushed on. A minute later we came across a bullock cart steered by two teenage boys emerging from a tiny track. I asked for Sengwa Gorge, and without hesitation they pointed back down the track. The more hesitant I looked, the more insistent they became. 'Sengwa Gorge, yes, Sengwa Gorge. That way.' There seemed little alternative. I slipped into four-wheel drive and put my foot down. Nomad accelerated down the trail, catching the late afternoon sunshine, before beginning a long descent into the dark valley.

As we passed through a small cluster of mud and thatch huts, some children rushed out, waving and shrieking with delight. Skidding to a halt, we asked for Sengwa Gorge. 'That way, down the hill,' someone called. We continued down the bullock track, now so narrow that bushes were scraping Nomad on each side. The next time we came to some huts, we tried a few tricks to make sure we were heading in the right direction.

'Is Sengwa up there?' asked Stu, pointing back up the hill.

'No,' came the reply, 'Sengwa Gorge is that way,' and the fingers invariably pointed downwards, further into the valley, further it felt into nowhere. After a couple of miles, the valley steepened and our track swung to the right before entering a patch of thick scrub. We pushed through the scrub and found ourselves surrounded by tall mopane trees. We crept slowly forwards until coming to an abrupt halt in front of a low circular wall constructed of stone with a neat thatched roof. A bucket hung on a rope from a cross bar. Two women with infants strapped to their backs were busy decanting water from the buckets into plastic containers.

'Jeepers,' said Stu, 'I wonder if Jack and Jill live here.'

It was the end of the road. There could be no mistaking that. Out of dogged cussedness, I asked one of the ladies for Sengwa Gorge. She raised her arm pointing along a footpath that led from the well into the middle of the dark woods. It was surreal – as if we had stepped into another world. I looked at Stu, who shrugged. Switching on the headlights, I eased Nomad cautiously along the path. We passed several large trees before the trail began to narrow: three foot, two foot, one foot…

'I wonder if we are going to find a house made of gingerbread down here,' said Stu.

Soon the little path had taken on the appearance of an erosion gully, then it ceased even to pretend to be anything else; finally, the erosion gully petered out. We were left sitting in the midst of a dark, dense wood without so much as an animal track to follow. I suppressed an hysterical laugh. Despite all the savvy that comes from 30 years of working in remote corners of the world, I had led our expedition into the plumb centre of nowhere.

'How on Earth did I manage this?' I asked.

'Dunno,' said Stu, 'shall we set up camp?'

I was thankful for his sangfroid, but wanted to make one more effort to reach Sengwa. We reversed up the hill, relocated the path, retraced our tyre tracks to the well, and from there headed back up the hill to the last collection of huts. A group of women appeared carrying loads of firewood on their heads. I asked for directions to Sengwa Gorge, and shook my head when they pointed down the hill. They turned and called out loudly. Eventually, a swarthy and rather corpulent farmer emerged from one of the huts.

'Where is Sengwa Gorge?' I asked whilst making frantic signs with my hands that were supposed to indicate a road crossing over a wriggling ravine. From the look on the farmer's face, he thought we were completely crazy. He pointed back into the forest from where we had just emerged, but then changed his mind, and to my great relief indicated that he would show us the way. He must be a man of courage I decided. We made room in the front and under his direction, began to manoeuvre our way in amongst the crowded huts, passing goggle-eyed children and impassive grown-ups, before turning hard about in front of some large trees, squeezing between two fence posts, taking a left at the storage bin, and beginning the crossing of a deeply ploughed field. I admired the young maize stalks and accepted the madness of our predicament without further struggle. Gingerly we inched along, keeping our eyes open for hidden stumps and antbear holes, until reaching a thick belt of woodland on the far side of the field. The farmer encouraged us forward. We began winding our way back and forth between the larger trees whilst pushing over smaller ones with the kangaroo bar. When you find yourself pushing down trees in a 4×4 you can pretty much guarantee you are nearing the end of your journey – whether you like it or not. Right on cue, we came face to face with a tall fence.

'Well that's that then,' said Stu.

It took a second or two but then hope sputtered into life. Tall fences in rural Africa usually mean game control, and that implies a boundary between an area of farmland and a game reserve. Now boundaries of game reserves are often demarcated by perimeter tracks. The farmer indicated right. There was nothing in that direction except for a thick screen of trees. I inched Nomad forward a fraction, then a fraction more, her nose tilted down and there immediately in front of the fence was a track. It was only a small sandy cut through the woods but it had all the allure of an intercity highway. We dropped down onto its hard surface and swung to the right before stopping to drop off our friend. He marched off with a big grin, clutching a can of Castle lager in his right hand.

Guessing that we had found the southern perimeter fence to Sengwa, I continued eastwards along the track until reaching a modest gateway with a small sign proclaiming 'Sengwa Wildlife Research Institute, Dept. of National Parks & Wildlife Management'. For the first time since leaving Gokwe I actually recognised where I was.

17

CAPTURE GAMES

As if the cottage was waiting for me

I was ready for disappointment but the pretty whitewashed bungalow looked just as I remembered. The only difference I could make out in the last of the daylight was a border of flowering shrubs that someone had planted around the edge of the well-watered lawn. I walked across the grass and stood outside the front door for a moment. It was strange to be here; almost as if the cottage was waiting for me. I turned the handle and pushed. Inside the green verandah floor was swept and polished, the walls freshly painted in white, and even the mosquito netting was in good repair. The glass in the windows and doors leading from the verandah was gleaming and unbroken; the heavy metal frames having proved their worth against time and termites. I walked over to my bedroom door and pulled it open. The two single beds were freshly made and covered with light woolly blankets. They were the same tan colour. A candle had been placed on a small table next to the bed standing upright in a jar filled with sand. I went back out to the verandah and walked along to the bathroom. There was a new bar of soap on the enamel basin and green towels on the rail. Someone had lit a fire under the kuni burner in the garden, so that hot water gushed from the tap into the bath. It came with the same helping of sand as before. In the kitchen, I found the standard issue crockery in the cupboard and a full aerosol of fly killer by the window. Someone had made an effort to welcome us and I was touched, remembering the tradition of hospitality in the wildlife department.

The first time I stepped foot in the cottage – that was back in 1974, at the beginning of all those adventures – I had been a graduate student newly arrived from UK and eager to make my mark in African ecology. The cottage was to be my home and it soon became my retreat from the authoritarian world of the research station that lay a few hundred metres to the west. I glanced uneasily in that direction. The headquarters was hidden behind trees and rising ground but I felt my shoulders tense just thinking about it.

Daily confrontations with senior staff who paraded about the research station contrasted with the natural peace and beauty of the surrounding wilderness. The director was an excellent ecologist but a strict disciplinarian with clipped mannerisms and Boy Scout uniform. He commanded an assistant director, two research officers, a station manager, accountant, 16 game scouts and a much larger number of unskilled labourers. Obedience was expected, and obtained from all. Every morning the African scouts turned out in their creased and immaculate khaki uniforms for formal inspection and every afternoon tea was served for the European officers in the library. The stilted conversations of the tea ceremony contrasted with the wild murmurings of the Sengwa Valley, audible through the open French windows. The untamed woodlands began just below the station and spread northwards in a wild panorama, all the way to the foot of Ntabamangwe, a flat-topped mountain high above the distant floodplain.

That younger self had arrived fresh from the anarchic campus life of Great Britain burgeoning with the 'way-out' euphoria of a '60s generation convinced that the future belonged to them. I had come to study the graceful impala antelope whose golden herds lit up the surrounding woodlands. Peter Mundy had arrived shortly beforehand to study four kinds of vulture – the little 'hooded' that was subordinate to the others, the 'white-headed' which often arrived first at a kill, the numerous 'white-backed' known to travel up to 700 miles in search of food, and the great 'lappet-faced' that dominated the kill, clearing all others from the carcass. The two of us entered a country still clinging defiantly to a colonial time warp that had its defining moment in 1923 when Anglo-Rhodesians gained internal self-government. Our long hair and unwashed jeans clashed with the authority's short back and sides and pressed khaki. The station belonged to the officers. It was their rutting ground – a place where they postured and strutted, and roared at subordinates. Peter and he had to toe the line there. But in the evenings, when entertained 'off-territory' in the senior staff houses, the atmosphere was cordial and even friendly. It was quite schizoid and difficult to manage. I remember feeling more at ease perched on a low stool in a metal hut eating sudza with the scouts.

For a time Peter and I avoided serious confrontation with the officers by escaping into the heady, adrenaline-charged world of the African bush where we noticed, much to our amusement, the research officers seldom ventured. It was an entirely different arena with its own rules and customs. I walked about on foot, exploring every valley, thicket and waterhole, intoxicated by the cocktail of beauty and danger. Most of all I liked to watch the large animals – the elephant, rhino, buffalo, zebra, sable, roan, eland, kudu, bushbuck, waterbuck, reedbuck, impala, warthog, hyaena, leopard and lion – which shared the wooded hills and valleys and which seemed to buzz with spiritual presence.

Matters took a turn for the worse after the director went on sabbatical leave and power shifted to the assistant director who had a penchant for cricket and crosswords, and a barely concealed scorn for our like. The man was out to make his mark and we felt his puppy-like eyes following us about, looking for any excuse to bear down. Peter was threatened with expulsion from the neighbouring cottage because of the mess made by a young vulture that perched on his verandah. Rather than capitulate, Peter and vulture moved to an empty hut midway between the research station and the game scouts' compound, where he serenaded the stars with his saxophone and entertained gorgeous women from the city with candles and a battery-driven record player.

With Peter ostracised, the heat turned on me. More than Peter, I depended on the wildlife department for my research, needing their help to capture and mark impala. I knew the assistant director was watching me closely, waiting for an opportunity to pounce, a single slip would do.

Stu went inside to find a couple more cans of Castle lager leaving me to lounge in an easy chair on the lawn with my memories and the night sounds for company. The Pleiades and Orion constellations hung above the far side of the valley and an almost full moon was rising slowly above the tree-lined horizon. Even the night sky felt familiar. The shadowy outline of the large Msasa trees on either side of my view, with a jaggedy 'baboon orange' in the centre, made a half-forgotten frame for the stars. As the cool night air stirred the branches overhead, I slid back again in time, slipping into my old life like a hand entering a well-worn glove. I found myself looking to the east, looking for someone…

If my cultural battle had been fought in the West then my emotional haven had lain in the east. Half a mile through the woods was the house where my neighbour Liz had lived. Soft-hearted but tough-minded, Liz was on a mission at Sengwa to civilise the single-tracked, male-dominated, scientific community. Bringing grace and wit to the dinner table she offset the starchy discussions on scientific rivals, office politics and peculiarities found in the bush, with her talk of far-off places, impressive people and the dazzling worlds of art and literature. She filled the room with her zest for beauty, romance and fun. Living in the African bush was not her choice of lifestyle, and I think she suffered more than others from the remoteness and tedium, but she rarely let it show.

I prized the occasional mornings spent chatting on her leafy verandah surrounded by elegant carvings and furnishings. Sipping freshly brewed coffee, I could escape for a few precious minutes from the regimentation of the office and the relentless grip of field work, and pour out my confused thoughts and feelings. I remember telling her about the animal welfare group I had joined so as to meet people who really cared about animals, only to end up cringing at their naivety when it came to dealing with livestock losses and other wildlife problems faced by rural farmers and, on another occasion, how I admired some of the park officers for their intrepid lives in the bush but flinched at the indifference with which they shot wild animals. I was like a cat on hot bricks flipping from one point of view to another. She would listen intently, frowning at my observations, a warm smile never far from the surface. Liz championed the cause of the underdog, whether talking about the historic struggle for Scottish independence, the ongoing struggle for Zimbabwean independence or the plight of some downtrodden employee threatened with the sack by the wildlife department. She instinctively took Peter and me under her wing, supporting our cause, tending our traumas and shielding us from the worst effects of the office oligarchy. Perhaps she saw it as a classic confrontation between the Bohemian and the establishment. What would I have done without her? She was my refuge from the world of science and authority, the prop I could always lean against and the very best of friends.

It started some months after the boma capture at a time when I was spending the whole day in the field watching impala. On that particular day, I had been sitting on a tree platform recording the build-up to the annual rut. The big males were roaring day and night, throwing back their heads with their handsome lyrate horns to bellow a challenge at rivals, and as a come-on to those lissom maiden antelope. They defended tiny territories in which they herded their harems in tight tawny bunches. But if a female was determined enough, she could break away either to find a better place to feed or an even more macho male consort. The other females would follow her, prompting general pandemonium with the herd male chasing the escapees, his rivals joining in, and adolescent males looking on and roaring in excitement. Meanwhile the youngsters skipped about with glee.

I was immersed in the world of impala from dawn to dusk, filling my notebook with observations, too distracted even to eat or drink. On the drive home I began to relax. I was looking forward to downing a couple of litres of freshly squeezed orange juice, soaking in a bath, and taking a beer out onto the lawn. Entering the house I smelt chocolate pudding, even before reaching the kitchen where the cook-come-housekeeper sometimes left a surprise. His main jobs were baking bread and peeling potatoes but sometimes Cook came up with a novel idea and I would be greeted by a pot of sudza or a casserole of stew. So I strolled into the kitchen and began looking around to see if perhaps he had surpassed himself and left a chocolate steam pudding. There was nothing on the kitchen table, in the oven, on the hob or in the kerosene fridge. I shrugged it off, put the potatoes on the stove, made myself a long drink of orange-juice and forgot all about it. Until the next evening that is, when exactly the same thing happened. This time the smell of chocolate pudding was so strong that after searching the kitchen from top to bottom I went through to the living room and searched that too, but without success. The third evening was no different, only now I had accepted the strange new smell as a permanent feature of the house. And in any case Liz had sent around a dinner invitation and I needed to hurry. I quickly poured a bath and washed in the hot sandy water; then ran about to dry off, pulled on a clean shirt and jeans and drove along the ridge to her house. Getting out of my Land Rover, I could see her working away in the kitchen. Knowing Liz, I guessed she would be preoccupied with preparing a sumptuous meal and easily agitated by anyone intruding on her turf. Smiling, I walked in the backdoor anyway and said, 'hello'.

'Oh Martyn,' she said. 'Do you know, I baked you a chocolate cake three days ago, and I've been meaning to bring it round everyday?'

Awakening to find the sun streaming into my old bedroom along with the plaintive cooing of rock doves, I leapt out of bed grabbed a sarong from my back pack and padded outside onto the lawn. The crisp morning air and wild panorama always energised my preparations for a day in the field, except occasionally when the bird song and tranquillity won me over and I stayed at home to organise my notes and enjoy the garden. In the wet season it was possible to grow radishes, grape tomatoes and even Cape gooseberries at the back. Today I dug out some Weet-Bix and dried peaches from Nomad's lockup and went back inside for breakfast and a bath. I pulled on my trusty black jeans and buttoned up my best shirt as I was planning to visit the research station later in the morning. Stu was still sleeping, so I fixed some coffee and took my laptop into the garden to catch up with my diary.

Walking slowly around the cottage, bare feet soaking up the memories of a thousand Sengwa mornings, I half expected the director to pull up in his Land Rover to find out where the hell I'd been all these years. The thought was unsettling. Returning to the garden table I sat down at my laptop and considered the task in hand. It was hard to concentrate. My memory of Liz walked over and sat down on the empty chair beside me. After a few moments pause, I carried on typing.

'Remember me?' she asked, 'I am going to keep an eye on you.'

My heart skipped a beat. She had been listening to my story all this time, without saying a word. Her presence was strangely reassuring.

The doe-eyed female impala, her inquisitive face poised above stilt-like legs, is the quintessential African antelope. When alerted to danger fluted ears prick up to form, with her delicate black nose, a perfect three-pointed star; when relaxed they flop backwards like those of a sleepy hare. She takes care that they don't become torn or punctured making it hard to find features that distinguish one animal from another. Her foxy coat is little help being devoid of stripes, spots or other marks.

I had found it hard to recognise individual animals in the dry season when groups could be observed out in the open, but with the coming of the rains it became next to impossible as the grass reached waist height and visibility was further reduced by layers of dense foliage on the bushes. With patience I sometimes managed to manoeuvre close enough to spy on one or two animals, but they were wary and sooner or later something, perhaps a whiff of scent or a stray sound, would disturb them. Then often what I had taken as a small group would turn into a herd of 150 or more. Visible for a fleeting moment, they rocketed across the open glades in a molten river of gold, only to disappear into even denser thickets on the far side. After a few months of frustrating effort, I accepted that separating female impala by natural features would be impossible even with the aid of a good spotting telescope on loan from the university. The animals would have to be captured and marked in some way. Without realising it, I had set in motion a train of events that would haunt me for years to come.

With the help of my field assistant, Christmas, I tried all sorts of tricks to mark the animals. Usually I dreamt up some outlandish scheme in the evening and Christmas would devise a cunning way of turning it into reality next morning. Christmas was a natural craftsman who could produce almost anything out of wood, wire and Land Rover inner tubes. To start with we tried paint bombs, but they were messy and ineffectual. Next we manufactured a variety of self-fastening plastic collars which we concealed cunningly along their favourite tracks in the evening. Showing off their uncollared necks the next morning, I could swear the impala were grinning at us. After that we tried to catch them at night using a powerful spotlight. Like the other ideas it sounded simple when hatched over a glass of homebrew but in practice – in the bush at midnight with wary animals – it was entirely different. Several game scouts volunteered to give a hand in the evening. One stood in the open back of the Land Rover looking for impala with a handheld spotlight. Once he had fixed a group in its beam, the rest of us would slip out the back, run silently forward and hurl ourselves bodily at the animals. With all the excitement and confusion, not to mention flying hooves, warthog holes, broken stumps and fallen branches, it was only a matter of time before someone got hurt. So we abandoned the method and instead Christmas set about constructing hides next to waterholes where I would sit for hours, dripping with sweat under the blazing sun, waiting for an opportunity to fire a tranquilliser dart. It became a game of cat and mouse: every time I moved a hide, the impala moved their drinking spot. And then a day came when the dart miss-hit a male impala.

In the end there was only one way left to catch and mark the hundreds of animals needed for a successful study, and that was to drive them by helicopter into a large net boma, much like a trained sheepdog will herd a flock of ewes into the shepherd's pen. The technology for capturing whole herds had been developed by the game department during Operation Noah when animals that had been stranded on islands during the formation of Lake Kariba needed rescuing. Later the same method was used for restocking private farms. The boma technique had worked well for some species, but it was not yet perfected for the highly-strung impala.

A friend from the UK turned up at about this time having hitched all the way from England. Chris was a brilliant mechanical engineer who helped design the compact black box equipment fitted to fighter aircraft on his first job after graduation. His arrival was a huge boost for the floundering capture operation and, just as important, it evened up the ratio of long to short hair in the officers' tea room. Over the next few months, we worked hard to devise a capture method that minimised the risk of injuring impala and reduced the chances of capture myopathy, a deadly condition akin to the muscle meltdown of stressed athletes.

Our strategy was to minimise the time each animal was restrained. Taking a lesson from Henry Ford, we planned a processing line. In the place of assembly technicians we would have an odd mix of scientists, park wardens, rangers, game scouts, labourers, family members and friends from Salisbury.[1] The idea was to carry impala down the production line on padded litters, stopping at

Herding impala into a net boma

Shortly before release

Early attempts at restraint

Collared female impala on the Lutope River bed

Kisimisi tending an impala ram fitted
with a rainbow radio collar

The top breeding impala ram

The collaring station

A golden herd

The quintessential antelope

Above: Kisimisi with the skull of a snared impala

Bottom: Sengwa is losing its wildness

Tree platform in the Cornfield

The darker side of elephants... but why?

Mavuradonha

Elephant lookouts

Nomad on the banks of the Zambezi river

Above: The author attempting to write his diary

Right: The river elephants used my camp whenever they pleased

Above: Inches from Nomad's flimsy window

Right: Zambezi river at sunset

Below: Elephants out on the islands

Bottom of page: Hippo grazing in the evening

Olduvai Gorge

Above: African buffalo with yellow-billed oxpeckers in the Serengeti

Left: Young Maasai warrior

Above: Topi are residential antelope in the central woodlands of the Serengeti

Below: Wildebeest, the archetypal migratory antelope

Above: Monsoon rains in the Serengeti

Right: Safari gear in the back of Nomad

Below: Last of the castellated islands

each station so that the animals could be provided with ear tags and notches, ID collars, penicillin shots and eye ointment, whilst collecting blood samples, tooth impressions and body measurements.

The director who was still on sabbatical leave authorised the department's special unit to undertake the boma capture but left all other arrangements to the assistant director. Sensing his advantage, the assistant director determined to whip Chris and me into line. His first move was to put the station's capture equipment, including ID collars, ear tags and veterinary supplies, off limits whilst at the same time refusing my request for funds to buy new gear. Christmas and the scouts were nonplussed by this foolishness, but powerless to help. Liz was furious and intervened behind the scenes but to no avail. The assistant director had smelt blood. One evening I jotted down all the gear that we required: a dozen animal stretchers, 500 ID collars, ear tags, tooth impression trays, tubs of dental alginate, boxes of syringes, antibiotics and sterile bottles. We also needed a portable centrifuge and a host of other equipment. I checked my bank account. There was the equivalent of 200 US dollars. It would be reckless to capture large numbers of animals without the proper gear and although I might be able to borrow some items, the outlook was bleak. I radioed through to my university supervisor who suggested I scale back the capture to 20 animals. It was not what I'd hoped to hear.

That evening I opened some bottles of homebrew and talked openly with Chris of giving it up. The constant struggle with research officers, the isolation of the station, the lack of official back-up and the technical difficulties of the capture operation were making life impossible. I admitted to myself that walking away from a safe studentship offered by Edinburgh Uni had been a mistake. On the other hand, it would be equally mistaken to walk away from Sengwa without a fight. And so I determined to put this matter to the touch of swords. Chris offered to work at the station as an engineer to raise some cash. Meanwhile I would go to Salisbury to look for equipment.

The next morning Chris made his request and the assistant director agreed to hire him at 30 dollars per month, the same rate as for unskilled labour. Still, 30 dollars would come in useful. Chris accepted but instead of being put to work on the impala capture, he was ordered to work on the assistant director's personal research. He resigned on the spot, walked down to the workshops, cannibalised some left-over building materials and set about building two litters that would be used to transport sedated impala on their stretchers. Christmas watched him for a few minutes then, getting the hang of it, started two more. Soon there were a dozen frames under construction. Once the first frames were complete, they tacked old lorry canvas onto the supports to make beds whilst using packing material for padding. Securing straps were made from inner tubes and handles fashioned from lengths of water pipe so that four people could carry each litter. As a final touch, Liz persuaded the women at the institute to part with their nylon tights to provide non-abrasive ties.

Whilst this was going on, I visited a maxillary surgeon in Salisbury who promised to design some dental trays for making impressions of the upper and lower mandible rows of impala teeth. I think my request tickled the quirky engineer in him. Next I contacted a veterinary friend who lent me a hand-operated centrifuge and all the syringes and sterile bottles needed for collecting and storing blood samples. I took out all of the money I had in the bank and returned to Sengwa. A collection of finely crafted trays arrived two weeks later in three sizes – for male, female and yearling impala.

The biggest remaining problem was to find suitable ID collars. These would need symbols that could be recognised from several hundred metres and yet be comfortable to wear and durable against sun, thorn and hoof. At more that 30 US dollars apiece for the professionally made deer collars, we could afford just six. Manufacturing 500 collars on our meagre budget seemed impossible; it crossed my mind again that we might have to give up.

After supper one evening, Chris cleared a workspace on the living room table whilst I opened up the last two bottles of homebrew and fetched a school notebook. We were determined to crack the problem of the collars. By 4 a.m. we had a plan. It was wild but it never occurred to us that it might not work. Four hours later, I was on my way to Bulawayo to find a vehicle scrap yard. The scrappie charged 80 dollars for two large boxfuls of secondhand seat belts. The next morning I went to the farmers' cooperative and bought a thousand nuts and bolts, a large reel of tough nylon thread and several square metres of woven plastic sheeting in different colours. The bill came to 40 dollars. By late afternoon I was back in Sengwa where I found Chris working on a contraption that could melt symbol shapes out of nylon belts. He had first bent lengths of packing case steel into the shapes of ten symbols, H, T, V, X, ✚, I, –, ▲, ● and ■, which looked like so many pastry cutters. Then he welded these onto a heavy metal plate using a cool oxyacetylene flame. It was a delicate job requiring a deft touch to avoid burning through the symbols. The heavy plate was set on legs that raised it about six inches above the ground. Underneath it was an iron tray, about four inches deep.

Chris' idea was to heat the heavy metal plate with burning coal until the pastry cutters were hot enough to melt symbol shapes out of the nylon car seat belts. As I had forgotten to buy coal in Bulawayo, Christmas suggested we try the heavy brittle wood of the mopane tree. He hefted an axe and walked down the road looking for some likely firewood. After a few hours he returned with a heap of chestnut-coloured chips. These were packed into the tray. Chris poured some kerosene over them and threw on a match. The chips caught and burned fiercely, but after two hours of constant stoking, the temperature of the pastry cutters was still not hot enough. Chris frowned and went back to the cottage. The next morning he set about making some bellows with Christmas. Soon they were ready to try again. They lit the fire afresh and took it in turns to fan the flames with the homemade bellows. The fire burnt furiously and after a few minutes, the cookie cutter symbols began to glow red. We were in business.

It took a couple of days of hot and smelly work but eventually we manufactured a large pile of seat belt cut-outs, each five inches long with two neat shapes, melted through the middle. The next job was to sew these pieces onto three-foot strips of seat belt that would be the collars, and in the process sandwich rectangles of woven plastic between the pattern and the belt. Each impala would be identified by two coloured symbols. And we would need to do this twice per belt so that the symbols could be seen on either side of the animal. Attaching the pattern pieces would be a big task in itself requiring a powerful sewing machine.

Christmas said he knew someone who might help, so we drove out of the research area, along the perimeter track for a few kilometres, and down a footpath that led to a traditional thatched hut. We were greeted by a smartly dressed schoolteacher who owned a heavy duty, pedal-driven, Singer sewing machine. After some negotiation the schoolteacher agreed to sew all the collars, starting immediately. The price was fixed at 80 dollars which cleaned me out. A fortnight later there was a tinkling ring outside the cottage. The teacher was standing by his bicycle, wearing a big grin, and holding a box of 500 expertly sewn wildlife collars. Through a telescope, the coloured symbols could be picked out clearly from 400 yards.[2]

'What a stonking morning,' announced Stu blinking in the sunlight. 'Fancy a cuppa?'

'Coffee would be good,' I replied, blinking in mild surprise at the sight of Stu and Nomad. 'I'm getting nowhere here anyway.'

Stu disappeared inside re-emerging with a couple of mugs of instant coffee. He plonked himself down in a canvas chair. 'Are you writing your diary?'

'Every time I begin, I find myself back in the past.'

'Huh, you're living backwards then like the White Queen.'

'You know this place really brings back the memories. I was just thinking about the impala capture. That was in 1975.'

Stu pulled out his tobacco pouch and teased out a suitable plug. 'I've always wondered about catching impala. I bet they kick like buggery?'

'They can jump 10 feet from standing.'

The capture team arrived at the station a couple of weeks later in a powerful four-wheel drive Bedford Truck; the chief set off immediately to search for a boma site. After a few hours he had found an ideal spot: it was in a grove of tall trees with the Sengwa River forming a natural barrier on one side. A dense thicket occupied the centre offering shade and refuge, and next to it was a small pool where the animals could drink. The capture chief worked with his crew to pass a wire cable in amongst the trees, about eight feet above the ground, making a complete circle with a diameter of 100 yards. Then he hung sisal netting along the cable, leaving a 50-yard gap on the southern side to form the main gate. Once the impala entered through this gate, teams would close it by sprinting from either side dragging light-weight woven sheeting suspended from hoops running along the overhead wire.

As the hour of the capture drew nearer, so my anxiety about the assistant director and his machinations intensified. Liz had been passing on information about his plans and now confirmed that he was determined to be seen as the man in charge. I didn't mind the posturing so long as it didn't interfere with the research. Liz organised a barbecue that evening, inviting the capture chief who was a tough veteran admired by all in the department. She alerted him to some of the station shenanigans. Next day the maxillary surgeon and vet arrived from Harare, joking that they couldn't trust Chris and I to do the job properly on our own. Finally the helicopter arrived, stirring up excitement and tension. At the briefing that night, the capture chief asked us to drive to the boma site an hour before first light and conceal ourselves along the net which was now rolled up on the ground under the overhead wire. He emphasised that no one was to move until they had heard a pistol shot from the chopper – the signal that a herd of impala had entered the gate.

On the way home from the briefing I stopped at the workshops to fill up with petrol, finding a large padlock and chain locking shut the outlet valve of the petrol storage tank. The assistant director had found another way to force our capitulation. I seized a metal hacksaw and began cutting open one of the links on the chain. Chris disappeared into a storeroom emerging moments later with the skull of an enormous bull buffalo which he strapped onto the bonnet with the last piece of inner tubing. It was a declaration of war.

At five o'clock the next morning we careered down to the boma site in our ghastly Viking chariot. About 50 people were milling about, illuminated by the headlights of half a dozen vehicles. The assistant director glanced at the great skull but made no comment. Minutes later the vehicles were ordered away and the whole crew disappeared from sight. Christmas and I joined Samson, the strongest member of the Sengwa labour force, and sprawled out by the net in a bed of aromatic herbs. Time passed slowly. No one spoke, not even in a whisper. No one smoked. No one so much as moved. Such was the authority of the capture chief. After a while we felt something stirring in the distant hills. It transformed into the steady "choof-choof-choof" of chopper blades, which came louder then quieter on the still morning air as the sky-dog worked the impala herds along the Lutope River.

The Polish pilot dipped the chopper in and out of the trees, sometimes leaning it right back to direct blasts of air from the main rotor into the herd. The animals would stream forward, gather in a tight bunch, stall, then when urged sufficiently, stream forward again. Only the older males would not be herded. Slowly but relentlessly the helicopter shepherded the females and young towards the boma, swinging one way then another, and sometimes having to spin rapidly back to stop a break away. On approaching the thickly wooded site, the pilot dropped the machine through tiny gaps in the canopy, until the rotor blades were chopping off the tips of branches on all sides. It was extraordinarily risky flying calling for immense skill.

At the sound of the pistol shot, we jumped to our feet heaving the sheeting above our heads. As if from nowhere a solid white ring materialised in the woods surrounding 150 impala; they backed away from the walls and edged into the central thickets. I felt a surge of jubilation.

An hour later, the first animals were passed down the production line without incident. Soon 10 impalas with bright ear tags and smart ID collars were standing quietly in a curtained enclosure awaiting release. I stopped to watch the last one running off and walked after it for a few metres to gain a better view. There on the ground was a collar; it had a bolt hanging from one end but no securing nut. I felt a twinge of self-doubt. Could it be that my system for securing the collars was not working after all, or was it a spare one dropped by the collar team in their excitement? I picket it up and walked quickly over to the large chart. Liz was in charge of the coordination station and I handed her the collar without a word. She took it and rapidly checked the symbols.

'It belongs to an adult female that's just been released,' she said quietly, looking me straight in the eye. A hasty search amongst the shrubs and forbs revealed another collar lying a little further off. It was the same story with this one. Clenching my fists in frustration I sought out the assistant director who had earlier insisted on taking charge of the collaring workstation. 'What do you make of these?' I asked, proffering the two collars. The assistant director stared at me with barely concealed scorn, and then walked off without a word. I remained standing there for some moments, puzzled and tense. Only the day before, I had demonstrated how to tighten the first nut against a flat washer, how to tighten a second locking nut against the first by using two spanners, how to crimp the thread above the nuts with pliers so the locking nut could not work loose, and how to safeguard the whole assembly even further by applying a drop of super-glue to the threads. Christmas touched my arm and whispered urgently that the assistant director had only been fastening the nuts finger tight... Sabotage!

Striding across the capture area, I cornered the man in front of the boma. 'What the hell do you think you are playing at with these collars?' I demanded, dropping all pretence of civility.

The assistant director stiffened and turned slowly to face me, eyes bulging in anger. 'One more remark like that and I'll order you back to the office!'

I realised that my research programme might hang on this moment, but was too far committed for caution. 'We can all pack up and go home,' I shouted so that the entire company could hear, 'if you're going to fasten collars finger tight.' In the hush that followed, I saw the arrogance fade from his eyes. And as the silent condemnation of the capture chief and fellow officers sank in, a pink flush crept over his petulant boyish face. Muttering something about making a radio call, he stalked from the boma, got into his Land Rover and drove off. It was the last we saw of him at the capture site.

Chris quietly took charge of collaring and Liz volunteered to run a final check on each impala before it was released; the others returned to their stations as before. Soon a new batch of animals had arrived. One impala followed another down the production line, each lying quietly on its green canvas bed until released into the surrounding bush. The maxillary surgeon perfected the technique of making hard stone plaster-of-Paris tooth impressions. They would form the basis for estimating the age of each animal. The vet took blood samples, separating them by hand centrifuge into serum and red cells, which would later be used to study the genetic structure of the population. Peter Mundy and Naboth, one of the longest-serving scouts, weighed and measured each animal so that later I could check the relationship between size, dominance and mating success. The capture chief was delighted at the data gathering system, which appealed to his sense of practical organisation. But it was too good to last.

My vet friend, Andy, had been following standard practice in administering a sedative as each impala was restrained and thereafter monitoring vital signs. As the day warmed up, the impalas' body temperatures started to rise and one or two animals began to pant. Air temperature and body temperatures continued to rise, and not long afterwards Andy noticed that some of the animals were growing listless. He suggested we call a halt and concentrate on the sick animals. We carried the worst affected animals into the shade and began dowsing them in cold water. But far from responding, the impalas' breathing became shallower and more irregular. It suddenly occurred to me that the animals were dying. And with an awful sinking feeling I realised they were developing capture myopathy. One of the females gurgled and rasped for breath. Andy stuck a syringeful of adrenaline straight into her heart. She didn't even react. In that moment I saw, as if from a distance, my real role in the drama. A burning ambition to become a field biologist had impelled me to kill the very animals I professed to love. For a long heartbeat I looked at myself as a stranger. Casting about for help, I saw the rest of the capture team ignoring the ailing impala; they were processing the last few in the production line as if all was well. Didn't they realise the animals were dying? Perhaps they thought that animals always collapsed during capture operations; it was just a routine part of the tough world of wildlife biology. Or maybe they were in awe of the park officials, like visitors to a hospital in front of busy doctors. More likely, I guessed, it was for my sake they pretended nothing was happening. As events continued to spiral out of control, I wanted to scream at my helplessness.

At about 11 a.m. the remaining animals in the production line were released and the crew went back to the station for lunch. Andy and I stayed with the stricken animals determined to do whatever we could. We didn't have oxygen but we kept on dowsing them with water, rubbing it into their belly fur. Liz returned with some canvas screens which she set up to provide more shade. When these measures failed, Andy tried heart massage and finally the adrenaline. One by one the animals succumbed. The beautiful wild creatures were dying at my hand. I took a deep breath and made my decision. We would release the remaining uncollared animals in the boma and abandon the capture. It might mean sacrificing my study but the alternative – to put on collars as animals were dying – would forever taint my work. I told Andy who was at my side assisting one of the surviving animals.

He considered for a moment. 'I think it's the sedative I've been using; it's making matters worse.' He explained how the drug was known to interfere with the heat regulation centre, and that this side-effect was almost certainly contributing to hyperthermia in the captive animals. 'If we abandon the use of the sedative and restrict operations to the cooler hours of morning and evening, it should decrease the risk.'

I grabbed at the lifeline: 'We could open up a second collaring station and drop some of the body measurements. Would that help?'

'The shorter the handling time, the better,' Andy confirmed. 'Why don't you write up a new protocol and we can discuss it with the others at the station.'

Later that afternoon the new fast-track procedures were explained to the crew who had been working on the production line. Everyone was keen to help and the capture chief offered to set up a generator and lights to allow us to work after dark. We decided to leave the captive impala in the boma overnight to rest: Christmas and two scouts stayed with them to keep a lookout for leopards whilst the rest of us retired early. The whole team assembled again before first light the next morning. Working quietly and purposively, we began sending animals down the line, refining our technique until the time from first restraint to release was reduced from 45 to 15 minutes per animal. By 9 p.m. that evening, we had released over 100 collared impala without a single casualty.

Stu had been listening without interruption, smoking the thinnest of roll-ups to ration his supply. Now he asked, 'What happened to Liz then? I mean she sounds such a fantastic person.'

'She was,' I replied. 'Beautiful, tender, poetic... full of pride for other's achievements... She died recently... Fucking cancer!'

'Shit!' said Stu. 'You should write about her Martyn.'

But I was feeling churned up. I couldn't concentrate. The past was catching up with me too fast. Grabbing my binoculars, I headed off for the main station leaving Stu to relax at home.

The path wound its way along the edge of the valley, passing through several dense thickets, before climbing a slight rise. Unbidden, my footsteps followed those of my younger self. The air was thick with the smell of the bush, the atmosphere taut. It was good to be back in the world of large animals. I inhaled the aroma of a Brachystegia tree with newly flushed leaves, and kept one eye open for buffalo which can be easily overlooked in dense bushes. Stepping out from the shrubs, I found myself directly in front of the H-shaped office block sitting above a small escarpment. The walls were newly whitewashed and the eves and window frames freshly picked out in dark green. The narrow terraces of well-watered lawns were just as before. The place was bursting with memories. I walked slowly up to the entrance and stopped, and then went round the side to the verandah where we had melted car seat belts into impala collars.

'Mr Martyn!'

I turned at the sound of that familiar voice. Kisimisi Dube stood stocky and crooked with an enormous grin stretched across his affectionate grizzly face.

'Christmas!' I beamed back at my old friend.

18

THE QUINTESSENTIAL ANTELOPE

She regarded me closely

Amazingly Christmas' smile grew even wider, showing a prominent gap where one of his teeth had jumped ship.

'Aaah, but you are older now,' he said.

'Neither of us has grown younger,' I replied, noticing the lines of tiredness under his eyes and the added prominence of hard cheekbones, and wondering why the past seemed more vivid than the present. 'How is your family?'

'They are well. My daughter is married now."

I recalled the morning that Christmas and his shy wife had walked through the bush to my cottage to show off their baby daughter who had been wrapped up tightly against the sun. It didn't seem so long ago – as if Africa has been sleeping in my absence, or was it I that had been sleeping? We began to make sense of the intervening years, walking slowly about the station. I noticed that the mast for radio-tracking elephants was bent and the aerial wires were frayed. There was little sign of on-going research.

'Look here, Mr Martyn do you see this one?' asked Christmas, pointing to a sizeable tree at the back of the office. 'It planted itself in 1975 when we were cleaning the stomach of that impala.'

'The tree planted itself?'

'Ja, it did.'

'That day when we were collecting rumen samples?'

'Ja. The same.'

'Well that's ecology for you.'

'Ja, look at it – this big tree.'

'Hey, do you remember that time I drove into a tree?'

'Ja, that was a bad day. You were bleeding from the head. You didn't want the others to know about it.'

Christmas had carefully washed the wound and applied a dressing from the veterinary kit. When it finally stopped bleeding, he prepared some soup. A warm feeling of comradeship stole over me as we recalled our shared adventures.

'Christmas, I hope you can spend the day with us. Do you think we could visit the impala study area together?'

'I will talk to the officer in charge,' he replied formally. Then added with a smile: 'You can meet me at the game scout compound.'

A short while later, Stu and I collected Christmas, now toting an AK47 rifle and 30 rounds.

'What's it for?' asked Stu nervously.

'Oh mainly for form's sake,' I replied, 'but we might come across lions or armed poachers.'

'Flippin' 'eck! What are you getting us into?'

We took the track leading down the mini-escarpment on the west side of the station. As a student, I had plunged down the hill each morning in the cool dawn air, singing at the top of my voice, with trees rushing past overhead and gravel scrunching under the tyres of my Series II Land Rover. With the roof removed, there was nothing between me and the wild Sengwa smells. In the woods I might catch the heady scent of flowering *Combretum*, the sweet odour of last night's kill, or the musty fragrance of elephant dung; out on the floodplain were aromas of tall grass and hidden waterways. Now Nomad followed the same route. We passed the cave where a leopard had stashed a large baboon and plunged into a belt of 10-foot high grass which could conceal a herd of buffalo, coming out onto open flats with their view of distant hills and escarpments; from there we crossed a dry gully that turned into a raging torrent after rain, rounded the side of a small glade where a cow elephant gave birth to her calf one night, and arrived at 'hole 20' – the big warthog burrow where three tawny lionesses once waited in ambush. A little further down the track, we reached the southern edge of the impala study area, which I had known more intimately than the streets of my home town. I had walked every winding game path, examined each browsed-over shrub, inspected the hundreds of pelleted dung piles and sniffed all the mud holes. Sitting on tree platforms day after day, I observed the daily rhythms of wild animals and learnt the seasonal pulse of the great valley ecosystem.

We pulled to a halt where 'transect 8' crossed the track and proceeded on foot, heading west towards the site of one of the 12 platforms.

'Over there,' said Christmas indicating a small herd of female waterbuck.

'Oh, they're really shaggy,' responded Stu beginning to relax.

'There are so many acacias here,' I said, struggling to find familiar landmarks in what used to be an open meadow. 'I think the tree platform was over there.' We walked on a few more yards. 'Is this the tree, Christmas?'

'Ja, this one. Do you see those steps?'

'Hah. Look there it is.'

'What, the tree platform?' asked Stu.

'Yep. See there are wooden slats going up the main trunk, and then out onto that big limb.'

'There was another main branch on this side,' said Christmas, 'but it has fallen down.'

'So this is my old tree platform,' I repeated slowly. 'Ahhh... this is where it was. Do you know Stu, there was a big male impala who lived here, and we watched him mate with 21 females in just 10 days.'

'Blimey, what a stud muffin.'

'There was a bunch of studs around here and each had his own trick for getting females. One of them used to keep his harem corralled between a steep river bank and a stand of tall grass. He was number two on the totem pole.' I rested my arm against the base of the tree and looked out over the old clearing. 'A third male used a psychological trick: he hid in some thick *Combretum* bushes and if a rival came close, he would give a deep roar and explode out of the thicket making a great racket that terrified the intruder. Another male stayed up on the mopane terrace where the females liked to go at night. But this chap here didn't need any tricks. He relied solely on fighting prowess.'

'Did he have a collar then?' asked Stu.

'Ja. His was "X over T black"' replied Christmas.

'He was the most successful breeding animal in the study area,' I added.

Sitting in this tree platform, I had noted down the minute-by-minute behaviour of the collared animals. A homemade electronic timer clicked at intervals, prompting me to take a sample of impala behaviour through binoculars by checking the activity of each animal and noting it down on a check sheet. Today, behavioural data are entered onto handheld computers, but the end result is the same – scanned samples that can be analysed with statistical tests. In this way I could calculate the energy cost of rutting by the top male whilst keeping tabs on the collared females. Lying flat on the logs, ignoring the lumpy bits sticking into my ribs, I would wipe the tiny sweat bees from my eyes, and peer through the telescope waiting for each impala to stand free of the bushes and her companions so that I could pick out the collar symbols.

On other platforms in the woods, Christmas and several game scouts did the same. Each impala had an ID card with its symbols and a picture of its ear notches. Day by day the animal's behaviour was entered onto its card. At the end of the study, the information was coded onto a stack of the punch cards that were used in the early days of computing and read into an enormous data file. I used the mainframe IBM computer at Cambridge University to analyse the groupings of impala. I was curious to know whether mothers stayed close to their daughters and granddaughters. The analysis revealed a different kind of society. Mothers preferred the company of their same-aged peers, the ones they had played with as frisky lambs. It was a gang world out there, with young gangs and old gangs hanging out in the woods and along the rivers – peaceable gangs though, which sometimes joined forces in the wet season to form super-gangs. I called them impala clans. They were the most stable social unit in the impala's world. The males left their home clan when one year old and seldom returned; others drifted into the area to live in loose male groups distinguishable from a distance by the forest of lyrate horns. A handful of the more dominant males graduated from these groups to herd females and young, seeing off their rivals in slow-moving rituals of yawning and posturing that occasionally erupted into fierce butting fights. During the rut a top stud would be exhausted after just one week of chivvying, chasing and fighting.

'Not much to see now,' said Stu from halfway up the tree, his cherry red T-shirt sticking out like the coat of an English foxhunter. Even his suede boots had bright red laces. He shimmied down and jumped to the ground.

Turning to Christmas, I asked: 'Do you remember the metal bands we attached to the horns of the first big males?'

'Hmmm, that first male was called "Ronny Baby",' said Christmas.

'That's right,' I said, astonished he should remember. 'Those animals disappeared. One night I was watching a group under the full moon. When they entered some shrubs all you could see were three silver bands moving about in the dark. I think the leopards must have followed the rings at night and taken those animals.'

'One time we recorded an impala which was staying just around here,' said Christmas. 'Then we found it over at Ntabamangwe; she went there in the dry season and came back in the rainy season.'

'That must be 10 kilometres from here,' I remarked.

I explained to Stu that the females mostly stayed put, but occasionally we found a lost soul wandering miles from home. Late in the dry season the impala travelled long distances to find water. Arriving at a waterhole in the heat of the day, members of a group would drink feverishly and then stand about dozing in the shade, ears drooping and heads bowed. Other groups would come from far off in different directions. After drinking they might move off again. If an impala was especially dozy, she would plod along with the wrong group and not realise it.

'She would get quite a surprise when she woke up,' said Stu smiling in amusement. 'I'd love to have seen that.'

'Mr Stuart, do you know before Mr Martyn put these collars on, I would think "Ahh, this is the same male staying with these females"…and yet not,' said Christmas, his voice lifting in surprise as he shook his head slowly. 'Now we have this new idea about impala. They are always changing. Ja, I thought I knew impala, but I found out, it was quite different.'

It was as if someone had switched on a light. Prior to the capture, I could never have guessed at the unfolding dramas filling the life of each impala. With the collars on, we could follow their fate and fortune and the woods lit up with stories. Those stories made up only one book. I wondered what it would be like to follow the lives of the other animals sharing the valley – to read from a library of books telling of individual zebras, warthogs, lions, elephants, vultures and so on. It was immense, yet this was the reality of the bush.

My eyes had first been opened to the power of individual recognition as an undergraduate when I studied shelducks inhabiting an estuary to the east of Edinburgh after fitting coloured rings to their feet. This was when the pioneers of field biology were amazing the world with their discoveries: people such as Jane Goodall with her account of wild chimpanzees in the forests of Gombe Stream, Roger Payne and Scott McVey with their discovery of humpback whale songs, and Iain and Oria Douglas-Hamilton with their intimate portrait of a wild elephant family. Everyone was finding the same thing. Large animals in the wild were individualised, capable of deep social bonds, aware and misunderstood.

In the late 1950s, as a young schoolboy, I had been fascinated by the 19th-century stories of gorilla hunters in the Congo and of whalers chasing Moby Dick. Neither my teachers nor I understood that the information on wild animals in these books was scant and narrowly focussed on the kill. Like others, I glimpsed another side to wild animals on reading Williamson's *Tarka the Otter* and Maxwell's *Ring of Bright Water*, but as a society we British were still very much in the dark as regards the true nature of wildlife. Field biology blossomed in the 1960s just as a whole generation was beginning to challenge the materialistic world of its time. Caught up in this youthful idealism, I had thought it inevitable that the flood of new knowledge would ensure the future of wildlife. In those days I hadn't a clue about Western economics; I was blind to its dazzling power and didn't realise how easily beauty and learning could be dismissed if they stood in the way of 'progress'.

We set off again down the barely discernible footpath walking as quietly as possible. It was like old times, save that now the path was so overgrown that only Christmas could follow it. Each of us was alert to potential danger. Unlike national parks that are networked with roads and signposts, the wild interior of Sengwa is dominated by animal paths. I listened for alarm calls and attended to the slightest movement in the veil of leaves ahead, lest we stumble on a buffalo or lion. There could be a puff adder on the trail. Awareness becomes a subconscious habit in the bush; it keeps you alive and it keeps you alive to your surroundings. My mental world with all its unsolved problems had faded; I was centred in the environment. And right now I was growing uneasy at the few signs of impala. There were no tracks around the muddy depressions and little sign of browsing on the favoured food plants. I had only seen a single dung pile.

'Impala,' whispered Christmas urgently. There was a glimpse of golden flanks and lyrate horns disappearing behind the bushes. And then one stepped into a clearing and turned: she regarded me closely. I looked back, equally closely.

'Are these the ones that you studied?' asked Stu.

For a moment I couldn't answer.

By the time we reached the site of the next tree platform, I was seriously concerned for we had not seen any other herds. Worse still, Christmas had found the skull of a male impala with wire twisted around the horns.

'Sometimes when we are collecting snares on patrol we bring back 500,' he said.

'Five hundred,' I repeated incredulously. 'That kind of poaching pressure will devastate the large animals.'

'Sometimes 100 or 200 in a day,' emphasised Christmas.

'Will the poachers try to shoot you?' asked Stu who was looking about anxiously.

'They run away,' said Christmas. 'But if we catch them we take them to the police, then the police take them to court and they are charged 2,000 maybe 3,000 according to the animal.'

'Is that a lot?' asked Stu.

'The judge says "How much will it cost to buy this animal". The poacher says, so much. Then the judge says "Now then you killed this animal so you should pay the same amount."'

Returning to Nomad we drove further north into the heart of the impala study area, between the double loops of the Sengwa and Lutope rivers, then set off on foot once more. The sun was now high and the heat was oppressive. A few guineafowls were clucking in the thickets but the rest of the bush was sleeping.

'I love that smell of elephant,' I mentioned as we passed by some large turds under a grove of tall trees.

'It smells like they digest only half of it,' observed Stu who was beginning to catch on to African biology.

'Do you see that clump of sansevieria over there?' I asked, 'looking like tall reeds with spiky tops? That's where we caught the impala.'

'Must have been quite something,' said Stu, passing Christmas a roll-up. Christmas lit up and beamed at the smooth taste.

'I still feel sick about those animals that died,' I admitted.

'What's the point of feeling sick?' Stu retorted. 'You figured out that we needed new knowledge about impala. You took as much care as anyone could in marking them. You produced a thesis crammed with new information about them, didn't you? They've all been poached anyway. End of ruddy story.'

It would have been good to go along with Stu: to let that guilt go. I felt the seduction of his way of thinking. Quite unbidden, an image came to mind of that Bushman hunter pursuing the rhebok lamb across the hidden rock wall in the Cederberg mountains. I could recognise myself as that hunter now, chasing after an animal with raised club, only in my case the hunt was for knowledge, not food.

'Knowledge has a price that is worth paying – provided it is not too much,' I said.

'What is too much?' asked Stu, 'When it is no longer sustainable?'

'Too much is when you stop caring about the price you are exacting.'

And there it was, the resolution I had been seeking for more than a quarter century. Bit by bit I had come to realise that my feelings on animal management were determined primarily by the care that managers give to the individual animals in their governance. It doesn't matter what kind of animal handling is involved, and the list is a long one: rearing livestock on the range; raising them intensively in factory farms; owning pets of one kind or another; training animals for sporting events; working with dogs, horses, elephants or dolphins; rearing animals for research; habituating wild animals for ecotourism; displaying them in zoos and aquaria; subsistence hunting; hunting for sport; culling or other forms of pest control. The relationship between the keeper and their charge is at the heart of the matter. If for example an owner loves their pet, then I feel reasonably happy about the animal's welfare; there might still be a problem but not usually so. If however the owner is careless or negligent then I am concerned for the animal. It is not so much why animals are kept, but how. Wild, domestic, working and experimental animals are not pets and the relationship between them and us is different. Nevertheless when a person is in charge of such animals, he or she may care about them as individuals, or be careless of them. It is not difficult to distinguish between the two. And once we care for them, can we take their lives lightly?

All day I had been looking forward to visiting Ntabamangwe,[1] the 'mountain of vultures'. Its enchantment lay not so much in its dimensions, a flat-topped mesa raised modestly above the surroundings, as in its location. Standing in isolation above the confluence of three rivers, it commanded wonderful views across the Sengwa Valley whilst containing an atmosphere of beauty and tranquillity. It was the place we used to visit for a break from our bush work, finding it the perfect spot to relax and commune with nature. That was what I wanted to do now. But my anticipation was tinged with apprehension at the prospect of sharing this special place with Stu and Christmas who would surely be out of synch with my mood. Nevertheless after some lunch and a siesta back at the station, we set off in the late afternoon hoping to reach the top of the mesa before sunset.

Below the station, we took the eastern track that leads to the Sengwa River. The ford is an 80-metre expanse of sandy mudflats crisscrossed by a tributary of streams. On the far side is a steep earth bank that leads up into woodlands. It looked treacherous when we arrived and there were no other vehicle tracks to guide our crossing; no-one had passed that way in a long time.

'We cross this?' asked Stu, with a touch of mutiny in his voice.

'Mmmh,' responded Christmas.

'Is that what you are saying? Is that where we go?' said Stu, pointing wildly across the river.

'Ja,' replied Christmas.

There was a stony silence from Stu. I changed into low-wheel ratio and edged Nomad down the bank onto the riverbed. I knew from past experience that the sand here was firm although there were other crossings which were more treacherous. There are even stories of Land Rovers disappearing into sinkholes. I took Nomad across rapidly, slowing as we approached the far bank and then gunning the engine for the climb. We lurched up the near vertical bank, hesitated for a moment with all four wheels spinning and began to slip sideways.

'Carnage!' yelped Stu.

Recovering on the riverbed we made a second attempt, this time clawing our way successfully over the top. The track led on through mopane woodlands, winding past muddy depressions and fallen trees, all the while shaded by an airy canopy of lime green leaves shaped like the open wings of countless butterflies.

'The elephants have been busy here,' I remarked, in an effort to relieve the tension.

'They've pushed down some big old trees,' agreed Stu.

'The males really enjoy it,' I added, as Nomad crunched and thumped her way across giant-sized footprints that had hardened in the sun.

'We ought to shoot the lot,' said Stu who was not going to be molly-coddled.

Periodically we caught a glimpse of Ntabamangwe's imposing cliffs through the trees. The track skirted round their base and entered a deep gully before beginning the ascent. We climbed through a belt of tangled scrub that completely engulfed Nomad, only breaking free when nearing the top where the thickets gave way to open *Terminalia* woodland. From here we followed the track westwards along a narrow promontory arriving finally at a dead end.

Relieved to escape from the atmosphere in the cab, I followed Christmas on foot past the broken aerial and abandoned research hut to the edge of an escarpment. We descended a slippery slope of tiny red pebbles to a narrow neck of rock, just wide enough for a single footpath that bridged a divide separating the main plateau from an isolated pillar of rock. I glanced at the vertical fall on either side: there was no room for error. Christmas strode easily across the bridge but on scrambling up the far slope, he missed his step. My heart skipped a beat as I leapt forward to give him a hand. He recovered without falling. Silently cursing myself for overlooking his advancing years, I took the rifle and helped him up the last bit. At the top he offered to wait for Stu whilst catching his breath. I nodded and moved on. Alone with my memories, I picked my way across the broken top of the spur to the lookout on the far side.

Standing on the edge, hanging in space above the confluence of two rivers, I marvelled again at the majesty of the view. In the distance, the plateau of Sampakwa floated on rolling hills cloaked with dark *Combretum* thickets that sheltered mud-grey rhinos and elephants. Folded along their base was an apple-green stole of mopane woods crisscrossed by silvery game trails. Nervous herds followed the trails down to sunlit pools that sparkled like gems in the rich grassy swathe bordering the Sengwa River. And where the Sengwa and Lutope rivers merged, the sandy confluence fashioned a woodland arrow that pointed to the spot where animals drank from shallow sip wells. It was deserted now. Light rain had fallen in the past few days leaving muddy pools in the mopane woodlands. There was no need to venture onto the riverbed unless you preferred your water filtered.

I felt Liz's presence even closer here and remembered the first time we came. The elephants had been playing in the river and the swifts were rushing past our heads. Friends have sat for hours in this mountain eyrie, chatting quietly or lost in private reverie; one burst into tears on first arriving. But not all are so moved, and it was not long before things began to fall apart. Stu and Christmas ambled over and perched themselves on a nearby promontory, taking in the view for a few seconds. Christmas rolled some coarse tobacco in a piece of old newspaper, lit the homemade cigarette, and coughed. A pungent smell spread around the outcrop driving out the subtle scent of river and woods.

In a low soulful voice, Christmas began telling Stu about the poacher. 'I found the camp near here. Down there, in that patch of mopane.' He gesticulated at the valley floor on the northwest side. 'They were after the rhino.'

'Oh yeah', said Stu. 'What happened?'

'We followed their tracks around the base of that hill.' Christmas indicated their route before continuing. 'I shot one of them.'

'Did he die?'

'Ja, I shot him here.'

This time I resisted the temptation to look at where Christmas was pointing.

'How did you feel about that?' asked Stu.

'He was a poacher!' replied Christmas, in a tone which suggested that far from regretting the incident, it was one of his proudest memories.

I, on the other hand, was annoyed. It was as if someone had spat in my soup just as I was about to drink it. I knew that Stu would be intrigued by the story, being fascinated by differences in moral outlook. But I was appalled that my old friend, whom I had helped gain promotion from temporary labourer to permanent scout, should have been led to such a bloody confrontation.

'Guys, would you mind talking about something else just now?' I asked politely. There was a moment of silence, as they cracked open some beers. I wondered if it was me who was being overly precious about this place. I did my best to switch off to my companions and opened up once more to the scene before me. A swift whooshed past.

Christmas began again. 'Have some snuff.'

'Thanks,' said Stu. The sound of sniffing and coughing followed.

'Do you see that plate?' asked Christmas pointing to a small bronze commemorative plaque close to where I was sitting. 'It is for Mr Coulson, the previous officer-in-charge. He died in a plane crash six years ago.'

I moved away from the others until I was well out of earshot, still hoping to recapture the peace and tranquillity of the mountain. I had known the man who died, a dedicated park warden who loved the wild places in Zimbabwe.

As the sun sank.towards Sampakwa, the still evening air carried a symphony aloft from the wild valley below. The beautiful falling cry of the emerald-spotted wood dove came from far away,

'*wau-wau,wau-wau,wau-wau-------wau----wau---wau--wau-wauwauwauwauwauwau*,' the final run descending quickly. Somewhere down below was a rustle followed by the rhythmic contact call of helmeted guineafowl.

I listened quietly, but my mood had changed, the magic gone. Reluctantly I took the camcorder out of my backpack to try and capture the changing atmosphere of the valley as night fell. The battery was flat and to my annoyance I found that I'd lost the spare. At that moment Liz, who had been by my side all day, laughed and walked away. Quickly I reached out, but was unable to touch her. She looked back… smiled one last time… and departed. There was nothing I could do. The mirage that was the Sengwa of 1978 wobbled, wobbled again, and collapsed.

With a heavy heart, I turned to face the present. In the far distance I noticed a line of smoke along the southern border where farmers were burning the stubble on their fields. Sengwa was no longer a remote wilderness area: it had become a wildlife refuge under siege. Worse still, I feared she was in danger of losing her soul.

19

MYTHS OF THE WILD

A wobbling orb of dung

'Look Stu! Do you see those broken mopane trees?' I shouted as Nomad lurched towards a clearing in the woods.

Stu flicked his roll-up out the window and glanced in the direction I was pointing. 'They've been flattened by elephants?'

'Yep,' I stopped for a minute in the centre of the clearing, 'and do you see all those new shoots sprouting from the fallen trunks?'

'I suppose that's an adaptation to being knocked down a lot?'

'Five years from now, they'll be young trees.' I breathed in deeply. 'Don't you find the whole place just reeks of big animals and wild bush?'

'A bit like a Bushman's armpit,' remarked Stu, as we continued down the dirt track.

'More like your armpit,' I retorted.

'We can park over here,' said Christmas, ignoring our conversation.

Leaving Nomad in the shade, the three of us pushed through a field of pungent herbs towards a large mopane tree that once held 'platform ten' in the midst of its outstretched arms. Some of the branches were leafless now and looked a bit suspect; avoiding these and the sharp snags I climbed up to the main crotch and wedged myself in. The platform had been just out of reach of an elephant's inquisitive trunk. I took in the wide sweep of riverine terracing known as the 'Cornfield'.

'Not much of a view,' I called down.

'Ja, it has changed so much,' agreed Christmas.

Stu climbed up beside me to take a look.

'Do you see all those young acacias?' I asked him. 'Look at them! They've sprung up everywhere.'

'The wispy ones?'

'They've all grown up in the last 22 years.'

'Blimey! Just like the weeds in my aunt's allotment.'

'That's the result of culling elephants.'

'I'll point that out to her,' promised Stu climbing to an even higher vantage point.

I remembered sitting in this spot watching a group of elephant bulls pushing down trees over to the east. Not the giants like the one holding platform ten, but still big enough to make a show. The crack of splintering wood echoed across the sleepy riverine terraces; it appeared to satisfy the elephants even to excite them to greater efforts. Some of the woodland groves in Sengwa were well worked over. The trees lay flat on their sides in beds of broken bark, roots exposed to the open sky. In these playgrounds, the great beasts had heaved and pulled and thrown branches and limbs about, and kicked and tusked and opened up the hard ground. And scattered about amongst the broken stumps, like so many discarded pots of compost, were heaps of elephant dung, any one of which might contain a dozen dormant seeds awaiting the coming rains. I found it life-affirming, like coming across a grassy bank filled with rabbit burrows, or a patch of ocean alive with diving gannets, or a tree in blossom humming with bees. Let the elephants trash the trees, I loved it.

The research officers had a different perspective on the elephant's unruly behaviour. One of them estimated that Sengwa bulls pushed down on average 1.6 trees per day. By extrapolation across the number of elephants in the reserve, this meant that 44,000 trees were pushed over by bulls each year, with cows accounting for an additional 12,000.[1] The parks' staff took this as proof that elephants had become a nuisance, blaming the recent increase in tree damage on the newly erected boundary fence in the south, which, they reasoned, would prevent elephants migrating out of Sengwa causing a build-up of numbers. It didn't seem to matter to their way of thinking that half of the trees pushed over were mopanes which readily coppiced from fallen trunks, or that many of the others formed dense scrambling thickets that recovered quickly after damage, or even that the end result of tree-pushing was an increase in the mass of new leaves at ground level, where it gladdened the hearts of hungry impala, bushbuck, kudu and elephants.[2] The staff were adamant that tree damage was harmful and particularly objected when one of their favourite trees – an umbrella thorn in the valley or feathery-leaved msasa in the hills – was floored.[3] I took them on once in a half-hearted way, writing a short statement about elephant populations and tree damage that questioned the need to cull. It received a frosty reception. Students were not expected to think about such weighty matters, let alone attempt to influence policy. The first cull of elephants at Sengwa began in August 1978, just a month after I had finished my impala study and left the country. A series of culls over the next few years halved the population, and then a further 250 were shot in 1991. The culls were kept quiet. When I learnt about them some years later, it made me feel ill. I wondered why the authorities in southern Africa were so trigger-happy when it came to wildlife management.

Concern about tree damage was being voiced all across Africa in the 1960s and '70s with many scientists calling for a reduction in elephant numbers. Culling operations in Kruger National Park began in 1967 with the aim of maintaining a ceiling of about 7,000 elephants. For many years this meant removing roughly 500 elephant per annum, along with numerous buffalo, hippo, wildebeest, zebra, impala, lion and hyaena. In Zimbabwe, the culling of elephants within national parks had begun a year earlier. Approximately 10,000 elephants were culled from the Hwange National Park alone from 1983 to 1987. The effect of elephants on woodlands was viewed in the same way as overgrazing of livestock on ranches. It was bad husbandry to let it get out of hand. The wildlife authorities would not tolerate range deterioration in the parks or countenance what they viewed as a waste of animal products (ivory, skin and meat) should there be a natural die-off. Others dissented, accusing those who wanted to cull of being bullish and unfamiliar with the natural rhythms of the African woodlands. It was the start of the elephant wars, which have rumbled on to the present day.

Elephant wars are just one example of a much wider conflict. Is culling justified? This is the quandary facing many wildlife authorities. What will be the consequences of not culling? Such questions have been asked of elephants, seals, antelope, deer, kangaroos, rabbits, rodents, badgers, hedgehogs, crocodiles and many others. The conflicts are partly generic and partly specific: generic in that people usually relate to wild animals in a predictable way – as pests for example or meat, or cuddlesome critters or study objects; specific in that each species has its own unique biology which affects its abundance and interaction with other species. If we wish to resolve management disputes, we need to understand both aspects of the conflict – the wildlife values that people hold and the biology of the organisms.

The most bitter controversy over elephant culling centred on Tsavo, a semi-arid area in the southeast corner of Kenya that is famous for its large bull elephants and red soils. For 2,000 years, it was the hunting ground of the notorious Waliangulu tribe whose lifestyle revolved around elephants. They killed perhaps 1,000 per year, using long powerful bows fashioned from five different woods. The bows had a draw weight of 170 pounds, and could dispatch a three-foot arrow, fitted with a vulture feather flight and poisoned iron tip, with sufficient force to penetrate the toughest elephant hide. Many of the Waliangulu were killed or maimed whilst hunting, but like the Bushman they revered their quarry, speaking of the elephant in human terms.

Once the Tsavo National Park was established in 1948, two African wardens, Bill Woodley and David Sheldrick, put a stop to the hunting in an intensive anti-poaching campaign that saw almost half the tribesmen put in jail. With some regret, those early conservationists recognised that they had delivered the deathblow to a unique society.[4]

The first report of elephant damage in Tsavo was received shortly afterwards. Soon there was emotive talk of 'unabated breeding' giving rise to 'devastated bush' and elephant 'slums', and calls for the control of numbers.[5] The Tsavo Research Project[6] was established in 1967 in order to investigate the problem. The principal scientist found that elephants bred more slowly as their numbers built up. When they were at low density, the mothers first gave birth at about 11 years old, but when numbers were high they delayed calving until reaching 20. Then, instead of giving birth every three years, they waited nine years between births. It meant that the number of cows pregnant at any one time was much reduced, dropping to about one-fifth.[7]

The extent to which reproduction slowed down was impressive, but even so the principal scientist knew it would take many years for numbers to decline as elephants are so long-lived. Although there was no scientific evidence, he reasoned that elephants must have emigrated out of high-density areas in the past allowing woodlands to recover. With human settlement blocking migration routes, he predicted desertification in Tsavo unless the elephant population was checked. He advised 'enlightened administrations' throughout Africa to deal with declining woodlands through elephant cropping.

The number of elephants in the Tsavo ecosystem at that time was estimated at 45,000. The principal scientist recommended an experimental cull of 2,400 elephants to obtain the data necessary to plan a much larger management cull. Others at Tsavo disagreed with him. The authorities had not expended all that effort to stop poaching by the Waliangulu only to turn around and begin shooting elephants themselves. There was a sharp exchange of views and those opposed to culling won the day.[8]

Events in Tsavo now took an unexpected turn. During a prolonged dry period in 1970 and 1971, an estimated 5,900 elephants died of starvation.[9] The calves were the worst smitten. Once the mother's milk dried up, the weakened infants were unable to keep up with the family group. The mothers were reluctant to leave their young so their condition also deteriorated. The younger animals who had been weaned by the start of the drought were not yet tall enough to reach the remaining foliage on the trees, so they also suffered. All the elephants were affected by heat stress. Many of the dying animals remained within their home territories along the Galana River, even although they were only 15 kilometres from an ample source of food further upstream. Anecdotal accounts from other drought-stricken corners of Africa paint a similar picture: elephants stay put when starving. There is just one report that mentions older matriarchs leading their families to safety. If we stick to the facts as known, it must be concluded that emigration by elephants out of high-density populations is at best a patchy affair that leaves many elephants to die at home.[10]

African trees are experts at survival. Even when all trace of them has vanished, they can sprout anew from buried rootstocks or from seeds that have remained dormant in the soil over several decades.[11] When the rains finally returned to Tsavo, it was hoped that the vegetation would recover. It didn't happen. Six thousand dead elephants is a disturbingly large number but it constituted less than 15 per cent of the total number in Tsavo, not enough to ease the pressure on trees.

Then the poaching began. A much greater number of elephants were shot for their ivory than had died of starvation. By 1988, when the killing spree was finally brought to a halt, the Tsavo population had plummeted to just 7,000 animals.[12] Now the woodlands began to regenerate in earnest, leading to a striking increase in trees fringing the Galana River.[13] These included acacias and a small thorny tree, *Commiphora myrrha*, which supplies the aromatic myrrh resin of the Bible.

Given the regenerative powers of these trees, could it be that pristine woodlands with few elephants and smashed-up woodlands with lots of elephants are two vegetation states united by a single ecological process? An eminent wildlife ecologist, Graeme Caughley, proposed just that. His hypothesis was that elephants on the increase thinned out the forest, and that this caused their numbers to decline due to starvation and a slowing in the birth rate, until eventually a point was reached at which the forest could begin to recover. This in turn triggered an increase in elephant numbers and the whole cycle was repeated. Caughley found evidence of such a cycle in the woodlands of the Luangwa Valley. By examining the numbers of surviving baobab trees of different ages, he estimated that the interval from peak to peak of the elephant-woodland cycle would be about 200 years.[14]

A sharp elbow of wood was jabbing into my right buttock prompting me to climb a bit higher to find a better seat. Stu was higher still and mulling over our discussion on woodlands and elephants.

'You think the evidence for woodland-elephant cycles is good? Or is it just a fancy idea?' he asked.

'We can't be sure,' I replied. 'There could be another explanation for the boom and bust in baobabs. Also some ecologists think that Caughley forgot about people.' I explained their view that humans have curbed elephant numbers over many thousands of years through hunting with arrows, spears and pitfall traps. It is only now with the protection of modern parks that elephants have been able to multiply. They fear that the parks have lifted elephant populations beyond a safe equilibrium. Other scientists reject the idea of a cycle altogether believing that from time to time droughts, floods, fire, disease and other catastrophes cause a collapse in both woodlands and elephants that is followed by a slow recovery. It's a chaotic kind of picture rather than a regular cycle.

'Sounds like a muddle,' said Stu. 'Where's your money?'

'I like Caughley's hypothesis, but the evidence is thin.'

'So it's all a big mystery – the interplay of woodlands and elephants?'

'The real elephant problem is our ignorance about change in the savannah. We don't know what triggers the conversion of woodland to grassland and back again, we are unclear about the factors promoting ecological stability and we can't predict the effects of climate change with any certainty.'

'That's not much help to the park manager,' said Stu climbing back down to the main crotch of the tree. 'If he wants to keep his woods, he is going to have to shoot elephants.'

'What we then have is management without facts,' I replied, slinging my daypack over my shoulder and descending to the ground.

'Without facts, the manager might as well shoot elephants,' remarked Stu.

'The tragedy is that Sengwa was the one place where we could have tested Caughley's hypothesis. We could have checked for migration out of the area by fitting radio collars and we could have tested whether elephants cause permanent damage by recording long-term vegetation changes.'

Christmas had been enjoying a ziz at the bottom of the tree, back propped against the trunk. Getting up now he slung the rifle over his shoulder and joined us. 'This was the first tree platform I built for Mr Martyn,' he told Stu.

'Wasn't it near here that Rodwell was chased by an elephant,' I reminded him.

'Ja, it was. He had to run. He ran back to the game scout compound.'

'But that's miles away,' said Stu.

'More than five miles, as the crow flies,' I chipped in. 'He had to zig-zag through the woods but the elephant followed his scent like a bloodhound.'

'Flippin' 'eck, talk about a waking nightmare.'

'The guy was in some state when he got home.'

'Ja,' said Christmas, 'he didn't leave his house for a week.'

'Come on,' I said setting off towards the west, 'let's walk over to the river.'

'You have to be kidding!' said Stu staring wildly about. 'We'll be massacred.'

'There're no elephants hereabouts,' I assured him with a sight more conviction than I felt. 'Who knows, we might see something interesting.'

We followed an old elephant path which crossed the Cornfield, descended an alluvial terrace and meandered through a grove of large riverine trees. No one spoke. I tried to avoid stepping on dry leaves or twigs which might give away our presence. From time to time Christmas stopped and listened. Elephants can move like ghosts and, despite my assurances, I knew we could stumble across a solitary animal anywhere. The path entered a patch of tangled scrub, the kind of thicket that elephants love. We stooped under the branches moving slowly. Stu looked nervous. I couldn't see a thing. Christmas stopped again. Sweat trickled down my armpits. It was like a recurring dream I'd been having for the last 20 years. I am walking through tangled scrub near to the river, on a mission and in a hurry, when elephants appear ahead of me. I search for a safe route past them, but every time I set off in a new direction other elephants appear, hemming me in. There are no trees to climb and no hiding places. I make a dash for the nearby riverbank but am spotted by elephants coming down the far bank. There is no escape. Forcing myself back into the present, I pushed on through the thickets until at last the scrub thinned and we reached a clearing; crossing that we stood at the edge of a riverbank. The sandy riverbed was empty, except for a heap of dried dung under an overhanging acacia. Next to it were some shallow depressions in the sand where elephants had been digging for water. A line of impala tracks led up the far side.

'This dung is old,' said Christmas.

'Yep,' I agreed. 'The elephants are long gone.'

'Maybe they've all been shot,' said Stu hopefully.

Management without adequate facts is a challenge but at least something can be done about it. Surveys, research and monitoring can equip wildlife authorities with all they need to know. Management by myth is another thing altogether. It blinds the authority even to facts. I was beginning to suspect that some kind of myth underlay the management of elephants in southern Africa.

Several summers ago, I was involved in some conservation work in eastern Mongolia. It was a country I'd never visited before. On the drive from Ulaanbaatar I was mesmerised by the steppe, which rolled endlessly from one horizon to the next without a house, fence or tree to interrupt the view. The wilderness was immense yet even in the remotest eastern corner unregulated hunting had caused a steep decline in gazelles and marmots. One of my tasks was to advise a group of Mongolian scientists on how to apply for international funds to support their studies on steppe monitoring. The scientists had been trained in the tradition of the Soviet Academy of Sciences but now needed to prepare Western-style research proposals.

They were a wild bunch, proud and independent, but always ready to give a helping hand. Despite the good humour, I came unstuck on the first day when introducing the idea of hypothesis testing – the single most important concept in the Western scientific tradition. The essence of an ecological hypothesis is the prediction, which relates one component of the ecosystem to another. For instance Brandt's vole, an abundant rodent of the steppe, is thought by some Mongolians to cause deterioration in plant cover, just as cattlemen in the USA once thought prairie dogs to be a primary cause of range deterioration.[15] This belief provides a hypothesis that can be tested by experiment (fencing out the rodents, for example).

The academy biologists would have none of it. In the place of hypotheses they propounded their notion of an 'ideal steppe' which they described in exquisite and minute detail, down to the exact composition of grassland species, the precise level of abundance of different invertebrates, the required density of Brandt's vole runs, and so on. As this ideal was itself not subject to change, it followed that my alien hypotheses – about one species bringing about change in another – must be irrelevant. In frustration, I labelled their belief in an ideal steppe as 'The Great Mongolian Myth'.

It was an impasse. I talked it over with a Canadian researcher who was helping to run the workshop; we wondered if the debate arose from a collision of opposing philosophies which, like two tectonic plates, had been crunching into one another for over two millennia. The philosophy of the academy biologists was inherited from the Soviet school of biology which was itself influenced by the architects of the Russian Revolution. From there, the concept of an unchanging ideal could be traced back to Plato's teachings on the ideal republic in ancient Greece. Essentially it is based on an untested belief; it is a myth. Against this school, my colleague and I were teaching in the Western tradition which could be traced back to Plato's wayward student, Aristotle, via his Renaissance critic, Francis Bacon. The tradition is based on the power of observation, its essence that something causes something else. Hypotheses are explanations for this causation and make up the stepping stones along which Western science advances.

Armed with this deeper perspective, we tried various arguments to win over the academy biologists but to no avail. Beginning to lose patience, one of the Mongolians explained: 'A horse tied up with a rope outside a ger is either there or not. You do not need to know why.' It was time to call a truce. We accepted that our viewpoints could not be reconciled; so we took three birthday cakes and umpteen bottles of vodka and set up camp in the wild prairie. In the daytime we concentrated on practising techniques for measuring plant and animal densities and, in the evening, on exchanging haunting folk melodies for songs from Abba and The Beatles.

That experience was a lesson in the power of myth in modern society. From then on I noticed the ways in which ideas are received or rejected. The physicist, Richard Feynman, considered doubtful hypotheses to be the source of all that was finest in modern society: 'This freedom to doubt is an important matter in the sciences and, I believe, in other fields. It was born of a struggle. It was a struggle to be permitted to doubt, to be unsure. If you know that you are not sure, you have a chance to improve the situation'.[16] In Feynman's terms, the essence of the scientific method was the testing of several doubtful ideas to see if there was one that we could end up being less doubtful about. Feynman was not dismissive of faith. He recognised that 'one needs one's heart to follow an idea', but he also admitted that therein lay a paradox: that whereas faith and love are the greatest sources of transformation in the world, they are also found at the centre of earthly problems. Could faith in some myth, like 'The Great Mongolian Myth', lie at the centre of the elephant wars?

We retraced our steps across the cornfield to Nomad and then followed the dusty track northwards to the confluence of the Lutope and Sengwa rivers. Grasshoppers were buzzing in the foliage as we walked quietly towards the meeting point of the two sand rivers. There at last we found some elephants: a family group of three cows, each with a calf at heel, standing in the middle of the dry riverbed. One of the mothers was siphoning up water in her trunk from a narrow depression, a sip-well[?] that must have penetrated half a metre into the sand. The two rivers were drier than I had realised. Through my binoculars, I made out her crinkly skin and such a mild expression on her face. The mothers took turns with their calves, which sank to their knees in order to reach the water. After a few minutes one of the cows lifted her trunk to test the air. Catching our scent, she turned quickly and ran towards the far bank, closely followed by the others.

It had been wonderful to watch them, but I felt a tinge of apprehension. The elephants must be breeding flat out, fuelled by the dry season fodder available from all those young acacias. I guessed it wouldn't be long before the managers developed itchy trigger fingers again.

The early afternoon sun was beating down remorselessly and by mutual consent we decided to find a shady spot. We were spoilt for choice. Each of the large trees along the Lutope River added its own character to the overall charm of the woods: the chunky-topped sausage trees, *Kigelia africana*, have long dangling fruits weighing up to four kilograms that give the tree a festive air; the charismatic flat crown of the umbrella thorns, *Acacia tortilis*, conceals pea-green pods twisted into tight spirals that tempt monkey and elephant alike; the elvish Ana trees, *Faidherbia albida*, have giant horizontal limbs that stretch across the sand rivers, creating a blue-green underworld beneath a canopy of fairy fronds. The Cape mahoganies, *Trichilia emetica*, carry a fat crown of leathery leaves that casts a dark pool of shade. As in the story of the Tsama melon seed, the shade is so black at midday that you can't see beneath them. A dozen of these trees creates a shady nook half the size of a football field. Elephants love to rest within these woody caverns, lolling in the heat and throwing dust over their backs. Lions too enjoy the shade. Not infrequently, the midday torpor along the Lutope River is broken by bouts of loud trumpeting and roaring as the two protagonists challenge each other's claim to the same shady spaces.

We found a grove of Cape mahoganies and lay back on the soft trodden ground. A breeze stirred the leaves above and then died away. The still air carried an occasional plaintive song from distant birds and the steady *sssssss* of insects. There was nothing human to hear: no cars, aircraft or humming machinery; no radio, mobile or doors slamming, just deep nature all around.

It is ironic that these magnificent trees, which shade and feed the Sengwa elephants, owe their existence to the European trade in ivory and the associated slaughter of elephants a hundred years ago. By the beginning of the 20th century the elephants in much of eastern and southern Africa had been reduced to a tiny number. Relieved of constant browsing pressure, the woodlands expanded and isolated clumps of trees sprouted all across the savannahs, leaving behind many of the fine stands that are highly prized today. The irony does not end there. The particular grove of trees in which we were resting reminded me of a luxurious South African campsite. With its hot springs, gurgling streams, and comfortable rondavels, they are a paradise for the weary traveller. Might the modern holiday resort be a throwback to the campsites of pioneering days? The Voortrekkers crossed the inhospitable highveldt in wagons pulled by spans of 16 oxen to escape British rule in the Cape. They endured exhaustion, malaria and thirst, not to mention the skirmishes fought with both Bushman and Zulu nations. When grazing permitted, they halted their trekking so as to fatten the livestock. The best camps would have offered shade, clean water and plenty of game. How they must have loved such places. Perhaps those pioneers developed a protective affinity for the most perfect camps, reinforced by their Dutch Calvinist sensibilities to protect the God-given Eden. Was a folk memory of the perfect camp passed down, first to traders and transport-riders who took their spans along the same routes as the trekkers, and from them into the heart of a nation's consciousness? Could it be that the yearning for camping paradise, arising from a pioneer's myth, now fuelled the regional antipathy towards high-density elephant populations, especially where the elephants inflicted damage on groves of tall trees along rivers or around springs? Perhaps it had seeded itself into the hearts of game department officers as an aesthetic value, spreading from there into the official policy on elephant management in the subcontinent? After all, the cull masters admit that the basis of the decision to shoot is essentially aesthetic.[17] How that younger self would have chuckled at the idea, even whilst recognising it as no laughing matter.

The former director of Sengwa would surely accuse me of overindulgence in my own myth, a romantic one that hearkens back to a Golden Age of harmony in nature, where real ecological problems have been spirited away. This might explain my attraction to Caughley's neat model of elephant-woodland cycles. I am not sure that I would altogether disagree with him. Myths crop up in all sorts of unexpected places. It is through our allegiance to myths that we develop wildlife values and choose the kind of relationship we will have with nature.

As the sun climbed down the eastern sky, we began to wake up. Stu went round to the back of Nomad to pour out some mugs of warm water.

'I think I'll do a spot of hunting and gathering,' he said, setting off to explore for bugs and creepy-crawlies. Christmas, handy as ever, sat down to repair a broken strap. I examined some elephant prints in the trampled ground under the trees.

'Yep, that's a fight,' Stu announced, stooping down to peer at something on the ground. 'The females are kicking the shit out of each other and the male's pushing like mad.'

'Ja, pushing hard,' said Christmas joining in this new spectator sport.

'Oh yes!' exclaimed Stu, 'No. Oooh! Okay, it's three males by the looks of things. This one's fighting the other two.'

I walked over to view the action and found a large dung beetle squatting on top of a wobbling orb of dung about the size of a tennis ball. Two other beetles were doing their best to take it over.

'Three males or is it three females?' cried Stu, now quite beside himself with excitement.

The top scarab in a supreme effort flipped his, or her, antagonist right off the dung pile and began rolling the ball through the grass.

'Did you see that?' asked Stu. 'There is a massive advantage to big size here.'

Undeterred, the dislodged beetle found its way back to the ball and began pushing in the opposite direction.

'That's what happens when you get two pushing at the same time,' said Stu, awestruck by the antics of these dung gladiators. 'They don't coordinate, so the ball goes in different directions.'

'It's much better when the female sits and the male pushes,' I observed pulling out my camcorder to record the struggle.

'Yep, that's my experience too!' smirked Stu.

'See another ball is coming,' announced Christmas in his deep voice, inspecting a fresh elephant's turd.

'Wicked!' said Stu.

Zaccheus was in the library when we arrived back at the station, chatting with the officer-in-charge and two other game scouts. Even when younger he possessed a quiet, dignified bearing but now, with a peppering of white in his beard and the creases of thought etched more deeply into his high brow, Zaccheus looked positively august. We chatted about the old days for a short while. As a self-taught botanist, he had been eagerly sought after by the scientists for his skill in plant identification; later, he came to be valued for his insights into the political currents running beneath the surface of the nation. The scouts held their companion in the highest esteem, choosing him to adjudicate in difficult disputes and accepting his counsel without demurral. Zaccheus extended a kind of moral compass to the community at Sengwa. Today he was the longest-serving member of staff.

'I am sorry to find so little research going on,' I said.

'It is a pity,' he replied. 'In fact the research and ecological monitoring stopped in 1994, at the time of the severe drought. With no food, the villagers were forced to come into Sengwa. They used snares and dogs to poach the game. Then after the drought, some of them realised that poaching was still a good business.'

'I bet they did.'

'You know these days a warthog's leg fetches 80 dollars,[18] so it is not so surprising.'

'And now there is no time for research?'

'Yes, you are right. Since the drought, the entire effort of the station has been diverted to anti-poaching patrols.'

'It must be an endless task,' I said. 'Dangerous too?'

'It is truly burdensome,' replied Zaccheus. 'And some of us are becoming old now. Christmas and I will retire soon, then it will be up to the next generation.'

His words caught me by surprise; the next time I returned, my friends and companions would be gone.

'What about the future Zaccheus?' I asked. 'What can be done about it all?'

Not one to dodge fundamentals, he talked freely about the political divisions that were undermining the nation. 'I hope that the future will bring reconciliation amongst all Zimbabweans. Then, God willing, Sengwa can return to its original purpose – the long-term study of plants and animals. All of us can play a part in rebuilding our nation's heritage.'

20

THE TOURNEY

Weaver nests

Leaving Sengwa early the next morning, we passed by the grassy vlei that sable antelope like to graze, manoeuvred around a sharp bend where Peter Mundy slid off his motorbike under the belly of a bull elephant, and exited by the main gate. From there we followed the southern boundary track to its crossing over the narrow Sengwa Gorge. One of the research officers hooked a crocodile in the deep pool 30 feet below using a blue water rod with a dove as bait. Not for the first time on this journey I regretted my leave-taking, but Stu had a plane to catch in Harare and Nomad and I still had a long way to go. Pushing back the memories, I accelerated up the far slope, taking the old road to Gokwe. Ploughed fields now pressed up against the game fence.

'What would you do with Sengwa, given the choice?' Stu asked.

'I like it pretty much as it is – as a wilderness area,' I replied.

'What about these farmers,' he nodded at some people preparing a field for planting. 'They have to put up with crop-raiding elephants.'

'You could bring in some tourists,' I suggested. 'That would provide something for the farmers.'

'You'd need a shit load of tourists to compensate all these guys.'

'And then Sengwa would be full of minibuses,' I conceded. 'It would lose its magic.'

Our road descended into Chief Sais' kraal, a grouping of thatched huts shaded by several old acacias. I stopped to make inquiries at one of the huts; Stu sat in the car fascinated by the comings and goings of a colony of weavers nesting in one of the trees. Back in Nomad we continued eastwards heading for an elevated plateau that had been covered in wild miombo woods.

'You know the main problem for the social weaver bird?' asked Stu.

'Snakes?'

'It's the antisocial weaver bird.'

Like many 'stuisms', this one could be taken at several levels.

It was slow going on the pitted road but even so I found it hard to recognise the surrounding countryside. After a while I realised that the miombo woods had been entirely replaced by farmland.

'What about project CAMPFIRE?'¹ asked Stu. 'Isn't that supposed to provide dollars as an incentive to keeping wildlife?'

'Wealthy hunters pay trophy fees – thousands of pounds – for shooting elephant and sable,' I agreed. 'Lions are pricey too. Then CAMPFIRE pays something to farmers with damaged crops. It works more or less I guess, even if it focuses on shooting.'

'And what's wrong with that? If the farmers are so hard up, why not shoot wildlife?'

'Critics of the project love the wildlife for its mystery and wonder.'

'So the poor old farmer,' said Stu, 'living on the edge of poverty and seeing his crops disappear down the gullet of a massive great elephant is supposed to tell his starving family: "but isn't it mysterious and rather wonderful?"'

'That's why CAMPFIRE supporters call their critics 'bunny-huggers' and question their right to push Western values over local African ones.'

'But you don't agree with them?' demanded Stu.

'It sounds convincing.' I explained how CAMPFIRE was underwritten by the same ironclad logic that the project manager had used to pin me down that evening in the Okavango Delta. And that furthermore it had the laudable, almost revolutionary, aim of transferring wildlife ownership from the distant executive in Harare to the local farmer. 'In some areas it has helped wildlife to recover,' I continued. 'No wonder it has become dogma in conservation circles.'

'You still haven't answered my question,' complained Stu who could spot a rhetorical trick a mile away.

'What do you think about it?' I countered.

'The conquest of the earth is not a pretty thing,' Stu responded, quoting Conrad. 'There's a whiff of something patronising about it. I can just imagine the district commissioner lording about and giving his orders, "This land is for growing maize; that bit's for trophy hunting."'

'You're not so far off the mark,' I replied, slowing down for a tractor that was bouncing along unsteadily in front. Four grinning chaps were clinging on to precarious handholds. 'The basic concept was dreamt up by a group of Anglo-African intellectuals. At its heart, it grants exclusive rights to market a product – wildlife trophies. That's Western thinking.'

'Basically you don't like sport hunting, right?' Stu challenged.

'I get too much pleasure from observing wildlife to enjoy hunting for its own sake.'

'You keep telling me what I know already. Come on. What's your real bitch about CAMPFIRE?'

'It's heavily one-sided; it's too Westernised. Wildlife should be more than a cash crop of meat and fur. It should be more than economic ownership.'

'What more do you want?' asked Stu. 'What more do they want?' he nodded at the tractor as we overtook it.

'It's our relationship with animals. The Bushman hunter had an intimate connection with the game animals. He felt that he was in the presence of God when he was with the eland.'

'You keep banging on about Bushmen. They are just one out of a thousand human societies.'

'It's the same with Native American societies.' I did my best to recite a quote from the Ojibwa Chief, George Copway: '"There is not a lake or mountain that has not connected with it some story of delight or wonder, and nearly every beast and bird is the subject of the storyteller."[2] He didn't mourn the loss of their hunting grounds on economic grounds, it was a spiritual loss – almost a loss of identity.'

'You're just dreaming about the ancient past. You need to wake up Martyn.'

'You find the same thing today. In Ghana, the villager who slays a bongo fears for his life lest its spirit exacts revenge. He has to bathe in a special medicine or risk going mad.[3] Even in Botswana, elephants are protected from hunting by the laws and traditions of the chief.'[4]

'So CAMPFIRE isn't spiritual enough,' asked Stu. 'Is that the main problem?'

I wondered if Stu would even admit to a spiritual dimension in life. 'If you observe wild animals closely and you get to know them, that in itself evokes a feeling of connection. When you understand nature that much, there is a greater incentive to care for it.'

'You think CAMPFIRE doesn't recognise these wider kinds of sentiment?' asked Stu.

I looked at the game fence on our left as we crossed the Manyoni River. Just a few miles downstream there was an acacia-clad floodplain. It was rarely visited. Under the canopy the light was bluish-violet, a colour that blended with the mauve-grey coats of the bull kudus that haunted the glades. I loved to visit that place but I hadn't known what to do with the emotion. How much would the CAMPFIRE hunters pay for one of those kudu trophies? How much would the farmer get?

'It's a bold initiative but a narrow one. It doesn't unite people with wild animals; it reinforces their supremacy over them.'

'I see,' said Stu, fiddling with his minidisc recorder, 'so you think the CAMPFIRE people are spreading a Western economic meme in Africa and their critics, the so-called bunny-huggers of the West, are pushing a hunter-gatherer meme about oneness with nature?'

'The critics are only trying to protect their spiritual connection with game animals.'

'Has anyone stopped to ask the local farmers what they think?'

'Not often enough,' I accepted, 'but a friend came out here a couple of years ago to find out.' I told Stu how she had met a local family in one of the CAMPFIRE areas and been invited to live with them. She was given her own hut, cooked with the family and helped look after the youngest infants. She also worked alongside the women in the fields and went to some of the village meetings with the men.

'Did she ferret out their innermost secrets then?' asked Stu, making it sound a bit sleazy.

'She became a friend and was trusted,' I retorted stiffly. 'The farmers told her that they liked to have elephants around. They begrudged the crop damage and worried that someone might be injured, but they still thought of the elephants as friends.'

'I bet if push came to shove, they'd rather shoot them. Look at the trade in wild meat around here. It's huge. People love meat.'

'There's a beautiful Bantu legend about elephants descending to Earth from heaven on a staircase of stars that is the Milky Way.[5] The farmer's view is not one-sided. He sees the elephant as both friend and enemy. He's not so different from the Bushman who sees the sacred game animals as meat.'

'So where does that leave CAMPFIRE?' asked Stu.

'The local farmers thought very little of the project since they didn't receive a penny of the money. It all went to the project leader and to the fat cats in local government.'[6]

Nomad's tyres scrabbled on the loose marram track leading up a steep escarpment to the Charama plateau where we stopped to admire the distant view of Sengwa. Stu rolled up a wafer-thin cigarette, lit it and enjoyed the first inhalation. Then he opened up the tailgate to find some orange squash. I looked back towards the Lutope River... the golden herds of impala... the elephant thickets... the mountain of vultures... the reserve of memories.

Sacredness. That is the element that best describes Ntabamangwe for me and I believe for others too. In the rural African tradition, Sengwa could be valued as a sacred park just as much as a hunting reserve and owe its existence to the ancestral spirits rather than to the revenue it brought in. It might sound unrealistic, even corny to some, but I believe that sacredness is an elemental part of our makeup. Certainly it is very far from corny to the rural farmer who believes in his imagination that elephants descended on the Milky Way from heaven. Surely it is the soul of Africa not her wallet that will ultimately determine whether Sengwa survives or disappears under the plough.

Getting back into the cab, we continued on our way to Gokwe. Nomad's tyres were humming over the sandy surface. I patted the dashboard. 'Sengwa is completely unique,' I declared. 'It's the only protected area in Zimbabwe that is legally established for the primary purpose of wildlife research; in fact, it's the only such area in Africa. As far as I know, it's the only such place in the world.'

'How does that help with its future?' asked Stu. 'It isn't as if there's any research going on at present. Even the foot transects have been abandoned.'

'But if the place is developed for tourism or for hunting, it will lose its uniqueness.'

'Out with it then!' demanded Stu. 'What's to be done with the place?'

'We need Sengwa as a reserve that generates sacred stories, both of the Selfish Gene kind and the Milky Way variety. Stories spun from scientific observation that can guide wildlife management, and stories arising from a deeper stream of consciousness that connects us with nature. That is what the game scouts want, the ones who have stayed at Sengwa through 30 turbulent years. All who really care for the place want that.'

In Gokwe we pulled up in front of a deluxe general store. Stu went in to find some lunch whilst I busied myself making notes. A couple of minutes later he came back out clutching a bag and two Cokes blinking in the bright sunshine. He had an amused look on his face.

'Thought you might like these,' he said thrusting a Scotch egg and an apple into my hands. I stared at them for a moment, gobsmacked. Gokwe had clearly arrived.

Back on the tarred highway, I put my foot down and Nomad surged ahead. Our conversation took a global turn.

'Rural Africans, Mongolian scientists and international conservationists all operate on the basis of myths,' I said. 'Western society operates within a myth-based information system, just as much as hunter-gatherer society.'

'So?' queried Stu. 'We need myths to provide us with a sense of identity and to interpret life's mysteries.'

'In that case our identities carry a whole heap of unwanted baggage. Myths cause endless disagreements in society. Look at all the problems caused by industrialisation.'

'What problems? You think industrialisation is the cause of all our woes. Personally I like the wealth it creates. I don't buy all this environmental damage.'

'You're like Adam Smith. You believe in an invisible hand that converts self-interest into public good.'[7]

'Maybe Adam Smith knew what he was talking about.'

'Industrialisation was imposed on Britain's agricultural society against the wishes of the majority. Farming in Africa is going through the same transition. Along comes an industrial myth about mechanisation and progress and, before you know it, intensive agriculture has taken over the fertile countryside and commercial hunting is taking over the rest.'

'No!' interjected Stu, 'you've got it the wrong way round. The idea that industrialisation is a bad thing is the myth. It goes against the facts, as measured by many reasonable indices, showing that the quality of life has improved through industrialisation.'

'Reasonable you say. Is it reasonable that the migration of Kalahari wildebeest was lost to increase profits in the livestock business, or that the wildlife of the Cape was almost eliminated for the same reason? In the 16th century we sent our biological diseases to the New World. That was bad enough. Today we are visiting our social viruses, on the same countries.'

'You're just ranting,' said Stu, 'and you're forgetting all the good things that industrialisation has brought. Several hundred million of us owe it a debt for our present lifestyles. We enjoy efficient transport, good health, brilliant leisure opportunities and delicious coffee.'

'You're forgetting the price.'

'What price? What's wrong?'

'How about the destruction of ancient forests that were once full of wild creatures.'

'What's your alternative then?' asked Stu. 'Don't develop?'

'It's how we develop that's important.' I outlined a classic example in economics of a paper mill: in buying timber, the mill pays for felling and transport but not for the cost of growing new trees; in manufacturing paper it discharges chemicals into the air and waterways without paying the cost of cleanup. 'It's the same with everything else. Regulations help but industry only pays a fraction of the environmental cost.'

'So you want a green economy then?'

'That's right.'

'You've swallowed a green myth then.'

'Not if the new economy is based on sound science,' I replied. 'If we put verifiable facts on the table, then we can provide an accurate costing and resolve disputes fairly. The problem is that no one is listening to the greens.'

'Maybe that's because the alleged damage to the environment is overstated. All this bullshit about carbon dioxide causing the greenhouse effect hasn't been proved, you know.'

'If the greens have abandoned science in favour of direct action, it's because they're frustrated.'

'What about the 320 billion dollars per annum for implementing the Kyoto agreement on greenhouse emissions? That's hardly something to get frustrated about.'

'The real action on this planet is in the market place. As of now the prices and rules don't add up to green economics; they don't ensure sustainable use of natural resources; and they don't support healthy ecosystems. Until that's changed, we will continue screwing our climate and shafting nature.'

'Lets face it, you're not going to be happy unless we all turn into Bushmen,' Stu pronounced.

'Post-industrial Bushmen – that's not a bad idea. We don't have to imitate their lifestyle, but we could achieve the same net result. We could develop a waste-free economy for a start. Look at all the energy escaping into the atmosphere from our cities and motorways.'

The sky had darkened and the 'hair of the rain' was descending towards the road from the eastern hills.

'Bushmen like to hunt,' said Stu, going for the jugular. 'Does that mean you would support the harpooning of whales?'

'I would keep the ban.'

'You're just like one of those missionaries. You start off with a preconception of what's good and what's evil, and you end up selecting the facts that fit your case. You wonder why conservationists get into fights about hunting. Don't you see? It's because both sides are up against the other's prejudices. It's a religious war. Why can't you stick to the facts?'

'The facts are that we've learnt a lot about the behaviour and intelligence of whales. That makes a difference. That's why I support the ban.'

'Even if it stops a valid research programme?'

I paused to think about this new strand of argument. The Japanese government had justified their annual whale hunt on the grounds that they needed to gather information on whale stocks, but I was dubious, as are many, about their motives.

'If we need information for proper management then of course we should get it, but how we get it is another matter. If there is no good or bad in what we do, there is no incentive to seek a better way. That's where postmodernism lets you down.' I paused to think about it. It seemed that our discussion was getting as dark as the sky outside. I switched on Nomad's headlights. 'I don't know much about whale biology but if we need to know about their diet or calving rate or whatever, then we should aim to find the answers using ethical methods. Perhaps we could develop hormone assays to test for pregnancy in the urine downstream of a swimming whale, or use acoustic imaging devices. Maybe body length could be used as an indicator of age, and faecal analysis could tell us something about their food.'

'Alright, suppose I agree with you about green economics and all that ethical management stuff,' said Stu, 'which I don't. How would you propose to change things around?'

'Look what happened to the Polynesians on Easter Island,' I replied. 'I bet someone warned against felling all those trees, yet their leaders didn't listen. Or maybe, the society just couldn't change direction. Without forests, crop yields plummeted, timber house-building stopped and everything it seems collapsed.[8] It's a sobering lesson.'

'Not to me it isn't,' said Stu barely concealing his irritation. 'I like money. It makes me happy as Larry. And you spouting on about Easter Island isn't going to change that.'

We were approaching Lake McIlwaine. Heavy clouds were boiling angrily over the hills and down into the valleys.

'Even as a capitalist bastard,' I replied, 'you must still be aware of harmful consequences. Our dominant myth, our top meme, is economic growth – the idea that our lives can only improve through ever-increasing use of the earth's resources. We are heading for a heavily controlled world with full-on industrialised use of nature. Wouldn't you prefer an alternative vision? One that embraces cultural values and local people caring for their own resources?'

The tops of the trees on the road in front bent and whipped as a sudden rain squall hit; bits of leafy canopy were whipped across the road. Nomad shuddered. The sleepy afternoon sunlight had been swept aside and the ominous gloom was deepening; traffic slowed to a crawl. There was a storm leopard about, searching for a victim: lightning was the flashing of her eyes, thunder was the crunching of bones. A Bushman would have attended closely to discern her mood. She was tracking us now.

What frustrated me was the knowledge that arguments couldn't change people's values. Behind the values lay our myths and traditions, and underlying those in the very workshop of our culture, lay something even more potent – our own storm leopard. Snarling and hissing it stood guard over the depths of the human psyche, giving Western economics an edge over more ethical ways of conducting business. It was feeding our own myths and priming our values. Year on year it had been growing more powerful, praying on our anxieties, and now it was operating at a global level. Maybe it was a hidden meme – an epic myth from pre-Classical antiquity supporting the Western way of thought – or perhaps something even deeper. Whatever it was, it had us spellbound. I had been half aware of it when first at Sengwa, sensing even then that something powerful underscored the fatalism of the old-timer. I hadn't made it out, and nor could I now. But I was following the pugmarks left in the sand. Faint at first, they were growing stronger. Soon perhaps I would know where to run without looking for tracks, like a Bushman hunter.

The storm circled above us as we reached Harare and took the road out to the international airport. Stu wanted to find a nearby room where he could organise himself for the morning's flight to London. We found a small hostel just as the downpour hit. A vision of femininity in tight black jump suit with short red hair and laughing eyes, ran to the gate to let us in. She smiled at Stu who grinned back. His luck hadn't deserted him. We jumped out of Nomad and ran after her, Stu with his few belongings all contained in a single black shoulder bag.

21

MAGIC OF FACT

Bush hat

Striding towards the gate in pressed shirt and khaki drill trousers, the director looked as lean and fit as ever. In matters of dress and discipline he was cast in the same mould as the assistant director at Sengwa, but the outward appearance concealed a more worldly nature that was not without its empathetic side. He greeted me with a familiar tight smile, and waved Nomad into the driveway of his leafy suburban home. I'd managed to track him down whilst staying with friends in Harare and he'd immediately asked me over. I wondered what Stu would have made of this encounter. Formality wasn't his forte.

'What brings you to our neck of the woods?' the director enquired as we walked over to the house.

'I'm on safari,' I replied, keeping it vague. Absurdly I found that the secretive habit acquired all those years ago had stuck. Realising this wouldn't do, I opened up a bit: 'Actually I've just returned from Sengwa.'

We joined his wife, who was sitting in an arbour of bougainvilleas on the front verandah and began chatting over sundowners, one of the more pleasurable colonial traditions which seems to have stuck. She had me sized up in a few minutes. 'So you've been on a pilgrimage to Sengwa have you, Martyn?' she enquired, with a raised eyebrow and knowing smile.

'Err yes,' I stammered, slightly taken aback. 'I suppose it was a kind of pilgrimage. There were some memories…'

'It was a wonderful time for us,' she said, ignoring my embarrassment. 'Life at Sengwa was…' She hesitated, 'well, simple, before all the politics and troubles descended.'

Leaving this poignant thought hanging in the evening air, she excused herself to see to some preparations for dinner. The director had been watching me closely, the way a bird of prey might watch an intruder on its territory. He was curious. Willing to be friends but ready to strike. He was well aware that we had different philosophies when it came to wildlife management. His was ordered and tidy whilst mine was wild and free. It was the difference between the neat borders of Kirstenbosch botanical garden and the untamed heights of Table Mountain. His way was gaining favour in government offices around the world; in time I feared it would smother the wild spirit of Africa. Now he cleared his throat and looked me in the eye.

'How was Sengwa then?'

'As magical as ever,' I replied with a smile. 'Save for the farms packed along the southern boundary. The external pressures are growing.'

'I've heard that,' the director nodded, sipping from a glass of brandy and ginger. 'The miombo woodlands are being cleared across the country; the pockets that remain are now isolated.' His voice had lost none of its crisp commanding tone.

'Otherwise.' I continued, 'the most noticeable change is the dense growth of acacias along the Lutope River.'

'Yes,' the director nodded, 'the *Acacia* and *Combretum* woodlands have regenerated well.'

'The woodlands are really thick. In some places you can hardly see 10 metres. With visibility that poor, I couldn't repeat my impala study today.'

'Really!' For a moment the director was taken aback, but he recovered quickly. 'The previous officer-in-charge must have overdone the fire protection. He was a bit fanatical about it. Sounds like he let the woodlands get out of control.'

Bush fires slow down the recovery of woodlands. By burning back young trees they allow browsing ungulates, like kudu and impala, to reach their tops. This retards tree growth. But the director knew perfectly well that elephants were the prime agents of change at Sengwa.

'There's been no fire management at Sengwa for six years,' I pointed out. 'It's the lack of elephants that brought the trees back.'

'That was the whole idea of culling,' the director responded. 'We now have the result we were looking for.'

I took a gulp of my beer, wondering how far to go. There seemed little point in shilly-shallying. 'In my opinion, the policy to cull was wrong.'

'The decision to cull was not taken lightly,' the director replied curtly. 'As a result of poaching in the north, more and more elephants were moving into Sengwa. They destroyed a parkland of acacias that stretched the length of the Lutope River. In the 1960s it was a magnificent corridor.'

'You're ignoring the other consequences,' I replied feeling my anger rise at the indifference of managers to the animals they culled.

'Such as?'

'For a start there's the disturbance to elephants.'

'We removed entire family units to minimise that problem.'

Both of us were aware of the mechanics of elephant culling. A helicopter or light aircraft is used to spot an elephant herd and relay its location to a ground team. The hunters then approach in vehicles or on foot. Using semi-automatic weapons, they begin by shooting animals on the outside of the herd, aiming to kill the entire group. Sometimes a marksman in the helicopter singles out the leading cow and shoots her in the brain. This brings her family crowding around, making easy targets for the ground team. Invariably the infants stand by their fallen mothers in a state of shock and are usually the last to be shot. It is a brutal, ugly business that takes an hour or more, even with aerial support and skilled hunters. It is highly distressing to the elephants undergoing the cull, and the loss must be felt for years, probably decades, not only by those family members missed in the round-up but by young males temporarily absent, and by members of neighbouring groups.

The matriarch of an elephant family in undisturbed territory may be 55 years of age. She has amassed a lifetime of information about the environment, which makes the difference between survival and death, especially for the young and old in her family who are prone to accident and starvation. She keeps track of individual elephants in her own and other groups, scenting their urine on her path and contacting them by 'belly rumbling' – a throaty growling that emanates from the larynx and trunk and keeps her in touch with other individuals even in the thickest forest. Family groups foraging on different sides of the Sengwa River used to meet up from time to time in this way, synchronising their activity so that they arrived at the river simultaneously. The matriarch can recognise calls from a hundred or more familiar elephants, distinguishing them from those of strangers.[1] Occasionally cows from another group will attack unaccompanied elephants, and may even abduct their calves. So when the matriarch detects a strange elephant, she signals to her family who form a defensive ring in which calves move to the centre. It is this response to danger that the marksmen exploit in their culling programmes.

Anyone fortunate enough to have spent time observing wild elephants knows that they are tactile, fun-loving and intelligent, and soon becomes aware of how mindful they are of other elephants, and even of other creatures. The studies by

Cynthia Moss and her colleagues reveal how family members develop lifelong emotional attachments to one another, through which they derive comfort, security and stability.[2] Their extraordinary attachments were evident to Daphne Sheldrick who raised many young elephants, some from only a few weeks of age. She noticed how the orphans mourned for their lost mothers, 'silently but deeply'.[3]

Evidently the director was unswayed by these considerations. I switched to ecology. 'Then there is the proliferation of thickets which has scuppered any opportunity for studying animal behaviour. Worst of all, we've destroyed our one chance of observing an elephant–woodland cycle, that's only the single most important event in the ecology of African savannahs.'

The director's face hardened and he leant forward in his cane chair, eyes glinting. 'Those woodlands are prime habitat not just for elephants, but for all kinds of creature. We now have hard evidence of fewer birds, and ants where elephants have knocked down trees.[4] We had a simple choice at Sengwa: cull elephants or lose biodiversity.'

As if to reinforce his point a small vesper bat flew past the bougainvilleas and into our alcove; it flitted about above the table hawking for moths attracted to the wrought iron lamp on the ceiling. Perhaps it had emerged from a cavity in one of the old trees at the foot of the garden.

'We know exactly what needs to be done,' the director continued. 'Keep numbers below 0.7 elephants per square kilometre, or we lose the woodlands. You can't have it both ways.' His words were delivered with the smack of a heavyweight. He lent back in his chair before landing a parting jab. 'The elephants were moving into the farms at night and becoming a menace.'

The director's logic was, as usual, impeccable. There seemed no way to reconcile our differences; no hope of a meeting of minds. I was beginning to despair. In spite of the intervening years I was staring into the same philosophical void as that younger guy pinned down at the dinner table in the Okavango Delta.

And even before that…

Pouring myself tea in the library at Sengwa, I'd overheard the director talking to a research officer about the need to cull elephants. I understood their concern for the woodlands, but not the matter-of-factness of their tone. They were living amongst wild elephants. They must feel their immense presence. How could they sanction this killing so lightly?

I realised their thinking must be blinkered in some way, but even though the pieces were there before me, I didn't connect them. I didn't realise that in order to champion culling one must first dismiss the spirituality of animals from one's heart. The Scottish gamekeeper who poisons a falcon relates to it as a threat in an economic landscape. Grouse bring in cash, falcons reduce the cash flow. But equally, those who oppose culling can be dismissive. They ignore the serious threat to life and livelihood of the rural poor. To do otherwise might threaten their primary decision to relate to animals in a spiritual way.

There were two mythic worlds at Sengwa. The director and his staff lived in an economic world which now dominates Western society. At its centre is a marketplace where land inhabited by elephants is priced against land covered in maize, wheat or cattle. Usually the crops and cattle have greater economic clout but occasionally wildlife matches their worth through income generated by safari hunting or tourism. In this mythic world, hunting and culling keep the 'product' and profitability in tip-top shape. The other mythic world is a sacred place where rumbles reverberate along the riverbank and ivory gleams in the moonlight a yard in advance of a dark shadow. It is the ancestral land of both elephant and human, filled with wonder, mystery and biological richness. Knowledge is the key to understanding it; money is an irrelevance.

Back then I had barely distinguished these mythic landscapes and could not have recognised that each was but a caricature of reality, extracted from a still larger canvas. I could not bridge those worlds. What I did know was the research officers at Sengwa scoffed at my attitude to culling. So I avoided talking about it, hoped the culling would never happen and immersed myself in the study of impala.

The director was watching expectantly. Despite our past disagreements, I liked the man and admired his prowess in ecology. Perhaps it was here, in our mutual respect for science, that progress might be made. Richard Feynman once tipped his audience on how to resolve difficult disputes that have a moral dimension. He urged them to concentrate on the practical consequences of their beliefs, where there is a reasonable chance of reaching agreement, not on the reasons why there is disagreement in the first place.[5] In a dispute over religion for instance, progress is more likely if the debate centres on people's responsibilities and duties to one another, rather than on the primacy of their different beliefs. In relation to wildlife where disputes centre on our allegiance to different values, Feynman would surely have urged us to stick to verifiable facts in attempting to bridge the divide separating our heartfelt beliefs. The magic of a hard fact, by which I mean a clear statement that is transparently corroborated by all sides, is that it can put the lid on fanciful claims and counterclaims, no matter how vehemently they are supported. Facts provide a platform for building agreement and trust. There were some facts in ecology that the director and I should be able to agree on; they might just lead somewhere.

'If we were talking about the passage of a hurricane,' I began hesitantly, 'the fall of a giant forest tree, or the movement of a river as it meanders from one side of a channel to another, then we wouldn't worry about disturbance to the forest, for we know these events are associated with a recovery process.' I explained that when one bank of a river collapses taking with it the trees and understorey, others elsewhere eventually replace them. The sand and mud on recently exposed banks is first colonised by pioneering grasses, then by rapidly growing forbs and shrubs, and finally these are replaced by slower-growing climax trees. In this way the whole complex riverine community is conserved. If the river did not meander, then biodiversity would be lower because the pioneering grasses and shrubs would have no place to take hold. It is the disturbance created by a moving river that actually enriches biodiversity. 'It's the same thing in the savannahs,' I pointed out to the director. 'Elephants are the major source of woodland disturbance. From time to time we need lots of them in one place in order to keep our plant successions alive.'

'I would agree,' said the director adopting a more conciliatory tone 'that the real problem with elephants is not that they trash woodlands but whether those woodlands can recover afterwards. And by recovery I don't just mean trees growing back but the entire habitat with all its plants and animals. That will be difficult if the place is isolated.'

'Those woodland creatures are good at finding new homes,' I responded, happy to have a chance to engage in constructive dialogue. 'After all, they've had to cope with climate change in the past. I bet the most specialised insects – the ones that require a particular kind of plant for their larvae to feed on – will be the strongest fliers. They would have no problem finding woods that are recovering from elephants.'

'That may apply to some savannah species,' said the director carefully, 'perhaps most, but what about those that are both specialists and poor fliers. Such species exist and they have a restricted distribution in the country. They are at severe risk from elephant damage. You wouldn't want Sengwa's biodiversity to be permanently damaged by elephants would you?'

'I want Sengwa to have a truly wild ecosystem,' I retorted.

'If we don't set a 'preferred management density' for elephants; we can't ensure the future of our woodlands.'

'I don't think elephant culling ensures anything. The acacia umbrella trees would have regenerated along the Lutope floodplain in one of nature's own swinging cycles, and the seed predators and other specialist insects and birds would have returned. You cause more damage by imposing a 'preferred management density' than by leaving the place alone. You put nature in a cage.'

'Do you really expect us to sit back whilst whole communities of plants and animals are wiped out?'

'We could protect key areas from elephant damage,' I suggested. 'We could fence off dense thickets to provide cover for birds; and we could propagate rare food plants to conserve endangered butterflies. We could study the options scientifically.'

'We don't have resources to fund research in that depth,' the director pointed out, leaning towards me in an effort to get his point across.

'Then why not just surround some areas with electric fences when the elephant density is high?'

'We don't want fences all over our national parks. It's bad enough that they are multiplying across the rest of the country.'

'Just small areas,' I suggested, 'like the elephant exclosure in Mana Pools National Park. It's only a couple of hectares but the acacias have sprouted from root suckers and there's a riot of trees and bushes inside.[6] Just a few of those would guarantee the survival of your specialists. Even single-strand electric fences can stop elephants and giraffes. We wouldn't need big boundary fences.'

The director walked through to the living room to recharge our glasses, whilst mulling this over. It was dark outside now, darker than usual because many of the streetlights were out. The infrastructure in Harare was steadily decaying. But it allowed the stars to twinkle all the more brightly in the night sky. It was strange to be here with the director, cocooned against time and space by a small light and the bougainvilleas. Not so different from enjoying a drink on his verandah in Sengwa. I was having to get used to time travel on this trip.

'Maybe it could work,' said the director handing over another chilled beer. 'It would be simple enough to set up some experiments to see what size of area is required and what type of fence is needed. Some of the specialists would, as you say, only need a small volume of intact woodland.'

'We could survey trees for holes and hollows, and protect individual trees that are important for roosting or nesting,' I suggested.

'Yes,' the director agreed, with growing interest. 'I think there is scope for that kind of approach. You're talking about a network of mini protected sites. Now I think about it, there was something along those lines at Addo Elephant National Park.[7] A similar plan might work elsewhere.'

'We could back it up with protected sites in the agricultural lands. That would give dispersing animals, like birds and bats, a place to forage and find shelter.'

'It still leaves the problem of the large parks where the woodland is spread out over a vast area. The elephant herds in Hwange are so numerous they affect whole landscapes. There are 28,000 there now. We need to bring the numbers right down and then keep them level by culling each year.'

'Surely you don't want a management action that locks itself into place permanently.'

'The department can't just sit back and do nothing,' said the director.

'Why not? Trashed woodlands may look devastated, but it's more of an aesthetic judgement than a biological one.'

'It is an aesthetic judgement, and the judgement is that we don't want to see trashed woodlands.'

Alarm bells began ringing as our conversation drifted back to the realm of immutable beliefs. I paused for a few seconds to think carefully. The bat was back, fluttering about overhead.

'Am I right that the elephants in Hwange do most of the tree damage in the dry season when they stay close to pans with water?' The director nodded his assent. 'Then, I have another suggestion.'

'You'll need to be quick, or we'll miss dinner,' said the director nodding to his wife who was signalling from the kitchen.

'Why not move the pumps supplying water from underground aquifers every 15 or 20 years to a new set of pans, allowing the former ones to dry up? The elephants will move to the new site allowing the damaged trees to recover.'

'You're looking to create a rotation in the use of woodlands? That's not so different from ranchers rotating their pastures.'

'It would be a manmade system,' I agreed, 'but then so is pumping water at a fixed location. It's surely less invasive than culling.'

'All very well in theory,' said the director, 'but in practice there are hotels and lodges around the pans, and the companies that own them have made a substantial investment in tourism.'

'True,' I admitted slowly. 'That really is a problem.'

'On the other hand, your idea might fit in with the new thinking on tourist accommodation. There's a move towards permitting only non-permanent structures inside parks with operating licences of 10 or 15 years.' The director stood and began pacing up and down on the verandah, hands held behind his back. 'It would have to be carefully tested. You might need three sets of pans to give a 60-year rotation. That would do it. The problem here is the politics. It has become almost impossible to get permission to conduct research in the parks. Still, things may change.'

'That's great,' I said, delighted at the guarded enthusiasm in his voice.

'We could combine your rotation plan with culling outside of the parks,' he finished.

My delight died a little. In seeking a solution to tree damage, I had forgotten the kernel of the conservation problem – the deep and unyielding conflict between wildlife and farmers.

22

Hot Shit

Tracking elephants

The soft cooing of a laughing dove, rising then falling on the chill dawn air, awakened me to a perfect African morning. After a few days relaxing in Harare, I was anxious to get back on the road to make the most of the high pressure that was once again sitting over the Kalahari, pushing back the storm clouds and allowing dry weather a temporary respite. It wouldn't be long before the 'intertropical convergence zone' arrived, sucking in moisture from the Indian Ocean and releasing it as monsoon rains that render off-road driving impossible. On the next leg of the journey I would be accompanied by Guy Parker. I'd helped him with his undergraduate project a few years back; now he had invited me to spend a couple of days at his research camp in the Mavuradonha Mountains on the edge of the Zambezi Escarpment.

Guy arrived a few hours later at the wheel of a Toyota pick-up loaded with provisions for the field. He jumped out with a big grin and strode across the forecourt looking cool in khaki shorts and Italian shirt, brushing aside large and small dogs. Somehow he managed to combine a rugged lifestyle with an easy grace and charm, and seemed oblivious of his classical good looks.

'Hey Martyn, how's the safari going?' We shook hands like Livingstone and Stanley grinning at the fun of it.

'No punctures so far,' I replied. 'You look well kitted out.'

'I've got the medical supplies in the back, just like you ordered.'

'Hell Guy, I thought you were getting me some local hooch from the valley.'

'The hooch is for later. First I want to show you the project.'

'Does that involve chasing elephants?' I grinned in anticipation of our bush adventure.

'They're the ones doing the chasing,' he replied with only half a smile.

For the past four years, Guy and his research partner, Loki, had been helping small-time farmers to ward off crop-raiding elephants which caused havoc around harvest time. They were testing a combination of traditional and high-tech methods in the hope of developing a viable alternative to 'Problem Animal Control', the game department's euphemism for shooting crop-raiders. Invariably it took place several days after the event and as often as not the elephants shot were innocent bystanders. It mollified irate farmers, but in parts of Africa more animals are now being eliminated by control shooting than are lost from ivory poaching. It has become the primary cause of declining numbers. It was a dilemma that struck at the heart of the human relationship with wildlife, and I was keen to see how Guy and Loki were tackling the problem.

As we drove north out of Harare in convoy, a text message came through.

> Howdy hoe daddyo! how u doin? I just had my haircut, took 4ever! 2 day is really cold. How u doing? love u lots isla xox

I stopped a little way down the road and keyed in a reply.

> Hello my marula piekin, leaving Harare now. 2 day is really hot. Guy has promised we will radiotrack elephants 2 morrow! Miss u lots, love Dad xox

I wished she could have been here for these few days at least. It would be cool up in the hills and she loved camping in the wilds. I had hoped that the next generation of youngsters would be taught more about nature than ours: enough to understand that wild animals are neither humanised Disney characters nor cute props for TV celebrities. They should not be reduced to commercial products in factory-farms like those black rags in Mariental, nor demonised as pests in our fields fit only for extermination. They need to be understood for what they really are. Every child would surely benefit from the opportunity to observe the individual lives of wild animals in the company of an expert naturalist. Even in the largest cities there are squirrels, foxes, kites, storks and pigeons along with suburban garden birds, which could serve. Children might then learn to respect our shared planet with its many strange creatures each with its own private way, and understand that we depend on them for our peace and prosperity as much as they depend on us.

We made good progress on the fine tarmac road, passing through mile upon mile of commercial farmland. Despite the break in Harare I was dog-tired from all my travelling but, happily, Guy was keen to demonstrate that field work doesn't have to be Spartan. He stopped at a roadside kiosk and brought over a container of Mazoe orange juice, squeezed on the spot, then at another where he loaded up with freshly picked fruit and vegetables, and finally at a third where, to my amazement, he acquired hot chicken pies. As we commenced the long climb up to Mavuradonha we left the tidy world of farms behind, and entered a wilderness of miombo woodland. We arrived just after sunset to a warm welcome from Guy's research assistant, Ignatius, and the camp attendant. I pitched my tent on a small hill that overlooked the neat lawns below, and sat out front in the twilight for a few minutes, soaking up the atmosphere of the Zambezi Escarpment. It was cooler right enough, and the air smelt sweet; the Southern Cross stood out brilliantly in the heavens. After a few minutes, I scrambled down the slippery path to join the others.

Guy's little team had gathered in the communal dining hut – a large thatched shelter with an open kitchen at one end. Most of the space was occupied by a wooden table with a deep chestnut-red surface that reflected the light of oil lamps. It had been made by a local craftsman with rounded angles and carved fat legs that imparted a homely feeling. Guy was talking to the camp attendant about some problem that had arisen in his absence. He gave the task his full attention, asking for details and checking he hadn't missed anything. Satisfied that all was well he took over the kitchen, chopping up vegetables and frying mince like a celebrity chef; by and bye he produced chilli con carne with salad and homemade dressing, served up with ice-cold beers. Silence descended for a few minutes – everyone was hungry and the food tasted fantastic. After dinner, we took our beers outside and sat on the lawn under the stars. The peeping of tree frogs and the monotonous si-si-si-si-si of crickets provided a hypnotic background for softer chirpings that occasionally emanated from the darkness of the surrounding woods.

'Would you like a demonstration of our secret weapon?' asked Guy.

'You have my undivided attention,' I replied, 'for about one hour, after which I shall fall asleep even if you are detonating elephant farts.'

'Right,' he said 'don't move a muscle.' And he disappeared into the night, emerging a few minutes later with a large brown cylinder of organic matter.

'Is that what I think it is?' I asked.

'This …' Guy paused dramatically, 'is known as Mavuradonha Hot Shit.'

'No kidding!'

'Here it is,' Guy continued, brandishing the object in the air, 'a number one dung briquette made of pure elephant shit, and the hottest chillies this side of Mexico.' He commenced throwing it from hand to hand like a juggler.

'*Pure* elephant shit, is it? None of that diluted cow crap, then?'

'One hundred per cent,' confirmed Guy with a grin. Hunkering down with the briquette he applied a lit match to the edge.

'Go on, put me out of my misery,' I said. 'Exactly what have you got there?'

'Do you remember how Loki developed a chilli grenade?' asked Guy, now striking three matches together to increase the chances of combustion. Right enough, I remembered Loki telling me about a device he had invented that could propel a canister into a field of elephants where it released an aerosol of capsicum.

'It contained the ultra-strong chilli stuff?'

'The very same. When elephants catch even a whiff of it, they snort it out and run from the fields.'

'The inner lining of the trunk must be so sensitive,' I remarked taking a gulp of beer and wondering how I would feel if the inner lining of my nose extended for several feet.

'It scares the elephants but doesn't cause them any harm,' said Guy who was now using five matches at a time. 'It works a treat so long as the wind keeps blowing in the right direction.'

'I'm guessing the farmers can't afford them?'

'Even the simple aerosol is beyond their pockets. We were stuck until my other research assistant, Kinos, came up with this idea.' Guy again brandished the briquette, which was now giving off a thin plume of smoke. 'Last year he saw some farmers throwing raw chillies onto a fire to drive elephants from a field. The smoke was noxious enough, but it didn't last long. So he came up with the idea of using dung as a burning matter, and mixing chillies in.' By now Guy had used up half the box of matches but the dung was again in danger of going out. 'We experimented for a while to find a successful recipe. Basically you grind up the elephant dung into a messy paste, throw in dried chillies, compact the mixture in a large tin, and leave it to dry in the sun.' Guy tried blowing at the base of the smoke. A corner of the briquette glowed brightly and burning pieces of dung scattered into the night, but it refused to catch properly.

'Is it a bit wet?' I asked.

'I think so. It's a shame Kinos isn't here to demonstrate. He's a master of the art.' Guy blew again. 'Do you see the smoke?'

'It smells quite pleasant,' I replied sniffing the breeze. A bit of chilli caught in my throat.

'Normally farmers would chuck one end into the fire at the start to get it going properly.' Guy was blowing harder now. Gulping in some smoke he broke into a rasping cough. Recovering, he blew harder still. The dung glowed and spluttered, casting an eerie light over his face. He blew once more and a mass of flame and sparks scattered into the night.

'Ah, dragon's breath!' I said.

'Haven't cleaned my teeth today!'

'What kind of whisky do you drink?'

'I'm going to light a fire and do this properly,' laughed Guy.

Soon he had a small fire crackling away. He held the briquette in the flames and a thick plume of grey smoke billowed forth.

'We are talking serious shit here,' I said.

'Yeah, it just needed to get hot. Now take a look at that smoke. Would you care to sample some, Sir?'

'By all means; allow me a whiff.'

Guy held up the burning dung and the smoke surrounded my face, tickling my throat and causing me to cough.

'It's acrid but not painful, kind of catches at the back of your throat.'

'I think this one is a bit weak.'

'Maybe, but I get the idea.'

'We are still in the R&D phase. We need to find out exactly how many chillies to stick into one of these things to get it to work well.'

With the demonstration over, my exhaustion returned and I decided to turn in. As I climbed up the small hill to my tent, a bushbaby screeched in the woods, complaining at the chilli smoke. Further off, an owl hooted… Something was scratching away at the back of my mind.

In the morning the surrounding forest came alive with bird song and I'd already seen my first butterfly by the time I slithered down the hill to the dining hut. A night at Mavuradonha had gone a long way to recharging my batteries.

'Do you fancy a short walk before breakfast?' asked Guy, as I splashed my face with cold water from a stream running along the edge of camp.

'You're on. Where are we going?'

'Eagle's Crag,' said Guy, pointing to the top of a hill some distance to the west, now bathed in morning sunshine.

'I'll get my binoculars.'

We crossed the road and followed a narrow footpath that descended into a valley of scrubby trees and abandoned fields, ending at a pool of clear water where several brown dragonflies darted about the reeds. We crossed just above the pool and began climbing a narrow ridge. At the top Guy led the way to a 12-foot aluminium mast with two pairs of antennae sticking out like old-fashioned

TV aerials. 'This is the tracking station we use to locate our elephants,' he said, pulling a radio receiver out of his backpack that fitted comfortably into one hand, and plugging it into a lead. He busied himself with searching for a signal whilst I looked around at the view. Between the trees, I caught a glimpse of the escarpment stretching westwards in an unbroken line of thickly wooded hills.

Chink...chink...chink... the urgent radio pulse of an elephant broke into the gentle melody of nature, sounding something like a hammer tapping on a half-full wine bottle.

'Who's that,' I asked.

'It's number three... a cow... I imagine she's down at the Muzengezi River. No... further east. She's close actually, definitely within line of sight.'

'What sort of range do you have?' I asked, gazing through my binoculars at a deeply forested bowl, supposedly favoured by bull elephants.

'Our record distance is 90 kilometres,' said Guy, packing up the receiver, 'that was for a bull shot by poachers.'

We set off in a northerly direction along the top of Eagle Crag, walking at a fast pace through the open understorey. On the way, we came across a 30-foot sapling with its bark entirely removed by elephants. Its crown of chartreuse green leaves was supported on a milky white column. A fairytale tree, but doomed.

'That's a *Julbernardia globiflora*,' said Guy, 'very recently stripped as well.'

I walked closer, noticing the fresh creamy smell. The bare stem felt moist. Finding a small piece of bark, I chewed it to test the flavour.

'Acquired taste?' asked Guy.

'Not much taste, but it's moist. The bark must have been running with sap.'

A little further on, we came to an abrupt halt at the edge of a sheer drop. It was as if some giant had pared off the end of the ridge with a knife. Guy lay down on a rock jutting out over the abyss and peered down.

'How's your head for heights?' he asked.

Taking Guy's place, I edged my way out on the overhanging rock and peeped over the lip. There was a breathtaking drop of 250 feet to the forest canopy, which then tumbled steeply downwards three times that depth to a muddy river. As it flowed back and forth across the canyon floor, the river sculpted twin shorelines from the forested slopes on either side. For a moment, I had the eyes of an eagle. Beneath me birds skimmed above the forest canopy as I soared aloft, winging it high above the heartland of wild Africa. Warm currents rose from the valley below carrying the rich smell of newly flushed trees and hidden vines; the rising eddies played in my hair. Scattered in amongst those trees were rocks the size of cottages. It dawned on me that they must have crashed down from this very rock wall. Glancing to the side, several other overhanging rocks caught my eye, holding on precariously to the crumbling cliff edge. Some were clinging by a toehold.

'What the hell am I doing?' I shouted, suppressing a mad laugh, and easing quickly backwards.

On the walk to camp, Guy told me about his vision for conservation in the Zambezi Valley. 'We have many different types of land use here – private farms, communal farms, wilderness that is scheduled for farming, hunting reserves and national parks. Until recently, the presence of tsetse fly kept the land wild irrespective of who owned it.'

'I suppose the elephants are used to wandering across the landscape, blissfully unaware of all the human stuff.'

'The eradication of tsetse fly has put paid to those halcyon days. The farms have expanded every year and now they are threatening the elephant migration. We want to involve the farmers in developing a management plan that will protect wildlife.'

'You'll need some kind of corridor then?'

'That's critical. We've mapped the villages and fields as they will appear in 10 years time. The farms link together in a continuous belt that lies between the wildlife areas along the Zambezi River and those up here on the escarpment. We need a migration route that allows elephants to cross over.'

'Will the farmers give you land?'

'We have one more secret weapon here,' said Guy with a grin. 'Sacred sites. We hope they will come to our rescue.'

Conversation was interrupted for a minute as we scrambled down a steep slope with loose scree. I grasped wildly at small saplings to slow my descent.

'What's so sacred about them?' I asked at the bottom.

'The river gods live in them. They're quite small, usually just a grove of trees. I'll show you tomorrow.'

'Are they very sacred? I mean do the locals keep right away?'

'People collect medicinal plants and firewood in them. We've spoken to some headmen about using them as stepping stones on an elephant migration route. They agree with the idea in principle, but we haven't got down to the nuts and bolts yet – which bits of land, what kind of restrictions, and so on.'

At the base of Eagle's Crag, we stopped for a drink at the pool. Some large blue dragonflies had joined the smaller brown ones. I dunked my head right under, enjoying the sensation of cool water trickling down my neck. Then we headed down the small footpath leading to camp, with Guy in front. We hadn't gone far when I noticed him stiffen, before edging cautiously forward peering into the bushes on our left. Looking in the same direction I spotted the problem: an elephant bull in a thicket about 75 yards away, and close to where our path was leading. I came up behind Guy, keeping quiet. The elephant stood still, trunk swinging, and then took a couple of paces forward to get a clearer view of us. He began feeding again, pulling at the shrubbery with his trunk, taking his time. He knew we were there watching him but he wasn't about to give ground. Checking about, I could see no obvious place of safety: the trees were flimsy and the boulders too small to dodge behind. Out on foot near to elephants, you understand what it means to be exposed.

'He's very assertive,' I whispered to Guy.

'These bulls know the farmers. They don't give ground.'

After about 10 minutes the bull turned and, raising his ears and tail, walked silently into the woods. Just a short confrontation, but he had made his point. I could see why the farmers feared elephants; it seemed even more marvellous that they still regarded them as friends.

Back at the dining hut, Guy threw together a late breakfast, spreading avocado onto fresh rolls and sprinkling the whole lot with Tabasco sauce. I'd never had such tasty food in camp. Afterwards he showed me around the vegetable garden. Chillies predominated, both the African variety and Louisiana long peppers, but there were also green beans, tomatoes and pawpaws. Afterwards we drove down to the fields on the lower slopes of Mavuradhona.

'What are those?' I asked, pointing to a couple of large muddy termite mounds with wooden structures on top.

'Lookout towers. In March and April they're manned all night by schoolkids. That's one of the hidden costs of wildlife conflict – all those months lost from school.'

Leaving the Toyota, we walked passed the towers and down to the river where we found Ignatius and three farmers standing next to a small square of cut thorn bushes. Inside were several beds of chilli seedlings looking like rows of dwarf beans. An old bucket lay in a corner. Someone must be carrying water up from the river each day. The experts call it bucket irrigation.

'We've developed a new strategy for protecting crops,' explained Guy. 'These farmers will plant a barrier of spiky sisal around the outer edge of their fields. Inside that they'll leave a 10-metre wide strip of bare ground, then plant a ring of chilli peppers, next tobacco or some other cash crop and finally, right in the middle, will be maize and melons.'

'When do you plan to get started?' I asked, stooping down to inspect a row of young plants. They were about six inches tall with pea-green, ace-of-spades leaves.

'We'll plant these out as soon as the rains come.'

'And you think that will deter the elephants?' I queried.

'It doesn't stop them but they can be spotted crossing into the field which allows the farmer to raise the alarm. Just as important, neither elephants nor bushpigs eat chilli so there's always one crop to harvest.'

With Ignatius acting as translator, I asked the farmers what animal caused the most damage. The three talked amongst themselves for a moment, and then the oldest one stepped forward in his faded orange overalls and old army hat, frowned and answered.

'The main problem here is elephant, then wild pig, and the next one is baboons. They are coming after our maize and cotton, and our groundnuts and sweet potatoes.'

Looking at his gnarled hands and worn clothes I wondered what it must be like to have the security of your family entirely dependent on the crops you have toiled to grow, and then to see wild animals coming to take them. 'What methods do you use to protect the crops?' I asked.

'We use fire and we bang on things... but the elephant... ahh, he keeps coming,' the farmer replied with a big grin.

'Is that right? Well what about the bushpigs and baboons; are you more successful with them?'

'On these two, the baboons come in the day. When the dogs are barking they run away. The wild pig comes at night – even now he is coming to take seed out of the ground – so from this time on, we are sleeping down here with the dogs.'

A friend of mine measured crop damage in Zimbabwe and found that elephants caused less damage than the other crop-raiding animals. If a rodent caused the same amount of damage as an elephant, few would pay it much attention.[1] 'Would it be right to say,' I asked 'that wild pigs and baboons cause much damage but you can control them, whereas elephants come only occasionally but are difficult?'

Ignatius held a long conversation with the three farmers and then turned to me. 'They echo your sentiments,' he said. 'The elephant is the main problem because it can chase you, and that will be the end of you. Whereas with bushpigs, provided the dogs are there, the farmers know and can chase the pigs. Now dogs can also alert you if there are elephants, but dogs with elephant, ahh...' and he smiled at the picture, shaking his head, 'they are not good friends.'

'Is that so?'

'Ja,' and he frowned for a moment. 'Maybe the dog will get killed.'

'Or worse,' interjected Guy with a grin, 'the elephant will chase the dog back to you!'

'Ja,' agreed Ignatius grinning in response, 'the dog is running away from the elephant, going back to its owner... then the two of you, you are in for it!'

'But the dog can run faster than you can,' I said, picturing a wee dog scooting under its master's feet to avoid a rampaging elephant.

'Ja, Ja! So really you are the one who is in for it.' Ignatius agreed, translating rapidly for the farmers who joined in the laughter.

On the way home, Guy suggested we make a detour to a small waterfall that tumbled down the escarpment through a series of plunge pools carved out of smooth granite rocks. We scrambled down to the first pool for a swim. Floating on my back I peered through the curtain of falling water to a fireball lily lodged in a crevice, its opulent flower bathed in a constant mist. It was cool and refreshing. The tension generated by days of heated debate with Stu slipped away, circling once or twice with the foam before overflowing into the pool below, from whence it tumbled down a wet and slippery chute, and jetted out across the great Zambezi Valley.

Back at camp Guy went straight to work in the kitchen, making another cracking-good dinner. This time he cooked up beef stir-fry with chilli and mashed potatoes, liberally sprinkling in Tabasco sauce. Silence descended at the homemade table as his troops relished their evening meal. Afterwards Guy and I carried canvas chairs onto the lawn to enjoy the light breeze coming up from the valley. A curtain of stars hung from the night sky.

'How do you think we're doing?' asked Guy.

'The stir-fry was great.'

'I'm a slave to my calling.'

'I think you're right on course. "Hot shit" is a great idea. I can just picture those marauding elephants high-tailing it from the fields. But even if it doesn't work, or if it only partly works, it's your approach that I like.' I thought about it for a moment… scratching my head… wondering where to launch in.

The heart of the matter is the human relationship with nature. It has many aspects. For years I'd struggled to make sense of it but I'd kept missing the one viewpoint which might have helped. The way that Bushmen lived, whether in the arid depths of the Kalahari Desert or the mountain fastnesses of Lesotho, embraced a balance between people and their environment. It is so profoundly unlike our way of living that, lacking the requisite experience of such a lifestyle, we fail to fully appreciate it. Still, with Guy encouraging me on I am going to try to unscramble it.

It begins with a simple premise: our place in the living world, whether Bushman or Western-man, is defined by our relationship with nature. In the case of the mobile Bushman that relationship can be divided into three primary elements. The first concerns the harvest. In taking what is needed for subsistence, no useful part of the plant or animal is wasted. And as for shelter, a simple grass hut is sufficient. Care, thrift and an eye for the future are hallmarks of the first element of the Bushman's relationship with nature.

The second element is their understanding of nature. Bushmen have an intimate knowledge of plant ecology and animal behaviour and they understand the principle of cause and effect in the ecosystem. Living within nature, they are constantly aware of its state of health. They accommodate a shortage of food by varying what they hunt and gather, by adjusting band size, or by migrating elsewhere.[2]

The third element is less easily described but as far as I can make out it is closest to the core. The Bushman's world is imbued with ancestors as much as by their living family. The distant ancestors – members of the Early Race – are shared with ancestors of the living animals and plants, so the fate of people and nature is intertwined from the outset. Moreover the spiritual world shadows the material one: powerful spirits haunt the deep pools of the hill country and may draw close to watch from shadows around a Kalahari campfire. The great God, /Kaggen, accompanies the hunter 'unseen but felt' protecting his beloved eland from hot-blooded, human excesses. These deeper mysteries of the spirit world move the Bushman's mind and fill it with awe. They are not spoken of lightly but held secret until initiation in the appropriate dance.[3] So the Bushman inhabits the spiritual and corporeal worlds, and their stories interweave from one to the other.

From what I can see, looking at it from the outside, the mobile Bushman's relationship with nature might appear something like this:

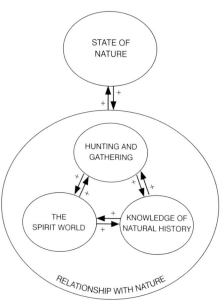

The 'Hunting and Gathering' and 'Knowledge of Natural History' elements of Bushman society mutually support one another. For instance, the gatherer determines where she may find the plumpest roots by discerning the past pattern of rainfall, and then gains yet more knowledge of natural history from the character of her harvest; the hunter gains a similar kind of feedback from the game animals. Other interactions are also synergistic. A deepening knowledge of natural history kindles a reverence for nature. Spiritual beliefs encourage sustainable harvesting which in turn reinforces the sanctity of the bond with nature. That bond might be epitomised by the bull eland which had great spiritual significance to the southern Bushmen of the Maloti-Drakensberg Mountains, being portrayed repeatedly in their rock art. Each element builds on the strength of the others to generate balance in the relationship between people and nature. In their world, as in ours, the state of nature begins to mirror the underlying human relationship with nature.

In the West, our relationship with nature is less intimate. We depend on industrialized farming and fishing for our subsistence and on a building industry for our habitation. The connection with nature is dispersed through complex trading routes. In consequence perhaps much produce is wasted either through over-production by farmers or over-purchase by consumers. Our knowledge of the environment is amazing in its brilliance and ignorance. We monitor deforestation by satellite and factory emissions by sensitive chemical analysis, yet we know little about the ecology of the tropical trees we exploit or the spawning behaviour of the marine fish we eat. It seems that we find it easier to construct advanced models of ocean ecosystems, or to map an organism's genome, than to observe life and ecology in our neighbourhoods. Science for us works best at a distance.

The soulful element is where we and the Bushmen differ most in outlook. Our 'use' of nature is now largely based on economic self-interest; we show her little respect and look the other way as traditional customs built on centuries of spiritual, cultural and historical ties, unravel. We are losing our sense of place in the community of living things. Our predominant relationship with nature may look something like this:

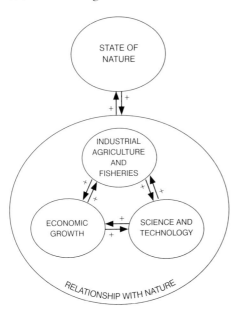

Urged on by agro-chemical science and advanced technology on the one hand and by the drive for economic growth on the other, our farms and fisheries produce food in abundance at the expense of wildlife populations and natural habitats which continue to decline across Europe[4] and the rest of the Westernised world.[5] The deer that once had value as friend, now only has value as canned venison, a trophy fee or a tourist attraction. The state of nature increasingly reflects our economic relationship with nature. As in the monster created by Dr Frankenstein, fragments of human, mechanical and scientific worlds are harshly juxtaposed. Despite enormous efforts by conservationists to ameliorate impacts, the Western economic model of development has failed to deliver environmental balance. It is just what the old-timer predicted. The need for clear thinking on these matters has never been greater.

When first challenged by the old-timer's fatalism, I felt sure that the West would, in time, restore harmony in its dealings with the environment. But the deeper understanding of nature that arose from the flowering in field biology turned out to be insufficient. Here in the Zambezi Valley, Guy and Loki are following a different line: they are directing science towards lessening the conflict between elephants and farmers. In a wider sense, they are attempting to resolve a conflict between two environmental values: the economic value that views elephants as pests and the aesthetic value that sees elephants as sentient creatures.

A similar approach could be practised in the British countryside. Surely, for example, it would not be impossible to study the transmission of infectious wildlife diseases like tuberculosis so thoroughly that we could devise management plans based on simple husbandry or inoculation that powerfully protected both dairy herds and wild badgers? The wider scientific challenge would be to develop an array of methods that delivered profitable yields of crops, livestock and fish whilst minimising harm to wildlife and natural habitats. We urgently need a fully fledged ethical science of resource management.[6]

Local ownership of wildlife resources has enabled game animals to increase on farms and ranches in Zimbabwe and other parts of southern Africa where formerly they were rare. The approach has much wider potential. As an example of how it might work in a European context, local fishing cooperatives could be granted long-term resource-harvesting rights to particular fishing grounds or fish species.[7] Furthermore they could employ their own biologists who might work jointly for a government specialist institution to give advice on sustainable methods of fishing. Working closely with the fishing community, the biologist could be responsible for monitoring the health of commercial fish stocks and the species caught up in the by-catch, as well as the marine habitats on which the food chain depended. Information could also be gathered on the way in which fish were caught, killed, stored and distributed. Members of the fishery would gain an incentive to fish sustainably in their own waters and they could trust the accuracy of the information produced on fish stocks by their own biologist. In the process they would learn more about the role of the marine ecosystem in their livelihoods, and that in turn might lead to improved management.

The concept of environmental balance needs to be so deeply embedded in our thinking that society resists strongly whenever it is threatened. Nature-friendly resource management could look something like this:

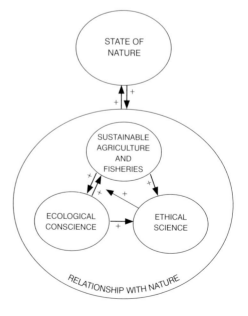

210

In this kind of future, society heeding its ecological conscience[8] ensures that farming and fishing are managed profitably but sustainably by regulating market forces and giving resource tenure to local owners and cooperatives. It also ensures that applied science is no longer the servant of government agencies working under a centralised brief to deliver economic growth at all costs, or of large corporations representing disconnected investors, but the handmaiden of a society insisting on environmental balance through its ethical relationship with nature. The supportive network in the diagram creates positive feedback in our relationship with nature, building a strong economy that is underpinned by a conservation ethic, as typified by the efforts of Guy and the Zambezi farmers to develop prosperous agriculture and wildlife in the same valley.

The night breeze carried the deep hooting call of an eagle owl summoning her mate in the valley below. Guy was looking at me expectantly. I scratched my head again.

'As I see it, you are attempting to reconcile differences between the needs of farmers and the ethical concerns for elephants.'

'And you think that's different from other conservation projects?'

'You only have to compare it with the kind of management in vogue today. Animals have to "pay to stay", that's the primary justification for their existence. It's an economic rationale. The typical solution here would be to organise safari hunting. The elephants would take on a cash value. The local cooperative might make a living out of their exploitation, even a good one, but in the process they would belittle the standing of elephants. Their feeling for them as sentient animals would be weakened.'

'So what does that mean as regards the direction of our work?' asked Guy.

'You're building a forum where people with different needs and different wildlife values can hold civilised meetings. That's right on target.'

'But what should we do with these meetings?' Guy wasn't going to let me off the hook.

'The local farmers and the district council trust you. That's a great start. If you can keep going, keep on testing wildlife-friendly techniques, keep on helping the farmers, then with a bit of luck you and the local community will develop a new form of elephant management. It will be cost-effective for the farmer yet more ethical than that practised elsewhere in Zimbabwe, or perhaps anywhere in rural Africa. If it works you can be sure it will be copied. Now that would be really worthwhile.'

Guy thought about this for a moment, frowning at the practical difficulties ahead of him. 'I'll show you our other study area tomorrow,' he declared. 'It's on your way west towards Mana; it will give you an idea of the wet season part of the elephant's range.'

'I'd like to stay longer,' I replied, thinking how satisfying it would be to roll up my sleeves and really help Guy and Loki, 'but if I'm to reach the Serengeti before that storm leopard catches up with me,' I glanced again at the southern horizon, 'I need to push on.'

I wanted to keep moving on my own journey too. I felt the need to immerse myself in nature for a few days, and I knew just the place to do it.

At first light I bundled up my sleeping bag and tent, threw them in the back of Nomad and joined Guy in the dining hut. He was rustling up some scrambled eggs with chilli. All this chilli I decided was having a good effect on me. Guy insisted that I top up my tank with 20 litres of petrol from his precious store, knowing that I had to travel the full length of the mid-Zambezi Valley before finding other supplies.

It was still cool as we headed down the escarpment in convoy, stopping at the office of the district council to drop off more petrol for the agricultural advisor. From there we proceeded westwards on dirt roads heading for the second study site. On the way we passed a track leading to an experimental impala ranch that produced game meat. It was supported by the French government's premier research organisation. The idea of turning the most sensitive and exquisitely beautiful antelope into meat made me feel sick: I made no attempt to investigate. A few minutes later Guy branched off the main track and led our convoy through the bush to the edge of a river. The crossing was about 30 metres wide. On the far side was a raised terrace with tall acacias interspersed with sausage trees. I parked Nomad on higher ground and walked over to join Guy, leaving a trail of footprints in the mud. 'Is this one of the sacred sites?' I asked.

'I've seen a hundred elephants congregate here on their annual migration,' he replied. 'We're going to talk to the traditional leaders about this place.' Guy pulled off his boots and waded across the river checking for soft patches. Satisfied, he returned to his pick-up, engaged the front hubs to enable four-wheel drive and crossed the river briskly. Nomad took the plunge just as gamely. About an hour later, we turned into a large field that had been ploughed in readiness for planting, driving towards a tall, spreading ironwood tree in the centre. High up in the canopy was a wooden platform with a tracking mast half-hidden by the flush of pale green leaves; down below, taking advantage of the thin shade, were a few tents.

'Welcome to camp number two,' said Guy, before introducing me to his two research assistants, Violet and Noah.

'It is much lower and hotter here and the field is dusty,' apologised Violet. 'It is a difficult camp and the farmers are not the best of company.'

Looking around I could see what she meant, but with no hills in the vicinity this tree was the best option for tracking elephants. The team had already demonstrated their worth by showing that elephants used the area for much of the wet season.

We walked over to the edge of the field to meet one of the farmers. Mr Dengi was tinkering with a hand pump next to a paddock full of noisy sheep. He was a handsome man in his late 40s with fine Arabic features, laughing eyes and a short dark beard. To my surprise he spoke excellent English and, but for the torn bush shirt and rural setting, could have been mistaken for a university lecturer. Guy told me later that many of the farmers in the valley were highly educated, so my surmise may not have been that wide of the mark.

'It must be hard work, making a good farm out of the bush?' I suggested after our introductions.

'Ahh yes,' said Mr Dengi, 'farming here is hard, but if you do it right it is not so hard. It brings me peace.' He glanced at his flock of ewes with evident pride.

'Could you tell me about the elephants?' I asked, trying to ignore Guy who was taking photographs for the project newsletter. 'How do you protect your crops?'

Leaning one hand against a tree, Mr Dengi tugged gently at his beard. 'We are beating the drums. We are putting fires in the boma. But we are failing at that. They just come to the fire. They just come straight to the person who is beating the drum. We are fearing them.' He laughed, acknowledging their helplessness in the face of such a formidable opponent.

'So how big a fire do you make?' I asked looking towards the field and wondering what it would be like in the dark with elephants on the rampage.

'A big fire! Even this height,' said Mr Dengi holding out his hand at about shoulder height. 'It is a flaming fire.'

'But they still come?'

'Ayih! the elephant is not used to it at first. When the farmer wakes up during the night-time, hearing them coming, he grabs the fire and tries to chase them whilst they are still in the bush. Ayih! The elephant goes around and tries to find another place, a good place. He just gets in there.'

'So if you make a big fire, the elephant will leave you?'

'Ja. But if they have a taste for the plants,' said Mr Dengi with a wide grin spreading over his face. 'Ahh-Ja! It will be very harsh. They can come at any time, they just keep coming, coming, coming.'

The menace of elephants may sometimes be exaggerated. A farmer's wife in Botswana once told me how a huge bull stood directly outside her thatched hut for the whole night in a deliberate attempt to intimidate her. But underlying such stories is a genuine danger. Every year elephants injure many rural Africans; the threat posed by elephants is one of their paramount concerns.

'Has the project told you about this new idea to protect crops using chillies?' I asked, glancing at Guy who was now recording our discussion on a camcorder.

'We want to plant chillies in the buffer zone,' Mr Dengi replied. 'I think the plan will work if we follow the instructions properly. We will try the line with bells. If an animal hits the line then the bells will alert us. We will also use some of Mr Guy's bangers and maybe the chilli bombs.'

It was going to be an action-packed summer. 'I'd love to give you a hand,' I admitted. 'Will you have a big celebration after you harvest?'

'If I harvest,' Mr Dengi threw back his head in laughter, 'I will give these scientists a goat to eat.'

'I'd like that big black one,' said Guy with a grin pointing to the noisiest goat in the flock.

'It's an important project for these scientists,' I said to Mr Dengi. 'It may be small, but it's forward-thinking. They are trying to solve this problem with elephants but they will need support from you and the other farmers.'

'Ja. I will try to support them. I can work some overtime. We will try.'

'What will happen,' asked Guy, 'if the project does not work and you do not harvest your crops.'

'Doesn't work? Ahh well,' laughed Mr Dengi shrugging his shoulders. 'We will just have to discuss what to do with you. It will be harsh!' he opened his hands in mock helplessness, the merriment shining from his eyes. 'Ahh! But if it works, I want to have a *mabiko* here. Do you know *mabiko* Mr Guy?'

'No,' Guy shook his head. 'What is *mabiko*?'

'Aha! a celebration. Everyone comes for a celebration. Cooking things, eating, drinking and whatever it is.'

'Sounds good to me,' said Guy, 'especially the "whatever it is".'

Later, back at Camp 2 we gathered in the shade of a long thatched shelter, seating ourselves on upended logs and enjoyed the cool breeze coming through the open sides. I asked the team about their future plans.

'The problem here,' said Guy munching on a cheese and ham sandwich fortified with fresh chillies, 'is that the land is uniformly suitable for farming.' He sprinkled a few dried chilli pieces into his sandwich and offered some to me. I declined the generous offer, being somewhat concerned about the state of my various orifices. 'What we have,' he continued, 'are numbers of isolated farming settlements surrounded by bush. It is hard work clearing the trees but even so the fields keep expanding.'

'This one grows by two or three hectares each year,' said Violet pointing to the surrounding field. 'The people don't want fences or rows of sisal to keep the elephants out because their farms will become limited by them.' She cut some more slices from a freshly baked loaf of bread to make a second round of sandwiches.

'That's right,' affirmed Guy. 'At present they shoot about four crop-raiding elephants each year through an agreement with the district council.'

I thought about the elephant-farmer conflict and how it might develop in the future. The families would keep growing and the farms would keep expanding. 'Suppose you perfect your chilli technique and manage to keep elephants out of the fields,' I said to Guy, 'and then persuade government to stop shooting, the situation will not remain static. The number of elephants will increase and the bush will shrink. Eventually the difference in quality between heavily browsed wilderness and young crops may overwhelm your aversion techniques. What would happen then?'

'It is a real worry,' replied Guy with a frown. He explained how they would like to keep the project running over the long-term so that they could respond to each new problem as it arose. One option was to place single-strand electric fences around farms on the front line; another was to provide contraception for elephants by vaccination, although there were difficulties there. Meanwhile there was the possibility of creating a wet season elephant reserve in the valley to match the dry season one at Mavuradonha. Hopefully tourism would provide an additional source of revenue. Perhaps with a combination of these techniques, and the goodwill of the farmers, they would be able to conserve the elephants.'

It was time for me to leave if I wanted to reach Mana Pools before nightfall. Guy sketched a route on the back of a school notebook, and Noah gave me a large bag of dried chillies to take along, just in case. I wondered what I was supposed to do with them if confronted by an angry bull elephant.

Soon I was heading east along the valley making good progress on the dry dusty tracks. Entering a belt of mopane woodlands, I was beset by the deafening whine of cicadas with its strange Doppler-like cadence that penetrated right through the cab. I wondered what Stu would have made of the racket. I missed the humorous asides that peppered our conversation. Still it was useful to have some time alone to mull things over. This afternoon I was musing on the divide which has grown up between 'man and nature' in the West. Our political leaders are skilled in advocacy, some have religious leanings, but few are schooled in environmental science or have personal experience of farming and wildlife. How many farmers are versed in ecology? How many spiritual leaders understand agribusiness? And how many of our scientists live the faith that begets great miracles on earth? They might each be competent professionals within their own domain but something whole has been lost.

Small wonder then if our fragmented society is losing touch with the natural environment.

Here on the floor of the Zambezi Valley, half-deafened by cicadas, it felt a long way off in the bush but, nevertheless, a small step was being taken by local farmers and conservationists that might just lead in a new direction. It would probably look kind of quirky to some, and barely relevant to problems back home, but I had a feeling it might just be the key to the whole shebang.

23

CAMP ON THE ZAMBEZI

cape buffalo

The noise that had roused me from my tent continued unabated, 'che-sploosh… che-sploosh… che-sploosh…' rhythmic and heavy, apparently coming from the other side of the narrow channel that separated my camp from a low-lying island. The pale wash of the Milky Way gave just enough light to silhouette the riverside trees against the night sky above but left the island below in complete darkness. A matching rhythm emanated from further downstream: it must be hippo I decided. Perhaps two bulls were tramping up and down, marking out their territories, each one forcing the other to keep a grim, all-night vigil. At intervals from further afield came the wheezing inhalation and rapid 'heh-heh-heh' honk of bulls surfacing from deeper water. And from somewhere behind me, a hyaena stirred the air with its mournful cry – a long musical 'whoo' rising quickly at the end. Almost immediately it was followed by the explosive 'wha-hoo' of a dominant male baboon. Guineafowl added a plaintive cackle from their nocturnal roost and closer to hand was the constant background chirruping from crickets. I checked the gully at the back of my tent, which looked a likely route for hippo intent on visiting the campsite. There was nothing to be seen other than bare mud walls. It should be safe enough up here, I thought. There was sufficient space for a large animal to walk around my tent without tripping over guy ropes or pegs, and in any case there was virtually no grass left in the woodlands to attract them.

Another strange noise caught my attention. This one was coming from the canopy of the giant fig: a slow puttering sound like the rotor of a tiny helicopter. It sounded something like a bull hippo spreading dung with its whirring tail, not that I expected to find one of them up there. I shone my torch at the tree hoping to spot something but the light merely vanished in a dense leafy void. No reflective eyes stared back at me. Nothing moved. I persisted with my search and after a few minutes spotted the silhouette of a large fruit bat circling in the dark; probably there were others up there, gorging themselves on the crop of wild figs. That sound was being generated by their wing beat, and the regular peppering of material on my fly sheet must have come from other bats roosting above the tent. I climbed back inside and lay awake for a few minutes listening to the night sounds. An owl hooted. Something grunted, perhaps a buffalo. From time to time, a bat dropping hit the fly sheet and fig seeds sprayed across the nylon. At one point I heard a soft step and wondered about the padded footfall of elephants. Then quietness again.

In the night, animals are alert to the contest between predator and prey, and they understand that silence is their best weapon. Here, in the heart of the Mana Pools National Park at the end of the dry season, the game was being played fiercely. Only the crickets chirped on unconcernedly and, once every long second, my resident hippo took his stride, 'che-sploosh... che-sploosh... che-sploosh...', lulling me eventually to sleep.

Awakening at first light, I lay dozing in my bag until a new sound jerked me to my senses. Something large was munching just outside the tent. Peaking out the doorway I was greeted by the sight of a massive bull elephant towering above me. I felt like a mouse that had peeped out of its hole and found a huge cat's paw just a whisker away. A copious secretion was running down the elephant's face from its temporal gland. It might signify a mild state of elephant anxiety but looking up at the huge tusks it was hard to imagine anything in me that would cause him alarm. On the other hand, the fluid might indicate that he was in musth, in which case I was confronting both enormous size and fickle temper. Either way my heart was beating rapidly and my anxiety gland was in full flood. Being trapped within a flimsy tent was making a bad situation worse. I had to move. In one rapid motion, I unzipped the door panel, stepped outside, stood up naked in front of the elephant, opened Nomad's door, hopped inside and closed the door. The bull reared up in surprise, ears opening wide as he turned, head lifting, until two large ivory tusks pointed straight at me. He shook his head in anger. I sat tight, transfixed at the sight. Where did I put those bloody chillies! After a few seconds he relaxed, stretched his trunk into the bushes above the tent, and broke off a large branch which he proceeded to devour, consuming leaves, bark and a long piece of the branch itself. Then, noticing some figs lying on the ground, he walked off a few yards to gather them up, grasping each individually with the pointed lips at the tip of his massive trunk. After a minute I judged there was enough of a gap between us for a quick getaway. I wound down the driver's window to clear the windscreen, which had misted up with my urgent breathing, and pushed the keys into the ignition. It was then that I noticed the soft hiss. Leaning out I saw that the front tyre was partly deflated. 'Not now Nomad,' I groaned.

The bull was in no hurry. I sat still. Nomad hissed gently. Eventually the elephant finished the figs and without so much as a backward glance strode jauntily out of camp. Back in the tent, I pulled on some shorts and fastened my boots; the day had certainly begun with a surge and I was wide-awake. I soon found the cause of the problem: a huge thorn was embedded in the tyre between the treads. I pulled it out with pliers, roughened the edges of the hole with a rasp, and thrust a rubberised repair cord into the puncture with the requisite tool. The leak stopped. I was amazed, being used to the conventional method of separating tyre from rim and repairing the inner tube with a patch. By comparison this was easy. I pumped up the tyre and drove over to the giant fig.

Having fulfilled her role as nocturnal refuge, Nomad, now doubled as a mobile kitchen. I parked her next to the concrete picnic table, lowered the tailgate and rummaged through the food boxes. Not much had changed there. I pulled out a yellow plastic cereal bowl, a packet of long life milk, and a box of Weet-Bix. I found a tea bag and the kettle but, search as I might, I couldn't find the mugs. They must have been left on the drying rack of my friends' house in Harare. I pulled out Geoff and Sue's large thermos jug. It was really too big to serve as a cup. What else? The empty tin of vegetable curry would be too sharp. Ah yes, a jam jar. Perfect!

After a bowl of cereal and some crackers with honey, I poured tea into the jam jar, screwed on the lid and walked a couple of yards to the edge of the terrace. In front of me the mile-wide Zambezi idled past, gurgling where an eddy had formed around a bed of rushes. The morning sky reflected off the blue channels that were interspersed with flat, hippo-grazed islets and occasional sandy bars tenanted by plovers and egrets. I had been told by the ecologist who used to work here that the islets were more than picturesque nesting grounds: they played a critical role in the long-term ecology of the riverine woodlands by protecting the seedling trees from fire and browsing animals.[1] Island life allowed the young acacias to gain a first footing. From time to time the main channel swung and then the acacias, having grown large enough to protect themselves, were reunited with the mainland woods. The mature trees on either side of the river testified to the success of this roving island strategy.

A movement at the corner of my eye caused me to turn and spot the last of a troop of baboons making their way into the canopy of the giant fig. At first they were quiet – although their presence was betrayed by the half-eaten figs that rained steadily down onto the dusty campground – but soon they abandoned caution and began chasing each other about, crashing noisily through the branches and filling the air with hoots and screams of rage. As this was going on, a small breeding group of elephants approached the camp, hesitated and then stopped to feed under a neighbouring tree. The leader had a tiny calf at heel, only about three foot high. The elephant group moved on, walking silently in the filtered blue-green ambience of the woodlands. As they weaved their way in and out of giant riparian trees, they stopped occasionally to pick up fallen figs and acacia pods.

Each of the acacias on the Zambezi's floodplain bears several hundred pounds of seed pods per year. When these are ripening and falling to the ground, my ecologist friend found that up to 23 per cent of the elephant's diet comes from seeds and pods.[2] In return the elephants deposit some of the seeds in fertile pots of dung thereby stitching themselves into the woodland fabric of the Zambezi Valley, as much a part of its biodiversity as its wonder.

Four warthogs trotted into camp, tails up as if on parade. Lowering their snouts to the ground, they vacuumed up the feast of figs that poured steadily down. Next, a young male elephant, about two-thirds grown, edged nervously around the back of my camp. He was so peaceable that on impulse I proffered him a succulent spray of fig leaves and fruits. He was tempted, holding out his trunk but too fearful to come close. I tossed the bunch onto the ground about 20 feet away. He approached gingerly, stopped with one foot raised, hesitated, then reached out his trunk and grasped my offering. It disappeared down his gullet. I picked up another stem and held it out. 'Come on "Woody",' I called. He watched me, then took a couple of paces forward – enough to make me realise how much I was going to have to trust this elephant. He might be a teenager but he could pick me up with one twirl of his trunk and pummel me to mincemeat. He took another step and for a moment I thought he was going to take the figs from my hand, but caution overcame valour and he backed away, shaking his head and scraping at the ground in frustration and mock aggression.

> Big, baggy, cowrin, tim'rous beastie;
> O, what a panic's in thy breastie!
> Thou need na start awa sae hasty,
> Wi' earlugs flappen!
> I wad be laith to run an' chase thee,
> Lest me ye flatten.[3]

I chucked another fig stem towards Woody and he came forward a couple of paces to take it. We played at this game for a few minutes: I trying to entice him closer and he maintaining a respectful distance but steadily gaining confidence. Eventually he lost interest, backed away and walked out of camp. Given time, I felt we might make friends with one another.[4]

All the while, the baboons had been covering my chair and table with fig debris and faeces; their constant grunting and screeching was becoming tiresome. I chased after one, a young male who was walking boldly across camp: he barked in alarm and took off. At once the whole mob came tumbling out of the fig, raced across 40 metres of open ground and scrambled up the next tree. All was quiet again. I cleaned off the chair and with a sigh of contentment settled down to write my diary.

The Zambezi rolled quietly by.

A huge old buffalo hobbled past showing off the wide span of his horns each equipped with a lethal upward-pointing hook. Covered in scars deep in the neck, he was surely a veteran of many hard-fought battles. Three kudu bulls walked by in a stately line, sporting long spiralling horns, elegant white chevrons on their noses and fine vertical stripes down their blue-gray flanks. They stopped for a few seconds to pull down foliage from some nearby shrubs. About an hour later, I noticed an elephant walking in the general direction of my camp but still someway upriver. I gathered up a leafy stem sporting a bunch of plump figs in readiness. Shortly afterwards I picked out two more elephants coming along behind the first one. There was a certain brash purposefulness in the gait of the leader which was familiar. As it drew nearer, it failed to slow down or show any other sign of nervousness, in fact its pace quickened. I recognised the bull elephant that had woken me that morning. He swung into camp and headed straight over.

I threw down the figs and grabbed my laptop from the tailboard, making ready to duck into the front of Nomad. The bull stopped and eyed me suspiciously, head swaying back and forth. I took in his huge bulk and two powerful tusks and nicknamed him 'Tom Cruise' for his testosterone-rich attitude. The other two bulls came in behind. Tom reached up with his trunk and pulled down a large branch from the fig. It broke with a crack and fell to the ground. He tore off a couple of sprays to eat, turned and chased one of his companions out of camp. At that moment, three more bull elephants appeared from the down-river side of the giant fig completing a flanking movement that closed off my line of retreat. One was even bigger than Tom. I had about two seconds to get into Nomad or risk becoming a human frisbee. Jumping into the passenger seat for the second time that morning, I shut the door just as a massive elephant walked up to where I had been standing the moment before. His right tusk was motionless inches from my face. It could punch right through Nomad's sheet-metal door and make nothing of the flimsy glass window. On the other side, a long trunk investigated the driver's door. A third and fourth elephant took up position directly in front of Nomad whilst Tom Cruise stood at the rear, rummaging amongst the breakfast things on the tailgate. I was surrounded by six bull elephants, all twice the height of Nomad; it was terrifying and exhilarating at the same time, but mostly terrifying. I was reminded of the scene from 'Jurassic Park' where two children cower in a jeep as a *Tyrannosaurus Rex* tries to get at them. The elephant on the driver's side turned violently around, head swaying from side to side, feet kicking up dust. My adrenalin level jumped an octave, until I realised that he was responding to the bull standing behind. And then quite suddenly, as earlier in the day, Tom Cruise had had enough figs. He coolly walked past Nomad and strode out of camp followed by the rest of his gang. I opened the door with a sigh of relief and walked around the back to assess the damage. The jam jar was a couple of yards away lying on the ground alongside the thermos. One or two other items had been knocked off the tailgate, but nothing was broken.

I settled down once more with my diary, leaning back on the canvas chair, jar of coffee to hand, laptop and a field guide to birds on the tailgate, kettle on the camping stand, glancing from time to time across the wide river and along the wooded terraces. As the sun reached its zenith, the riverbank grew quiet. The baboons were sleeping or drowsily grooming. The old bull buffalo was nodding under a tree. I was nodding under a tree. All along the Zambezi, great beasts were nodding in the shade. A warm breeze wafted into camp carrying the muddy-ripe smell of tropical river, tinged with the organic whiff of baboon faeces and the pungent odour of crushed leaves and fruit. Two fish eagles swooped down 50 yards in front of me. Gaining height again, one of them threw back its head and yelped a wild thrilling call, which was answered by other territorial pairs up and down the river.

The scene was idyllic, like a living Garden of Eden. And in this riverine garden, the community of plants and animals lived in a kind of harmony with one another. Floods might come, banks might wash away, elephants might descend in hoards and trees might be bowled over, but in time the floods receded, new mud banks emerged, elephant numbers subsided, and the young trees germinated and grew. Balance was restored. This magnificent tangled forgotten bit of Eden – humming with life that was free to come and go or just to be, that gave as much as it took each year in nutrients, nourishment and natural resources, that was home to so many of God's wonderful creatures – had sustained itself undiminished over countless millennia. Why couldn't we sustain our bits of the planet too?

My camp was set in the midst of this earthly paradise and it seemed as if every wild creature wanted to join me under the giant fig. I crooned a Scottish ballad, popped two tins of beer in amongst some reeds on the edge of the river to cool off and placed the solar shower in the sun. That completed my preparations for the evening.

Later in the afternoon, a steady patter of falling debris signalled a return of the baboons. Locating one high in the canopy, I stared at it aggressively. It barked in alarm whereupon several more panic-stricken faces appeared. I played at being a dominant baboon: moving my head rapidly forward and to one side, pausing to stare, and then moving it equally rapidly to the other side, raising my eyebrows, and grimacing, occasionally enriching this repertoire by ducking up and down and giving the 'wha-hoo' grunt. In this way I built up a chorus of alarm calls from the troop. Once a critical mass had sounded, pandemonium broke out with part of the troop rushing down the bowl of the giant fig and the rest flying out along the main limbs, to disappear into neighbouring trees. Satisfied, I paraded around the camp proclaiming my territory and whooping triumphantly.

The river was rising slowly. There had not been enough rain to warrant the opening of an extra sluice gate in the Kariba Dam, some 70 miles upstream, so I assumed it was some kind of daily cycle. My ecologist friend told me that when people woke up in Harare they switched on their electric kettles to make tea and the power station opened its gates a little to match demand. It then took some hours for the resulting rise in the Zambezi River to reach Mana Pools. I wasn't quite sure if he was pulling my leg. But he was being perfectly candid when telling me about a weekly cycle in which the water level at Mana Pools is lower on Monday reflecting the fact that many industries have been closed over the weekend. Apparently this is particularly noticeable over long weekends such as Easter. More than one canoeist has awoken on the Tuesday following a bank holiday to find that their canoe has floated off from their mid-channel sandbank, carried away during the night by rising water levels.

As the sun sank lower the mood along the river changed. The sky blushed apricot, and terracotta hippo climbed from shimmering silver channels to graze lovat green lawns on a thousand small islets. There was an air of expectation on the riverbank as if the curtain were about to rise for the final scene of a well-loved play. Two elephants waded across to one of the larger islets evoking perfectly the primordial atmosphere. A small herd of buffalo settled down on a grassy sandbar near to camp to chew the cud. A flock of 50 black storks flew silently overhead in close formation, keeping just above tree height. A plover piped intermittently from the sandbank opposite and then hushed as if by royal command. Silence stole softly across the valley until even our local pair of Egyptian geese quit their territorial honking.

The Zambezi rolled quietly by.

As darkness fell, a family of hippos surfaced at the far end of the nearby grassy islet and began walking slowly in my direction: 'che-sploosh… che-sploosh… che-sploosh…'. I grabbed my binoculars and hastily scanned the group. There was just enough light to make them out, and to see that the rhythmic noise was coming from feeding, not marching, hippo. By now, the Zambezi had risen about four inches, covering half the surface of the islet in the process. The hippo were feeding on the inundated section and the rhythmic 'che-sploosh, che-sploosh' noise was the sound of their massive heads swinging from left to right, like the pendulum of a grandfather clock breaking through the water at its lowest point. It must have been easier to grasp and uproot the grasses when they were covered in water. I walked over to the tent and climbed into my sleeping bag, listening to the hippo for some minutes before falling asleep.

The sound of baboons climbing quietly into the giant fig woke me at first light. It was a stealthy move. However they rushed off as I walked over to the picnic table to brew a cup of tea. The first part of my morning was spent intermittently writing and chasing baboons, but just as I was gaining the upper hand, a large elephant approached, walking rapidly and swinging its head as only Tom Cruise could. He breezed into *my* camp, although in Tom's mind it was clearly *his* camp, rocked up to within 20 feet, stopped, and looked straight at me. He was an imposing sight. I wondered if he was assessing me or just smiling to himself at my cheekiness in occupying his camp. He stepped forward with his ears out, his enormous body dipping down and up. This felt personal and I quickly retreated into Nomad. He walked to within an inch of the car and stood alongside to show me exactly who was in charge. I noticed the streak of fluid stretching from behind his eye to the underneath of his chin. It was an ominous sign but nevertheless I sensed that he wasn't planning on being aggressive, provided I accepted my subordinate station.

'Ok Tom, you are the boss,' I whispered.

Every detail of his fig-foraging was now visible. He used the sensitive finger and lower lip at the end of his trunk like fleshy tweezers to gather up one or two fruits from the bare earth of the campsite. Then he curled the tip inwards whilst rolling up the rest of the trunk; on reaching the appropriate height the tip was straightened to flick the fruit upwards, whilst simultaneously blowing it into the depths of his mouth. It was an extraordinarily dextrous manipulation for such a large animal. Standing alongside Nomad, I could hear his huge teeth milling the fruit. He certainly knew how to play the game of dominance.

Whilst this subdued confrontation was taking place, the baboons seized their opportunity and moved back into camp. Soon the figs started raining down again creating a constant banging on Nomad's roof, which quickly became plastered in bits of sticky fig and leaves, both fresh and partly digested. Tom enjoyed the ready supply and quartered back and forth across the central area of the camp. He and the baboons had stumbled upon the perfect strategy. Tom kept me pinned down, giving the baboons open access to the giant fig, and both parties got as much to eat as they wanted.

After an hour or more of this onslaught, I managed to sneak out of the passenger door, throw the scattered cooking pots and plates into the rear, jump back into the front and drive over to the tent. Looking back, I could see the camp teeming with baboons. Tom was standing foursquare in the centre, finishing off his breakfast. As I watched, his phallus emerged and several gallons of pee gushed forth in a great jet, like a fire hydrant, just where Nomad had been standing. This was followed by a large pile of dung and, in case I still hadn't got the message, Tom now had a whopping erection, penis extending a yard forwards. It jerked up and down twice in ejaculatory judders.

'Okay Tom,' I murmured, 'I get the picture'. Adding to the baboons, 'and I accept it boyos, total defeat!' and finally to no one in particular, 'and anyway that's the way it should be around here.'

Talking to animals whether wild or domestic doesn't seem strange to me. It wouldn't seem strange to Bushmen either who after all are descended from the Early Race. They expect animals to behave in fully human ways, sharing their emotions, powers of reason, tricks, plans and ambitions. In the Bushman folklore humans evolved from animals, but the corollary is also true, animals evolved from humans, and a pattern of their human past is retained. Thus wild animals have a language, they take an interest in human affairs, and they may even help or hinder us. In some provinces, their knowledge is greater than ours. They know for example about rain and death and what is going to happen in the future. This may seem exceedingly fanciful to us. But it should be remembered that Bushmen also hold that higher animals have long-term memories, lifelong bonding, experiences of pain and grief, and complex emotional lives. All of these are recent Western 'discoveries'.

Tom taught me a lesson today. As a wild bull elephant, he was not about to be tamed by me or anyone else. It made me realise that in throwing figs to Woody, I was not acting so differently from the farmer who throws grain to hens or beets to sheep. Such innocent beginnings beget domesticity. You start with a wild Serengeti ostrich but end up with black rags in Mariental. By providing food, we take away a little bit of an animal's independence, which is the very essence of the *wild* spirit that we so admire. We like animals to do our bidding, to come when we call, to take our offerings, and to perform at our request. We don't like to see them skinny or suffering. But can wild animals ever be truly wild, if we cannot first release them from our mental grasp?

When we enclose animals with fencing, even more when we trap, poison and shoot them, we also change something in ourselves. Consciously or unconsciously, we find ways to justify our actions so as to make them appear more reasonable. In weeding out the less healthy and desirable ones, are we not helping the animals? By reducing numbers, did we not improve their habitat? Will they not live longer? In any case, would they not otherwise have been a threat? Does not their damage cause human hardship? Do they not spread diseases? Are they not, in fact, mere 'vermin'? In making such justifications, we alter the quality of our relationship with wild creatures. Whether we like it or not, we become a bit thicker skinned, and a bit less sensitive. Our spiritual connection with wildlife suffers and we are left with a narrower appreciation of nature. We may even reach a stage where we no longer feel for the animals that we victimize. We become estranged from nature.

Hanging out on the riverbank for a couple of days had done me a power of good. I felt refreshed and ready to move on. I was ready to do some excavating, to delve about in our ancient human past. I felt something was missing in our understanding of the human–nature relationship and the hunch I was following led all the way back to our earliest roots, to the time that humans first walked on Earth. It would mean travelling up to Tanzania and continuing north across the country to Olduvai Gorge at the edge of the Serengeti Plains. That was where I had ended up after leaving Sengwa, when a second opportunity had arisen to study the biology of large African animals.

As I pulled up at the exit gate, a parks officer stepped off the verandah of the nearby office and came over to greet me.

'My God!' he said, looking over Nomad, now plastered in figs, latex and baboon turds. 'You've been having fun.'

'Just a little disagreement amongst friends,' I replied with a wry smile. 'Any news about the border crossing into Zambia?'

'Shouldn't be a problem. It's only an hour from here. If you step on it you could make Lusaka by this evening; after that, there's a new road that takes you all the way to Tanzania.'

24

THE LAST KOPJE

I heated up some coffee

The remarkable thing about Olduvai Gorge is not its size or grandeur, even on the rough dirt road the visitor to Serengeti National Park has only to nod off for a few seconds in the heat of their minibus to miss the shallow wooded depression. It is not the giraffe stretching for a green morsel from the umbrella thorn; nor the Maasai pastoralist, tall, proud and sculpted, who watches you pass in a cloud of dust; nor even the skull of *Zinjanthropus boisei*[1] one of our early human-ape ancestors so famously discovered by Louis and Mary Leakey in the crumbling clay sediments. What is truly amazing is that this modest gully, cut into the bed of an ancient soda lake, is a gateway into our distant past. It is a portal by which to enter a living Pleistocene world of migratory herds, large predators and untamed landscapes, where we can hear the thundering hooves and eerie night sounds, taste the sweet incense of flowering trees and the robust stench of decay, and know again the rhythms and pulses that defined the lives of our remote ancestors. Through it we may hope to better understand the forces that shaped the human mind.

When I arrived in 1985, the lodges were empty, the park authority was operating on a shoestring and the border with Kenya was closed. My reason for coming to live in this abandoned corner of Africa was to understand the ecology of grazing ungulates – the buffalo, hartebeest, wildebeest, topi, waterbuck, reedbuck, gazelle, hippo, zebra and others that make up the most diverse assemblage of large mammals on earth. By that time, the pioneers of field biology had completed their accounts of individual species but few had gone beyond to look at the communities of plants and animals sharing the same habitat. It was hard enough to follow the fortunes of a single species let alone a half dozen or more. Yet, that was what I hoped to do. Bit by bit, I meant to unravel the complex web which linked one species to another, hoping to lay bare some of the rules underpinning the glorious confusion of life on the savannah. I chose ungulates because they were well studied and selected the Serengeti because there the biologist can follow individual animals all day long. During the next four years, I mapped the minute-by-minute movements by animals of each species, calculated the energy they burnt every 24 hours, and counted the calories in the food they ingested. Slowly a picture emerged. One animal might make a living from a particular kind of pasture because of its size, or mouth shape, or digestive system, whereas another could not. Each was adapted to its own grassland niche. And once I knew the limitations acting on each ungulate, it became possible to understand how they influenced one another.

Crossing the gorge in Nomad, I stopped for a few moments to savour the familiarity of this world. The hills and plains had not changed. Gazelle still grazed in a shimmering sea out on the plains' horizon. Other ungulates would no doubt be grazing nearby in the woodlands. I reminded myself that I had returned with a different purpose in mind: to find out, in so far as I could, how another group of mammals, the hominids, had adapted to life in the African savannah a million years ago. That Pleistocene landscape was closely similar to the one spread out before me today. Our ancestors walked within a mosaic of woodlands and grasslands just like these and shared them with the same large mammals. It was at least possible that environmental preferences and biases evolved during the Pleistocene in this kind of landscape, that they were still alive today, and dramatically influencing our future along with that of all other life on Earth.[2] In looking to discover the roots of today's environmental conflicts, I was curious to find out how the early hominids fitted into their savannah landscape. Did they possess distinctive foraging strategies or embedded behaviour patterns that might be passed on from generation to generation? Some might reckon this as farfetched but the alternative – that our environmental behaviour is learnt from scratch each generation without any innate channelling – seemed even more fanciful to me.

It had taken a week of driving to reach northern Tanzania but the rains had held off and for the most part the roads had been in fair condition. It was good to be back in my old stamping ground. The sun was already low in the sky by the time I turned off the main Seronera road to follow the track leading west to Ndutu Lodge, formerly a hunting camp but now a privately owned safari lodge on the southern edge of the Serengeti Plains. I was looking forward to meeting Jon Cavallo, an archaeologist, friend and one-time Serengeti neighbour who had studied both the fossilised hominids of Olduvai and the living predators along the Seronera River. If anyone could help me decipher the ecological niche of ancestral humans, it was him. Large cumulus clouds had been building over the Ngorongoro highlands all day, but still the rains held off enabling Nomad and I to make good progress along the graded track. Arriving just after sunset, I parked next to the receptionist's hut and walked around the front of the long, palm-thatched building. Jon was sitting on a tall stool in white T-shirt, blue jeans and sandals, chatting animatedly to the barman with a glass of white wine at his elbow. He appeared unchanged by the intervening years: face creased with smiles, eyes still twinkling beneath Romany eyebrows as his mood shifted from laughter to intrigue to concern in a restless, roving capriciousness. As an Italian-American, he had acquired an erudite patois which was just as engaging at the bar in upcountry Serengeti as in downtown Manhattan.

'*Jambo bwana* Jon,' I called,

'*Jambo* Martyn! Hey, it's good to see you.'

'*Habari gani?*' I asked, using the common Swahili greeting for 'how are things?'

'*Safi kabisa!*' he replied. 'My, but you look even younger than last time we met!'

Jon is good with compliments like that, and we were soon catching up on the intervening years. We had one particular thing in common – we were both crazy about our teenage daughters, thinking them to be the most beautiful creatures under the sun. He once gave me his daughter's favourite shoes, which to her chagrin, she had outgrown within six months. They were black leather, Italian and stylish. This was a rare honour and they became Isla's favourites until she in turn reached eight. So we began with daughter talk. After a couple of beers we moved into the dining area, finding a table underneath the sweeping fossilized horns of *Pelorovis*, an extinct ungulate related to the present-day Cape buffalo. The conversation shifted to work.

Jon began his career as a graphic artist in the competitive world of New York advertising and was doing well until smitten with archaeology and the romance of human evolution. He packed in his job, enrolled as a graduate student and came out to the Serengeti. Not an easy thing to do at any age but particularly creditworthy for someone in his mid-50s. Jon's project was to study the fine detail of leopard predation. He was curious to know how they selected and killed their prey, what kind of trees they used for stashing the kill, and the manner in which they dismembered the carcass. The first thing he did on arrival in Serengeti was to go to the Seronera Lodge and get to know the local tour-bus drivers; the bar soon became a vital centre for information and ideas on leopard behaviour. If he wasn't there, Jon could be found somewhere along the river recording the history of leopard kills – noting where each bone fell, how it was marked by tooth and claw, and where it ended up after being scattered about by other animals. Then he took this information over to Olduvai and used it to distinguish between the fossilized remains of kills made by leopards and hominids one or two million years earlier.[3] He was constructing a bridge across the divide that separated the living ecosystem from the ancestral Serengeti adrift somewhere at the boundary of the Pliocene and Pleistocene epochs. It was this connection that I wished to understand.

I took a long draught of chilled Safari lager, eased back in my wicker chair and began the journey back in time. 'So how do you think the hominids fitted into the Pleistocene environment?' I asked.

'There were lots of big mammals in Olduvai at that time. Pretty much the same as today, but with a few extras like that extinct buffalo up there.' Jon nodded at the *Pelorovis* horns. 'All the big carnivores were here too, and a sabre-tooth cat. As for the hominids, my main interest is *Homo habilis*, that's the "Handyman". They showed up around two million years ago. Quite small. Maybe only this high,' Jon raised his hand to chest height, 'but they were fully upright and walked along like us.'

'Do you have any idea what they were doing? I mean what was their niche out there?'

'They were bipeds like us, but they must have spent a lot of time climbing trees. You can tell from their strong arms and curved fingers,' Jon bowed his own fingers in demonstration. 'The anatomy is about halfway between our own and that of a baboon. I think they scavenged meat from leopard kills by climbing trees to steal the stashed carcass.'

'Huh! That sounds pretty dangerous, especially for a small guy.'

'Not if you choose your moment,' Jon pointed out. 'In fact, it's easy to snatch a carcass without the leopard ever knowing who did it.'

'But leopards are not that common,' I insisted. 'Even if the Handymen were expert meat-lifters how could they obtain sufficient food for a family – let alone a whole band of hominids?'

'You have to remember that the riparian woodlands were extremely productive,' said Jon tapping out a Sportsman cigarette from a soft pack. 'There would be lots of prey available for the cats. I've seen a single leopard cache several kills when the game animals are around.'

I was fascinated by the thought of this creature, so different from anything out there today, yet it had carved out a successful niche. That same mode of living might even exist today – an empty niche awaiting some newcomer. 'So you think Handyman survived off leopard kills alone?'

'They had stone tools,' replied Jon, signalling to the barman for another round.

'Not very advanced ones I grant you – mainly river pebbles with sharpened edges – but ideal for cracking open large bones and skulls. With those they could get at the marrow and brains of the big prey animals left by lions. There are plenty of calories in marrow fat.'

This little biped had lived a risky lifestyle alright – pinching leopard food out of trees and lion food from off the ground. 'Wouldn't Handyman have caught something for himself?' I asked. 'Wasn't he a hunter as well as a scavenger?'

Jon paused to make room on the small tabletop as the barman arrived with our drinks followed by a waiter who set down the meal we had ordered with a big smile. There were not many guests about and Jon was evidently a favourite visitor. 'Not in a systematic way as they didn't possess real weapons. They could throw stones and wield sticks, but it would have been pretty feeble. It's the later hominids like *Homo erectus* that could bring down game animals.'

'Well I suppose the Handymen could at least gather roots and fruits?' I asked.

'Oh sure, and they could use their stone tools to crack hard nuts and pound up tubers. I think they would forage in much the same way as a savannah baboon. They'd have a number of sleeping groves on their territory but prefer the big trees down by the river.'

Whilst we were talking, three genet cats crept into the dining room and slunk along the roof beams in their bold spotted coats, each apparently pursued by a long banded tail with a life of its own. The night animals were coming out of hiding; now it was the turn of the day animals to be quiet and vigilant.

'They didn't move out onto the plains, then?'

'They would have stuck close to their sleeping trees for safety. Each morning they would quarter the surrounding area looking for food. If they came across a carcass, they would stash it in one of their own trees to keep it safe from hyaenas and vultures.'

'It sounds like Handyman was a kind of carnivorous baboon?'

'More like an arboreal hyaena!' laughed Jon. 'I'll show you their habitat tomorrow; that will give you a better idea.'

Helping ourselves to coffee from the thermos, we walked outside to enjoy the cool air drifting across from the nearby soda lake. We pulled up chairs around the campfire and leaned back to listen to the sounds of the African night.

My homely little banda at Ndutu reminded me of Sevilla cottage in the Cederberg Mountains which now seemed very far away. There was that same attention to detail and the same thoughtfulness that spoke directly to the guest – the choice of sketch on the wall, the spare torch battery, the bottle of filtered and boiled water by the bed, and the positioning of the generator so that it didn't interrupt the quiet sounds of the bush. After a night of luxury, I was ready to feast on the mammoth breakfast of mango, pineapple, water melon, rhubarb, millet porridge, scrambled egg, chapatis and toast covered in wild honey – all freshly obtained from the home farm in the Ngorongoro highlands. Even the coffee beans were home grown. Jon joined me halfway through and we discussed the likelihood of serious rain. He mentioned that a heavy storm had struck a week ago, rendering some roads impassable. The tracks had dried out again but he guessed that the monsoon rains were not far away. 'That's the last thing I need now,' I muttered. But as we both knew, you have to be ready for anything in the bush. Shrugging off the thought I went out to check Nomad's tyres. The puncture repair was holding up.

We set off a few minutes later with Jon leading the way in his white Land Rover. He headed east along the course of the Olduvai Gorge, passing first through acacia woodland then out across open grassland, until we reached one of the main archaeological sites. From here the view swept over a vast arid plain to a volcano visible on the far horizon, *Ol Donyo Lengai* the 'Mountain of God', a sacred place to the Maasai. It still erupted from time to time covering the plains with fine ash, feeding the grasses with salts and minerals that drew in the great herds of migrating animals. Leaving the vehicles under the meagre shade of an umbrella acacia, we slid down the broken clay slopes passing several geological horizons on the way, until reaching a layer of ash and clay known as Lower Bed II.

'We are now in the Serengeti as it was two million years ago,' announced Jon, looking straight at me to ensure I heard the import of his words. 'See these concretions,' he stooped to pick up a semi-crystalline ball of calcium carbonate. 'They show we are standing on the bed of an old lake, a shallow soda lake that stretched for 20 kilometres west towards Ndutu Lodge. It is fed by freshwater springs that bubble out at the base of the Ngorongoro escarpment, just like the present ones feeding Lake Manyara.'

I imagined blue water all around us studded with pink flamingos; grassy fringes along the edge grazed short each evening by hippo.

'Okay, I'm with you.'

'Now, what do you make of this?' said Jon, passing over a large bone.

'It's heavy, very heavy – it's amazing.' I looked in disbelief at the piece of femur in my hand, about the size of a large steer's.

'That's fossilized bone,' confirmed Jon. 'The light protein matrix has mineralised with silicon and must weigh six times as much as normal bone.'

'Look!' I exclaimed, 'there are more bones here, and more… there must be bones everywhere.'

'This is Olduvai Gorge,' said Jon with a smile.

'Do you suppose there might be hominid remains right here?' I asked, pointing at a nearby bank of clay which had several bones sticking out of it.

'We are not just guessing. We mean business here – that's Upper Bed II.'

'So there might be!' I was awestruck by this grey world full of fossils, having always assumed it took years of monotonous sieving to find a tiny fragment of anything. 'Look! There are more bones up there. Bones and bones and bones.'

'They all belong to one animal,' said Jon in amusement. 'Do you see how it's lying? It could be a giraffe.'

Calming down a bit, I looked at the half dozen fossilized bones sticking out of the clay and traced the pattern of a large animal lying on its side. 'Yep, I see what you mean now.'

'And do you see those pebbles?' said Jon, pointing to a bank of smooth round stones that varied from golf ball to coconut size. 'They've been rolled down a river.'

'So this is an old riverbed!' I exclaimed.

'Without a doubt. Upper Bed II was laid down in a drier period in which the lake disappeared. This giraffe may have walked down to the river for a drink and been killed by a predator. We would need to check the bones for claw marks to make sure.'

'Oh, now I see the fascination of this subject,' I exclaimed.

'Look at this,' said Jon showing me a lump of clay with several channels up to seven millimetres in diameter. 'These are fossilized root casts. They indicate dense vegetation growing along the river.'

I recalled the clear streams tumbling down from the springs above Lake Manyara, feeding the reed beds and groundwater forests with their mysterious yellow-barked fever trees, giant figs and dark mahoganies. Baboons and vervet monkeys loved those trees. Why not Handyman too?

Jon hunted about for fossils, pointing out various finds – the cheek teeth of a grazing ungulate, the incisor of a large cat, a section of horn from a bovid, more root casts, and a large lava stone that might have been used as a weapon. He replaced each find exactly where it came from.

'The magic of Olduvai is that it preserves all the details,' he said, pulling out his crumpled pack of Sportsman cigs and lighting up.

I looked around me with increasing respect for the work of archaeologists, recognising that a site as large as this could hardly be damaged by their painstaking excavations. In this gorge, they had opened a second doorway into the Pleistocene. What they had discovered might only be a shadow of its former self, but it was the shadow of a world at a unique moment in our history. The sediments, stones and fossils of Olduvai offered a glimpse of the early hominids in an environment that was as vibrant and alive for them as that surrounding us. It was as close as we were ever going to get to the daily lives of our distant ancestors. As the realisation sank in, I felt an urgent need to find out how they made that crucial step out of the forests and onto the open plains.

'Jon,' I asked, 'what do you think of the idea that the earliest hominids followed migrating ungulates across the plains to scavenge their carcasses, and that this nomadic lifestyle led to the evolution of bipedalism?'[4]

'Well, the line of hominid footprints that Mary Leakey found at Laetoli are about 3.6 million years old and clearly made by a bipedal hominid like Lucy,[5] so that kind of fits. But you have to remember that those ones, that's *Australopithecus afarensis*, didn't have any stone tools, and that would have limited them.'

'They could be driven off carcasses, you mean? In the way that wild dogs have to surrender their kill to spotted hyaenas,[6] and cheetahs to lions?'

'Lions would drive them off no trouble. They might even have hunted the hominids as prey animals. If you are talking about full emancipation from the trees, you have to wait for *Homo erectus*. Those guys were physically bigger, had larger brains and more advanced tools. They could control the site around animal kills.'

It was already midmorning and Jon had to leave for a meeting in Arusha. We climbed out of the gorge and I saw him on his way, promising to meet up again on my return journey south. Then I started up Nomad and headed cross-country for Naabi Hill which was visible as a small lump on the horizon. It marked the main gateway into the Serengeti National Park. Bumping across the rough turf, I thought about Handyman: bipedal but adept at climbing trees, stealing carcasses by day and taking refuge in the canopy at night, using tools but only primitive ones, playing a dangerous game of cat and mouse with big predators. Handyman was still tied to the trees, but one of his descendants had loosened those bonds and made that fateful transition to life in the open savannah.

Two hours later I turned off the graded road leading to the park headquarters and tourist lodge at Seronera, and joined a small track that provided a back entrance to the Serengeti Research Institute. Once world famous, the institute had been sadly neglected for many years although it still provided a focal point for long-term botanical and zoological research. The track wound along the boundary of the central woodlands and southern plains before entering a cluster of granite kopjes which concealed the station and several researchers' homes. Leaving the track I drove up the rutted airstrip, long abandoned even when I'd first arrived save by one quixotic film-maker, until reaching a gently sloping hillside of short grass that once concealed the dens of several bat-eared fox families. It was also the favoured haunt of a herd of hartebeest which came out at night to lie on the open ground. For an hour or two they chewed the cud and rested whilst keeping an eye open for nocturnal prowlers. Scanning these same slopes now with my binoculars, I wondered if the herd was still about. And then with a humph of satisfaction, I spotted some pale coats in amongst a tall stand of red oat grass.

Hartebeest are haughty antelopes, almost regal under their crown of pedicellate horns. But in their majesty they are not neglectful of vigilance, as I knew from the many hours spent recording their every step, bite and glance. One incident from that time made a lasting impression. I'd been observing a mother and her young calf on a hot afternoon in the late dry season. The mother looked thin, the outline of her ribs and pelvis showed clearly, and I'd wondered how the two of them would cope if the flush of rich grass that comes with the rains were to be delayed much longer. The day wore on and the temperature eased a little. As if from nowhere, I noticed a lioness. She was crouched low, perfectly camouflaged by the dry grass, staring at the two hartebeest. Gliding slowly between the yellowed tussocks, she began to stalk. Catching my breath, I watched her every move, admiring the flow of contoured muscles through my binoculars. Whenever her quarry's head went down, the lioness crept forward. Her focus was absolute. Even so, I knew she would have to be a superlative hunter to bring down this wary and fleet-footed adversary. Panning back to the hartebeest mother, I saw the first signs of nervousness. Every few seconds, she stopped feeding to look around, staring at anything that might be suspicious. Her cupped ears strained for the smallest sound and her flared nostrils tested for the hint of a scent that might spell danger. For a moment, she looked in my direction, both eyes holding mine in their binocular vision, shocking me with the penetration of their gaze. I noticed the quivering leg muscles, raised head and extended ears, but most of all those unwavering tawny eyes. A long pause followed. The air grew heavy, and the hartebeest dipped her head back into the sweetly smelling, red-oat grass.

The café au lait calf was indifferent to the unfolding drama, large ears flopping about as she nibbled lazily at a tiny green shoot some distance from the safety of her mother. The lioness drew nearer, taking advantage of the mottled shadows under an umbrella thorn; with each stealthy step she grew more wary. Her eye settled on the calf. Crouching still and taut, she awaited the precise moment to rise and sprint. A baboon barked and the hartebeest mother looked in the direction of the troop. Without hesitation the lioness rose and accelerated: powerful, low, formidable. Instantly, the mother's snort brought the calf running to her side and they fled together, wheeling, dodging and bounding frantically. I was utterly engrossed, not noticing the coffee cup knocked from the dashboard until later. Making a supreme physical effort, the lioness strove to close the gap, to grab or sideswipe the diminutive calf, but the young hartebeest never faltered, and after a few seconds the two antelope drew clear. The lioness slowed to a canter, then a walk. I relaxed too, and as I did, a mixture of emotions vied for my attention: anticlimax… relief… elation.

That younger self was so immersed in the science of nature that he'd thought only in terms of the animals. He saw the event as a contest between predator and prey, as one more piece to fit into the complex jigsaw of the Serengeti ecosystem. Looking back on the event today, I am more curious about its emotional impact. I'd been transfixed by the hunt, giving my allegiance at one moment to the lioness and at the next to the hartebeest. Was that because I shared with the lioness the capacity to be a predator, but equally with the hartebeest, the potential to be prey? Might the chase have triggered within me an instinctive response that had its origins a million or more years earlier? Perhaps we all possessed a Pleistocene wardrobe of roles that included the predator and the prey, the hunter and the hunted, the protector and the protected. Urgent need rather than casual inclination determined what clothes we wore.

Pulling into the parking lot in front of the abandoned office block, I was greeted by a rush of hyraxes running for cover in amongst the vehicle wrecks and granite boulders of the surrounding kopje. Some things never change. The buildings at the research institute had been just as dilapidated when I first arrived, but I'd found it exhilarating to follow in the footsteps of a previous generation, and to probe the ecological processes that orchestrated the most famous ecosystem on Earth. Walking past the laboratory wing, I took the path that led first to a defunct met station and from there across rough ground to a wooden stable where I used to keep the antelopes. The green canvas screens were gone and much of the wood used for the stalls had been vandalised, but my memories of the animals that lived there were as vivid now, as on the day I'd released them back to the wild. There were two shaggy black wildebeest, three chocolate brown topi, and a tall proud hartebeest called 'King'. One night a leopard tried to force its way through a gap at the base of the wall, spitting and snarling in fury before it was beaten back. On another, after heavy rains, a hoard of siafu ants scaled the sides in deadly cinnamon columns, dropping from the roof onto the panic-stricken animals. Emergency followed emergency until the stable hands and I were exhausted. But each morning we'd taken the animals out to feed on plots of carefully measured pasture, and every evening after leading them back, we'd learnt a little more about their foraging habits.

In previous years, I'd followed free-ranging animals out on the range. I could count the number of bites taken per minute and I could measure how far they walked in a day, but I didn't know the size of their bites or the proportion of young leaves and shoots in their diet. To gather this critical information I weighed the tame animals on a digital scale before letting them out to feed. After they had taken a thousand bites, I weighed them again. The balance was accurate to within 10 grams and the animals stood quietly on the platform whilst we took the readings. You could actually see the weight of an animal going slowly down as it lost moisture from its breath. We tested the animals on different kinds of pasture until I knew exactly how much grass each species was taking and what proportion of stem and leaf they were selecting. Finally I measured their metabolic rate – the amount of energy each animal was burning up whilst at rest – and added this to the amount of energy they used to walk about the home range. This gave us an energy budget for each species.

When the rains came and green grass sprung up in thick luscious swards, the animals had a surfeit of energy and their feeding habits were quite similar. But when the rains failed and the grass shrivelled, and the long drought set in, their survival depended on their feeding strategy – where they fed, how selective they were, and on how well they balanced a sparse food intake against their constant energy outgoings. It turned out that there were two different solutions. And those solutions I reasoned must have arisen in an ancient Pleistocene environment shared with the early hominids.

Arriving early at the park headquarters next morning, I discovered that the chief park warden had been called to Fort Ikoma in the night to deal with an accident, but had left a message to say that Mr Kisamu, the officer in charge of the community programme, would assist me. Mr Kisamu was courtesy itself, arranging tea whilst briefing me on the park's management problems. There were a host of pressing issues: the rapid rise in numbers of farmers and pastoralists on the periphery of the park, the increasing impacts of tourism, the spread of infectious diseases from domestic dogs to wild carnivores, and various illegal activities that included hunting, rustling, smuggling and banditry. Managing a large African park is akin to administering an entire region of a country with the added complexity of multi-cultural misunderstandings over the use of natural resources. Serengeti benefits from its international reputation and is fortunate in having influential friends, nevertheless its future has sometimes balanced on a knife-edge. Commercial pressure to build more tourist lodges inside the park had intensified over the years. There was a new threat to siphon off water from the springs that feed the Mara River to supply hotels being constructed outside the park. Worse still there were repeated calls to drive a trunk road across the centre of the plains to connect the thriving communities of Lake Victoria with the coastal capital, Dar es Salaam. It was a never-ending battle but Kisamu didn't seem dispirited. Perhaps this was because his own unit had worked wonders in winning friends from amongst former enemies in the villages that lay along the western border of the park. As I departed he proffered a hand-written letter that would permit me to travel in a remote region of the park, and wished me a safe journey.

Back at the research institute I called in on the lion house to see if anyone had been to the Milima kopjes recently. One of the biologists sketched a plan of the best route onto my large-scale map, marking four points where the track crossed drainage lines.

'These are the spots where you might get stuck,' he said. 'They're still wet from last week's storm. If you get past them you should be fine, provided the rains hold off.'

The sky looked bright enough to the east where I was heading, but was ominously dark in the southwest; there was a definite feel of rain in the air.

'Any chance you might be going out there in the next couple of days?' I enquired.

The lion biologist shook his head. 'I want to survey the Milima pride but I got stuck trying to get there just two days ago. I'm going to stay with the local pride and wait for the tracks to dry out a bit more.' He glanced at Nomad. 'I'd hold off for a few days, if I were you.'

Although Nomad didn't have the clearance of the lion project's Land Rover, we'd come a long way together and I decided to take the chance. With luck I'd be able to reach the drier region in the east before the big storms arrived. Thanking the biologist for his help, I climbed back into Nomad and set off.

The track to Milima followed a high sandy ridge that provided Nomad with plenty of grip when traversing the large puddles lying in the dips. The hot sun was evaporating the water as I journeyed, which was a comforting thought, and I ignored the dark clouds gathering in the southwest. After about an hour I came to the first of the marked drainage lines. It was a broad basin that had trapped an area of silt and moisture in its centre. There was no obvious way round so I kicked off my shoes, changed into shorts and waded in ahead of Nomad to check for depth and firmness. I could feel with my toes that there was hard sand under the oozing mud. It seemed fine and sure enough Nomad crossed without difficulty. At the next two drainage lines, the crossing was softer but I was able to pace out a firmer route higher up the slope. Progress was slow but uneventful and we finally made it across the fourth drainage line. Relaxing a little, and beginning to think that the track was not that bad after all, maybe even a doddle, I made a mistake. After navigating a deep puddle without difficulty, I swung around a rocky outcrop to find a marshy area before me. The track led down into a patch of tussocky *Pennisetum* grass, disappeared underwater, and reappeared again on the far slope. Still thinking I was past the difficult area, I switched on my camcorder to record the fun and drove recklessly forward without checking the crossing on foot. Halfway across, I realised that the two parallel ruts were deeper than anticipated. Nomad slowed. I threw the camcorder to one side and slipped down a gear. We crept forward reaching the middle of the swamp. By now I was down to first gear and gunning the engine, but despite every effort Nomad came to a complete standstill, leaning over at a forlorn angle. I swore at my stupidity, applied the 'diff lock', and tried to reverse out. I was stuck fast.

Switching off the engine, I climbed down into the muddy water to assess the state of stuckness; the soft mud squelched between my toes and the water came up to my knees. It was equally deep to the front and rear, reaching up to the doorsill on the side at which Nomad was down. I decided that the back axle must be sitting on the hard, grass-covered ridge that stood between the two muddy ruts not quite clear of the surface; that would lift the rear wheels and prevent them from gaining traction. At least I was carrying some basic emergency equipment. I went around to the back and rummaged about for sand ladders. Trying to avoid knocking myself in the shins, I wedged these heavy iron contraptions into the ruts immediately behind the two rear wheels, where hopefully they would deliver sufficient grip for Nomad to claw her way out backwards. Using four-wheel drive and low range, I tried reversing again. Nomad refused to budge. This was a bloody disaster.

It was hard to see what was going on underneath because of the depth of muddy water, so I pulled out a shovel and started to dig a small trench that would drain some of the surplus water into a neighbouring rut where the level was several inches lower. The wiry grass and thick rootstocks made the digging slow work, but at least it felt as if I were doing something useful. After half an hour of heavy labour, I was rewarded by a small flow of water running down the trench; I turned my attention to the hi-lift jack. It was a first-class bit of engineering that enabled the off-road motorist to ratchet up the end of a 4×4 by half a metre or more, lifting it clear of the softest ground. They are quite lethal if used incorrectly as the long heavy handle can fly upwards at a speed sufficient to break a limb. I refreshed my memory of exactly how it worked, then slid it into position and pumped on the handle. The higher I lifted up Nomad, the more the foot of the jack slipped backwards into the mud, and that forced the top of the jack up against the tailgate. The whole contraption was in danger of collapsing. Whilst in Cape Town, I'd meant to obtain a metal plate that could be placed under the jack's foot to increase stability. No use regretting that now. I tried one more time and succeeded in slipping the sand ladders a little further under the rear wheels. Hopping back into the driver's seat, I started the engine and tried reversing again. The wheels spun uselessly. By now, I was covered in mud and becoming a bit desperate. I tried again, this time recklessly driving off the jack. Nomad budged an inch and settled down as before. I switched off the engine to stop myself from digging her in even deeper.

My arms were shaking from the last couple of hours of spadework and jacking, and my eyes smarted from the sweat that was running down my face.

It was time to reassess the situation. I found a towel to wipe away the sweat then sat down in the back of Nomad under the open tailgate, dangling my feet in the water to wash them free of sticky mud. I downed three mugs of orange squash in quick succession, spread a thick layer of peanut butter onto some crackers, and carried my lunch over to a dry tussock.

When the dry season holds sway over the land causing the grasses to dry and shrivel, the hartebeest and other resident antelope continue to feed over the same coarse meadows, nibbling away at the brown leaves and peeling sheaths that cling to the stiff stems. They become experts at finding whatever green morsels remain, and ensure that this meagre fare goes as far as possible by dispensing with unnecessary movement. In severe droughts they even shutdown on reproduction, just like the Bushmen. Although the evidence was circumstantial, I thought they slowed their metabolic rate as well, entering a mini-hibernation. I reasoned that the overall strategy of the residents was to 'minimise energy losses'. That was their way of surviving hard times: it was a matter of tightening belts and holding on until things got better.

One day I witnessed a peculiar event that suggested an additional element in their strategy. I was watching a small group of topi that occupied a neighbouring territory to the hartebeest above the airstrip. The topi's territory boasted a fine standing crop of hay that was just sufficient to last them through the remainder of the dry season. The group was feeding quietly in the centre of their range when a herd of more than 500 wildebeest appeared over a ridge on the far side. This was the last of the migratory herds to pass through the area, the rest having moved on quickly to pastures in the Grumeti River basin, but it soon became clear that this herd was intent on feeding not migrating. They began to graze their way towards the topi. I worked out on the back of an envelope that the wildebeest could consume the topi's entire dry season reserve of grass in just a few hours. The dominant male topi noticed the intruders and stopped his feeding to watch. As the vanguard of wildebeest reached the dry streambed that marked the edge of his territory, he detached himself from the females and walked forward, nodding his head vigorously as a warning. He moved stiffly down the slope towards the invading column, angling his approach to come up from the side and rear, and then broke into a canter. Drawing near he accelerated, galloping fast along the flank of the wildebeest column which was now flooding over onto the topi's side of the stream. Soon he had the wildebeest running too, and just like a cowboy rustler he stampeded the column of shaggy black gnus all the way down his territory for half a mile. He didn't stop until they had run across the boundary at the far end. A few minutes later he reappeared walking steadily back to his females. His action appeared cool and calculated. Certainly the outcome could not be argued with: the topi's precious food reserve was safe. The motto of the resident might be, 'look after what you have today, for you will need it again tomorrow'.

Unlike the residents, wildebeest and other migratory antelopes made no attempt to sit it out on exhausted territories. They watched and sniffed the air for signs of greener pasture elsewhere. A flicker of lightning on the distant horizon of the night sky, or a suspicion of moist earth carried on the morning breeze, was enough to set them off on a journey to seek out the tender grass that sprouts forth in the wake of dry season rain storms. As they travelled the tendons above their hooves acted as springs, reducing the energy needed to maintain a rocking canter. Their muscles too were rich in the kind of cell that supports endurance running. On arrival they cropped the new grass flat, stripping the pasture bare before moving on in a ceaseless nomadic wayfaring. It was a hazardous lifestyle, what with the stumbling passages down ravines of crumbling rock, the risk of a surprise ambush en route, and the added danger of river crossings, but it was also richly rewarding. I supposed that the migrant's strategy was to 'maximise energy gains'. In order to survive, they powered their way through the lean times throwing everything they had into the search for food. Their motto might be, 'take all that you can today, for tomorrow we move on'.

The predators of the Serengeti matched these differences in their prey. The great stalking cats, the leopard and the lion, preferred to hunt in amongst the hillside thickets and riverine woodlands, ambushing unwary residential antelope; whilst the lean, coursing predators, the hyaenas and wild dogs, made free with the migratory herds. They were continually inspecting their prey, seeking out weak members, testing them if necessary with mock attacks. Once they had chosen a quarry, they pursued it across the plains, hoping for a stumble and a quick kill, but ready for the marathon. It was a satisfying insight into the survival games being played out each year on the African savannah. I did not guess then that the same divergent strategies might unlock part of the human story.

Munching slowly on the salty crackers, I wondered what to do next. It was 2 p.m. That still left me with four or five hours of daylight, surely enough time to get myself out of this hellhole. One option would be to jack Nomad up again and place firewood under the wheels. Probably a waste of effort. Another option would be to dig away the central ridge, allowing Nomad to settle back onto her wheels. But the ground was iron hard. Without a pick, it would take a day of bruising effort. Looking about I noticed that the clouds had been thickening, especially in the southwest where a darkening sky foreshadowed heavy rain.

There was no other vehicle in the vicinity. The lion biologists were the only people likely to use this track and they wouldn't venture out for several days, longer if rain came. It was such a vast and empty landscape. All at once, I felt quite lonely and vulnerable.

What the hell was I doing? Way out here… on my own… following in the tracks of that younger self on some stupid personal crusade. It would have been better to have left him to wallow in his own unsolved problems. As if I didn't have enough of my own. Suddenly the whole safari felt reckless. I clenched my fists in exasperation. What did I hope to gain from it all?

It had to be that bloody old-timer – that unyielding adversary, my wretched nemesis. *They will all disappear one day. Every single wild place.* Those words had nagged away at the back of my mind all through my life, appearing at the most unexpected moments. On the occasion of a culminating triumph – a paper accepted for publication, a grant proposal approved, a tough ecological problem solved – there he was winking and laughing at me, causing me to question the very soul of my work. Now look where he had got me. The little mud ditch looked futile, and worse was set to come. The rainstorm in the southwest was approaching rapidly, growing in size all the time. Under its shadow we were entering a twilight world. Thunder rumbled overhead in a continuous drumming roll. The storm leopard was nearing, growling and snarling, eyes flashing, dense rain hairs streaking down its brow in a broad attacking front. Shit! If that thing hit, we were done for. These tracks would turn into rivers rushing down into the marsh from either side. The water level would rise… in moments it would be flooding into Nomad. Time was running out for us again. If only Torran were here to lend a hand and a cheery smile. For the umpteenth time, I told myself to calm down… Face it! There never was any other option. The old-timer had to be taken on.

That younger guy would have loved this predicament, it had just the mix of danger and drama that he revelled in. I could almost hear him now, taking charge with that big goofy grin…

'Remember what Chris and I used to say back in Sengwa? When the going gets tough the tough *keep* going. Come on now, I know you believe that stuff. Look you said it yourself: the problem here is that Nomad's axle is grounded on the ridge. You've tried digging to lower the axle, and you've tried jacking to lift the wheels. Neither worked, so what other options do you have? You don't have to be a genius to work it out, man. Just lighten up. Get all that gear out. Once you take the weight off those springs, the axle will ease up a fraction by itself. And hey! Where did the smile go? Don't tell me this isn't bloody good fun!'

All of a sudden I felt very close to him. Lying down in the water, which had now lowered by two or three inches, I peered under Nomad. This time I could see the exact place where she was stuck, and realised that I would stand a better chance of freeing her off by driving forwards. And he was right; Nomad was carrying half a ton of gear. Hastily I began to pull every conceivable thing out of the back to lighten the load. As I worked, a thunderclap burst overhead like a detonating explosive. I looked up briefly, and then continued to unload furiously. Spare wheels, tools, jerry cans, food and freezer boxes, water containers, gas canisters, backpacks and tents followed rapidly one after another until the little island of higher ground was covered in debris. At last she was empty. I slammed shut the tailgate, cleared away the jack, rammed the sand ladders back under the rear wheels, this time from the front side, and jumped in the cab. The engine fired up. I engaged first and eased out the clutch. Nomad moved a fraction and settled back. I tried again. This time I caught the rock back, and exaggerated it by slipping into reverse, changing quickly to first to catch the forward motion. Flicking the gears rapidly from first to reverse, and back again, I generated a substantial rocking momentum. The rock lengthened becoming six inches, then a foot. Sensing my moment, engine revving madly, all four wheels spinning wildly, I held her in first and gave full throttle. The wheels spun even more furiously, Nomad lurched, scraped forward a foot, paused for an agonizing second, slipped sideways, and then surged forward bouncing along the track, water washing off the sides, bounding up onto the dry road on the far side. My relief was palpable.

Within minutes the heavens had opened and the deluge descended. I stood outside letting it wash the mud from my face, glorying in the flashing eyes and crunching bones of the storm. My luck had changed and with it my mood. Nomad fairly dashed along on the sandy surface, cavorting like a mad springhare whilst making for the lighter patch of sky that marked the position of the Milima kopjes. There was no chance of retreating to Seronera now, but I found the thought oddly liberating. As we headed eastwards, the rain eased, and then stopped. When at last I sighted the Milima kopjes on the near horizon, they appeared as fairy castles set on wooded islands in a sea of rippling grass with the sun glinting off granite parapets. Dotted round about was a great herd of wildebeest, the first to reach the plains this year. As if by magic, I was transported from the grim misery of the fifth drainage line to an outpost of sunshine and beauty. It was a moment of pure enchantment.

Driving across the open plains of Serengeti with the grass rushing towards Nomad and swooping by underneath was madly exhilarating, like sailing under a stiff breeze across the land.[7] I started singing wild songs. The castellated islands slipped by, each with its own profile of trees and boulders and, at the last, I found the ideal camp. On the lea side of a 30-foot-high whaleback were three umbrella thorns and a sycamore-fig covered in ripening fruit; the little copse enclosed a space just large enough for Nomad and my tent. Immediately in front of the trees and facing the wide open spaces, was a natural fireplace shielded from both wind and curious eye by a large stone. A sitting rock was set nearby. Manoeuvring Nomad into position, I pulled out my camping gear and pegged down the big red tent in soft earth. All the while, a herd of wildebeest was walking past, trekking westwards towards the storm clouds. My evening's repast was easily prepared: a tin of pasta, another of mandarins, and a handful of plain biscuits. I left them for later and took a couple of Castle lagers up onto the kopje to watch the sunset.

On top of the whale's granite back, inbetween the spherical boulders and flowering bushes, was a wild rock garden. Its little passages were bordered with aloes and spiky sansevieria and decorated throughout with dwarf grasses and flowering herbs. Nearby were one or two shallow puddles and a deeper rock pool with clusters of spear-shaped leaves that floated in curious geometric designs. The sycamore flowed over from one side, pale winding limbs hugging the grey stone. It was laden with milky green figs that were ripening to dark pink, offering a rare feast for roving doves. Scattered about this little paradise were the gnawed bones of antelope and the faeces of lions and hyaenas. I found a perch at one end and sat to watch the wildebeest trekking slowly past, their endless column fed by new herds filing out of the woodlands in the north. A warm breeze wafted their myriad base bellows and higher-pitched bleats to my roost. From far away a lion grunted rhythmically, adding its counterpoint to the wild concord. Gentle she-rain was falling all over the plains save for here at Milima, where the evening sun was casting a golden light over the primaeval landscape. It was the perfect place to collect my scattered thoughts.

The early hominids at Olduvai weighed little more than a savannah baboon and were adept at tree climbing.[8] With poor night vision and only stones as weapons they must have avoided the plains after dark for fear of encountering large carnivores. The same goes for Handyman, the first member of the genus *Homo*. Just under two million years ago, a more modern-looking hominid began to walk the African plains. As tall as a Maasai, leggy and muscular, *Homo erectus* possessed an arsenal of stone tools, including cleavers, picks and hand axes. In all likelihood, 'Erect Man' also fashioned spears, throwing sticks and other wooden implements that have not been preserved.[9] Some of their fossilized bones were found only 40 kilometres from this spot. I wondered idly if they ever slept here, in amongst these rocks. If so they would have encountered lion prides and hyaena packs. How they must have treasured those weapons with their power to transform a group of nervous scavengers into a band of proud hunters – nothing less than a metamorphosis of prey to predator. Weapons cut the umbilical cord tying hominids to trees and opened up the possibility of a fully nomadic lifestyle.

As hunter and alpha-scavenger, *Homo erectus* could have followed the wildebeest on their annual migrations around the Serengeti and beyond without fear of predators; and just as one wildebeest population can be migratory and another take advantage of year-round conditions to remain residential, so Erect Man may have developed both migratory and residential habits. Bands that specialised as mobile hunters would have developed different skills and survival tactics from those that opted for a settled lifestyle. Twin foraging strategies might have evolved, corresponding to those of the antelopes, with associated adaptations in muscle and mind that could be summoned to support the pioneering or settled lifestyles. Erect Man was the first travelling hominid, the first out of Africa.[10] As pioneers they would have taken risks in seeking out and conquering new resources, exploiting them to the full before moving on, eyes scanning the horizon for the next opportunity. As settlers, they would have harvested local resources with care, used them frugally and defended their feeding territory against intruders. No doubt they would also have selected the most rewarding prey to hunt, in terms of the time and energy expended, just like the G/wi people of the central Kalahari.[11]

When modern humans appeared on the savannahs, about 200,000 years ago, they surely inherited several key attributes from Erect Man: an athletic physique with the power to pursue prey and take on predators; a brain with the ingenuity to make tools, process food and lay an ambush; and perhaps also the inherent biases and preferences in behaviour that would fit them for pioneering and settler lifestyles. Could it be that the same foraging strategies that equipped those modern humans for life in the Pleistocene have emerged as the seeds of our contemporary environmental problems?

In today's world the pioneer's strategy may be revealed in our fascination for grand objectives... our yearning for distant horizons... our willingness to enter into high stakes contests... and in our adventurous and questing spirit. But that same strategy may also manifest itself in our tendency to deplete bountiful resources and pollute our surroundings without regard to the consequences. Commercial fishing and logging concerns exploit stocks to the limit and beyond, only to abandon them once exhausted to embark on the search for more profitable harvests elsewhere.

The settler's strategy may reveal itself in our yearning for security, our desire for exclusive land or resource ownership, and in the care we devote to tending animals and nurturing plants. It may also find expression in the measures we take to control pests. Farmers in Africa have found ways of controlling many kinds of animal that inflict losses on their crops, such as the damage to vegetable greens by antelope, grain by hares and mice, maize by baboons and bushpigs, and root crops by porcupines and molerats. Modern farming techniques take such controls to an even greater extreme, eradicating virtually all life other than the crop plant itself. In the West it seems that biodiversity has become the pest.

Could it be that overfishing, over-harvesting, and intensified agriculture are 21st century nightmares bequeathed to us from the Pleistocene? That the reason why Western society values economic growth above all else, even if it destroys life and depletes biological resources, is because an ancient voice from within urge us to guard our immediate survival? It is the snarl of the Western storm leopard holding us in a Pleistocene trap that has retained our million-year-old reactions to an ancient world with bountiful resources and infinite horizons, and released them into a modern overcrowded world of finite resources. Is that why we struggle so hard to look after the remaining wild places in Africa? Perhaps the old-timer grasped all this and reckoned we could never escape.

I lingered on the kopje until dark then climbed down to my camp. Someone, probably one of the lion biologists, had left two acacia logs as communal firewood, to which I now added my remaining pieces of mopane from the Zambezi Valley. It took my last firelighter and much blowing to kindle a blaze. I heated up the pasta and some coffee and sat on the sitting rock staring into the flames, aware of the beauty and terror in the encircling plains. During their self-imposed exile in the Namib Desert, Henno Martin and Hermann Korn concluded that our imagination can be placed at the centre of the human evolutionary process. If they were right, then has it not at least equal potential in determining the course of human culture? When picking up the gauntlet thrown at his feet by the old-timer, that younger self knew instinctively that imagination guided by science held the answer. By discovering more and more about wild animals, he felt sure we would learn to protect them. It wasn't enough. The Western imagination might have loosened up in the '60s but it was far from roaming free. Increasingly we have used our skills to devise more efficient ways to exploit nature for our own benefit, paying little attention to the damage inflicted. We take over habitats and we dominate wild animals. We ignore the cry of pain. We have broken our spiritual links with the wild. Stuck within that broken place, unable to reconcile economic and spiritual values, we have found there is no way out.

In seeking safety and protection 'modern man' has constructed a cocoon in which to fall asleep. We now increasingly live in the past and future where there is no sacredness. But natural man, whether Bushman or Handyman, must live in the present moment as alert and conscious as the animals themselves. And it is here, in that moment of heightened awareness, that the outer world may reach within to touch our inner world – the dream world, the realm of intuition, and for the Bushmen the spirit world of their ancestors. As our soul encounters nature, our relationship with the environment quickens. Dreams awaken. Imagination takes wing. Spiritual creativity is released and with it humankind's best hope for protecting both inner and outer worlds. It is in the creative alliance of spirit and nature that we may seek a way to both profit from and revere the wild. If we use our imaginations in this manner, if we are prepared to try hard enough, to be bold enough and open enough, we can start the healing process.

In applying our minds to solve the human environmental dilemma, we could start by moving beyond the protection of nature to the cultivation of our relationship with nature. If we base that relationship on one kind of value only, be it economic or ethical, we end up with suffering: on the one hand through overexploitation of nature and on the other through a vein sentimentalism that leads to human affliction elsewhere. If both values are accepted as valid then, with ingenuity and effort, bridges between the two might be built. And who could be better at designing those bridges than the pioneers? We need them to forge an ethical science of environmental management that delivers the understanding and methodology needed to manage resources without harming nature. They could seek ways to replace heavy-hitting control measures with targeted low-impact alternatives. Settlers might then substitute hot dung for rifles, Anatolian guard dogs for poisoned bait[12] and vaccination of domestic species for the culling of wild ones.

Back home in Britain, livestock farmers put up with the intensified rearing systems and mass culls that have been brought upon them by global markets and intense economic competition that are beyond their control. Yet for the most part they still love their animals, checking each one carefully every evening. Caring about animals is part of our humanity. Would we not all welcome a pattern of resource ownership that brought back a sense of friendship in our dealings with wild and domestic plants and animals? It would mean putting our relationship with nature at the heart of environmental decision-making. Rather than just weighing the environmental benefits and costs of proposed developments as we do today, it would mean pioneering an active process of seeking and perfecting more ethical ways of meeting our material needs. By such means we might take on the old-timer that lurks within us all and begin to nurture an ecological conscience in society just as we now foster a social conscience.

Full of these thoughts, I pulled a large log off the fire to conserve firewood and climbed up onto the kopje for a last look at the night sky. Jupiter was shining brightly in the heavens and I could make out some of its tiny moons through my binoculars. For the southern Bushmen it is the 'Dawn's Heart Star', the main character of a mysterious and revelatory saga in which people mingled their identities with wild animals[13]. A silvery light from the newly risen half moon spread across the plains. All was quiet save for the occasional soft grunting of wildebeest now bunched up for safety. Nearer at hand something breathy and fluting was flitting about above the fig; perhaps a nightjar. A tarantula wasp droned past with a deep rasping buzz. Silence descended again. A light breeze stirred the aloes in my wild garden, and beyond, out on the far horizon, lightning flickered where the storm leopard was hunting her prey.

Endnotes

Chapter 2

[1] J. Diamond. 2005. *Collapse: How Societies Choose to Fail or Survive*. Viking Books.

[2] George B. Silberbauer. 1981. *Hunter and Habitat in the Central Kalahari Desert*, p.271. Cambridge University Press, Cambridge.

[3] A.R. Willcox. 1956. *Rock Paintings of the Drakensberg*, p.46. Max Parrish, London.

[4] George W. Stow. 1905. *The Native Races of South Africa*, p.84. MacMillan Co., London. However Stow's interpretation has been challenged by P. Tobias, T. Dowson and J. Lewis-Williams. 1992. 'Blue ostriches captured' in *Nature*, 358:185.

[5] J.D. Lewis-Williams (ed.). 2000. *Stories that Float from Afar*. David Philip, Cape Town.

[6] David Lewis-Williams and Geoffrey Blundell. 1998. *Fragile Heritage – A Rock Art Fieldguide*. Witwatersrand University Press, Johannesburg.

[7] Recounted by George W. Stow. 1905. *The Native Races of South Africa*, p.230. MacMillan Co., London.

[8] To the delight of many, the anthropologist, Frans Prins, has recently been able to track down some descendents of Bushmen who once lived in the Maloti-Drakensberg Mountains, including one who was able to shed light on the meaning of paintings made by his father and grandfather (Frans Prins, personal communication; see article by Sue Derwent in *Africa Geographic*, February 2005).

[9] Formerly known as Hottentots, the cattle-herding Nama and Korana refer to themselves as Khoekhoen, 'People of People'. Alan Barnard provides an introduction to the Khoisan peoples of southern Africa including both the Khoekhoe or Hottentots and the San or Bushmen in his book, *Hunters and Herders of Southern Africa*. 1992. Cambridge University Press, Cambridge.

[10] The rhebok (*Palea capreolus*) is a long-necked mountain antelope, about the size of a small reedbuck or roe deer, with upstanding ears, spiked horns and short rabbit-like fur. It is only found in South Africa.

[11] Elizabeth Marshall Thomas. 1959. *The Harmless People*. Alfred A. Knopf, New York.

[12] Lorna Marshall. 1976. *The !Kung of Nyae Nyae*. Harvard University Press, Cambridge, Massachusetts.

[13] W.H.I. Bleek and L.C. Lloyd. 1911. *Specimens of Bushman Folklore*. George Allen & Co., London.

[14] Elizabeth Marshall Thomas, *ibid*.

Chapter 3

[1] George W. Stow. 1905. *The Native Races of South Africa*, p.35. MacMillan Co., London.
[2] The only exceptions are a small parcel of land in South Africa and another in northern Botswana, where Bushmen have limited hunting rights. Rupert Isaacson. 2001. *The Healing Land – A Kalahari Journey*. Fourth Estate, London.
[3] Sandy Gall. 2001. *The Bushmen of Southern Africa – Slaughter of the Innocent*. Chatto & Windus, London.

Chapter 4

[1] Henno Martin. 1957. *The Sheltering Desert*. William Kimber, London.
[2] George B. Silberbauer. 1981. *Hunter and Habitat in the Central Kalahari Desert*. Cambridge University Press, Cambridge.
[3] Assessments of personality in domestic animals have revealed consistent differences in temperament (F. Wemelsfelder. 2001. 'Assessing the "whole animal": a free choice profiling approach' in *Animal Behaviour*, 62: 209–220).
[4] Jonathan Kingdon. 1993. *Self-Made Man and his Undoing*. Simon and Schuster, London.
[5] J.R.R. Tolkien was born in Bloemfontein, just a few hundred kilometres away, but only lived in South Africa until the age of four. Perhaps he heard stories of Spitzkoppe and used them in later life as inspiration for the Lonely Mountain where Smaug, the dragon, guarded a hoard of gems and golden treasure. J.R.R. Tolkien. 1937. *The Hobbit: or There and Back Again*. George Allen and Unwin, London.
[6] A bakkie is the local name for a pickup truck.

Chapter 5

[1] Personal communication of Megan Biesele quoted by J.D. Lewis-Williams. 1996. 'A Visit to the Lion's House' in *Voices from the Past* (edited by Jeanette Deacon and Thomas A. Dowson), p.132. Witwatersrand University Press, Johannesburg.
[2] Mantis is another name for the trickster god, /Kaggen, who may often appear in the guise of a praying mantis.
[3] Pippa Skotnes. 1999. *Heaven's Things – A Story of the /Xam*. University of Cape Town Press, Cape Town.
[4] Wilhelm Bleek and Lucy Lloyd. 1911. *Specimens of Bushman Folklore*, p.431. George Allen & Company, London.
[5] J. David Lewis-Williams. 1981. *Believing and Seeing*. Academic Press, London.

Chapter 6

[1] Wilhelm Bleek and Lucy Lloyd, *ibid*, pp.251–253.
[2] Richard Katz. 1982. *Boiling Energy – Community Healing Among the Kalahari Kung*, pp.115, 227. Harvard University Press, Cambridge, Massachusetts.
[3] J. D. Lewis-Williams. 1996. A Visit to the Lion's House in *Voices from the Past*, (edited by Jeanette Deacon and Thomas A. Dowson), p.132. Witwatersrand University Press, Johannesburg.
[4] Wilhelm Bleek and Lucy Lloyd, *ibid*, p.187.

Chapter 7

[1] Laurens van der Post. 1958. *The Lost World of the Kalahari*. Hogarth Press.

Chapter 8

[1] Descriptions of the paintings on 'Male' and 'Female' Hills are provided in Ione Rudner. 1965. Archaeological report on the Tsodilo Hills, Bechuanaland. *South African Archaeological Bulletin*, 20, (78), pp.51–70. A more general account of the paintings on all the hills is provided in Alec Campbell, Robert Hitchcock and Michael Bryan. 1980. 'Rock art at Tsodilo, Botswana' in *South African Journal of Science*, 76, pp.466–478.

[2] L.H. Robbins *et al.* 2000. 'Archaeology, palaeoenvironment, and chronology of the Tsodilo Hills white paintings rock shelter, Northwest Kalahari Desert, Botswana' in *Journal of Archaeological Science*, 27, pp.1085–1113.

[3] Tsodilo was inscribed on the World Heritage List in December 2001. The nomination file contains a comprehensive introduction to the area and its conservation.

[4] Summarised by James Denbow in Jacqueline S. Solway and Richard B. Lee. 1992. 'Foragers, genuine or spurious' in *Current Anthropology* 33 Supplement, pp.187–224. See also J. R. Denbow. 1980. 'Early iron age remains from the Tsodilo Hills, northwestern Botswana' in *South African Journal of Science*, 76, pp.474–475.

[5] Alec Campbell, James Denbow and Edwin Wilmsen. 1994. 'Paintings like engravings: rock art at Tsodilo' in *Contested Images: Diversity in Southern African Rock Art Research*, edited by Thomas A. Dowson and David Lewis-Williams. Witwatersrand University Press, Johnnesburg.

[6] J. David Lewis-Williams. 1981. *Believing and Seeing*, p.65. Academic Press, London.

[7] J.F. Thackeray and J-L Le Quellec. 2007. 'A symbolically wounded therianthrope at Melikane Rock Shelter, Lesotho' in *Antiquity 81*.

[8] In the folklore of the southern Bushman, the dassie was the wife of the trickster deity /Kaggen. She was known as /huntu!katt!katten.

Chapter 10

[1] The G//ana and G/wi are both of the central language family of Bushmen and are closely related. !Kung speakers constitute the northern language family and !Xo speakers make up the southern language family, which includes the /Xam Bushmen who collaborated with Wilhelm Bleek and Lucy Lloyd. See Richard B. Lee and Irven Devore (eds.). 1976. *Kalahari Hunter-Gatherers*. Harvard University Press, Cambridge, Massachusetts.

[2] Introduction to J. David Lewis-Williams 1981. *Believing and Seeing*. Academic Press, London.

[3] The Central Kalahari Game Reserve was established in 1961 on the recommendation of the district commissioner and anthropologist George Silberbauer with the aim of protecting both the wildlife and the Bushmen of the Kalahari. It extends over some 52,600 square kilometres, an area somewhat larger than Switzerland or the state of Massachusetts.

[4] George B. Silberbauer. 1981. *Hunter and Habitat in the Central Kalahari Desert*, p.271. Cambridge University Press, Cambridge. Although the numbers of eland and other species have declined in the Kalahari Desert in the past century, Silberbauer estimated that the total kill by Bushmen in the 1960s was a fraction of that arising from outside poachers and game control fences.

[5] On the evidence of language, Bushmen only entered the Kalahari in significant numbers some 2,000 years ago (Alan Barnard, personal communication). See also A. Barnard. 1992. *Hunters and Herders of Southern Africa*. Cambridge University Press, Cambridge.

[6] Megan Biesele. 1993. *Women Like Meat – The Folklore and Ideology of the Kalahari Ju/'hoan*, p.45. Witwatersrand University Press, Johannesburg. Also see Lorna Marshall. 1976. *The !Kung of Nyae Nyae*, p.309. Harvard University Press, Cambridge, Massachusetts.

[7] Lorna Marshall. 1976. *The !Kung of Nyae Nyae*, p.295. Harvard University Press, Cambridge, Massachusetts.

[8] George B. Silberbauer, *ibid*, p.241.

[9]   Rogan P. Taylor. 1985. *The Death and Resurrection Show – From Shaman to Superstar*. Anthony Blond, UK.

[10] Subsequently I was informed that the Wildlife Department had reported the arrest of 14 Bushmen at Molapo for poaching eight giraffe, 14 eland and 26 gemsbok. Giraffe and eland are rare in the Central Kalahari Game Reserve and gemsbok can only be shot with a licence. Furthermore the animals were all shot with guns, not arrows, contrary to reserve regulations. The Bushmen claim that figures from the Wildlife Department are grossly inflated, that they had valid licences for the animals killed, and that 13 men were taken away from their village and systematically tortured by police and wildlife officials. The incident is reported by Sandy Gall (2001) in his book, *The Bushmen of Southern Africa – Slaughter of the Innocent*. Chatto & Windus, London. It was also investigated by Survival International.

[11] George B. Silberbauer, *ibid*, p.xiv.

[12] Jiro Tanaka and Kazuyoshi Sugawara, 'The G/ui and G//ana of Botswana' in *The Cambridge Encyclopaedia of Hunters and Gatherers*, edited by Richard B. Lee and Richard Daly. Cambridge University Press, Cambridge.

[13] Lorna Marshall, *ibid*, p.289.

[14] Bags or trousers made of gemsbok or springbok skin are thought to possess supernatural potency, as discussed by D. Lewis-Williams. 2003. *Images of Mystery: Rock Art of the Drakensberg*. Double Storey Books, Cape Town.

[15] L. van der Post and J. Taylor. 1984. *Testament to the Bushmen*. Viking.

Chapter 11

[1]   George B. Silberbauer. 1981. *Hunter and Habitat in the Central Kalahari Desert*, p.78. Cambridge University Press, Cambridge.

[2]   Wilhelm Bleek and Lucy Lloyd, *ibid*, p.395.

[3]   George B. Silberbauer, *ibid*, p.216.

[4]   George B. Silberbauer, *ibid*, p.269.

[5]   George B. Silberbauer, *ibid*, p.160.

[6]   Elizabeth Marshall Thomas. 1989. *The Harmless People* (Second Vintage Books Edition), Vintage Books.

[7]   George B. Silberbauer, *ibid*, p.156.

[8]   John Paul Myborgh. *People of the Great Sand Face*. Anglia Films.

[9]   /Kaggen is translated as 'the Mantis' by Wilhelm Bleek and Lucy Lloyd in *Specimens of Bushman Folklore* and by Dorothea Bleek in *The Mantis and his Friends*. Whilst he has supernatural powers and can appear as a praying mantis, /Kaggen is most commonly in the form of a man. His wife is the Dassie (rock hyrax) who is Mother of the Bees.

[10] Recounted by /Han≠kass'o in D. F. Bleek. 1924. *The Mantis and his Friends*. Maskew Miller, Cape Town.

[11] J. David Lewis-Williams. 1981. *Believing and Seeing*, p.124. Academic Press, London.

[12] The Central (e.g. G/wi) and Northern (e.g. !Kung) Bushman languages are as different from each other as, say, English is to Hindi. Nevertheless all Bushmen are generally said to share the same religion. Another name for the G/wi creator god is 'Pishiboro'. His trickster exploits are similar to those of Kaoxa, the trickster god of the !Kung, and /Kaggen, the trickster god of the /Xam (Alan Barnard, personal communication).

[13] George B. Silberbauer, *ibid*, p.233.

[14] E. Pennisi. 2004. 'The first language?' in *Science*, 303, 1319–1320. For another interpretation of the origin of language, see R. Dunbar. 2004. *The Human Story*. Faber & Faber, London.

[15] L. van der Post and J. Taylor. 1984. *Testament to the Bushmen*. Viking.

[16] P. J. Schoeman. 1961. *Hunters of the Desert Land*, p.118. Howard Timmins, Cape Town.

[17] Jonathan Kingdon. 1982 *East African Mammals Volume IIID*. University of Chicago Press.

[18] J. David Lewis-Williams, *ibid*, p.131.

[19] One rock painting in South Africa apparently shows a shaman in the form of a lion helping

Bushmen to attack a powerful enemy with many shields. G.W. Stow. 1930. *Rock-Paintings in South Africa*, Plate 12. Methuen, London.

[20] Richard Katz. 1982. *Boiling Energy – Community Healing Among the Kalahari Kung*. Harvard University Press, Cambridge, Massachusetts. The original source is Megan Biesele. 1975. *Folklore and Ritual of !Kung Hunter-Gatherers*. 2 vols. PhD dissertation. Harvard University, Cambridge, Massachusetts.

[21] Lorna Marshall. 1969. 'The medicine dance of the !Kung Bushmen' in *Africa* 39, 347–381.

Chapter 12

[1] Sandy Gall, *ibid*, provides a dispassionate account of the treatment meted out to Bushmen living in the Central Kalahari Game Reserve.

[2] George B. Silberbauer. 1981. *Hunter and Habitat in the Central Kalahari Desert*, pp.218–219. Cambridge University Press, Cambridge.

[3] Edwin N. Wilmsen. 1989. *Land Filled with Flies – A Political Economy of the Kalahari*, p.121. University of Chicago Press, Chicago.

[4] Essay and commentary in Jacqueline S. Solway and Richard B. Lee, Foragers, genuine or spurious? 1992. *Current Anthropology* 33, Supplement, 187–224.

[5] K. Abernethy, personal communication.

[6] J.M. Orpen. 1874. 'A glimpse into the mythology of the Maluti Bushmen' in *The Cape Monthly Magazine*, 9, 139–156.

[7] Dates calculated from analysis of human mitochondrial DNA indicate several parallel colonisations of the Americas from out of Beringia, a continental refuge created by low sea-levels some 22,000 to 30,000 years ago. This was shortly before the Last Glacial Maximum blocked access. A synthesis of current genetic information is provided by Stephen Oppenheimer. 2003. *Out of Eden – The Peopling of the World*, Constable and Robinson, London.

[8] Archaeologists have found evidence that humans killed mammoths and mastodons but little evidence for hunting of the other Pleistocene mammals. It is likely that mammoths and mastodons would have dominated the vegetation, creating openings for many other herbivores. Extinction of the giants might have created a knock-on effect, ending in the extinction of other species. Until we have more evidence, the North American overkill will remain enigmatic. The influence of big herbivores on vegetation is described in Norman Owen-Smith. 1988. *Megaherbivores: The Influence of Very Large Body Size on Ecology*. Cambridge University Press, Cambridge.

[9] Evidence for the depression of favoured prey species by Native Americans is provided in C.E. Kay, R.T. Simmons (eds.). 2002. *Wilderness and Political Ecology: Aboriginal Influences and the Original State of Nature*. The University of Utah Press, Salt Lake City.

[10] A brief account of the sustainability of hunting in human history is provided in: M.G. Murray. 2003. 'Overkill and sustainable use' in *Science*, 299, pp.1851–1853. See also related correspondence in *Science* 301, p.309. The problem of why some *agricultural* societies have persisted, but not others, is superbly analysed by Jared Diamond (2005). Collapse: How Societies Choose to Fail or Survive. Penguin, London.

[11] Calvin Martin. 1978. *Keepers of the Game – Indian-Animal Relationships and the Fur Trade*, Berkeley, University of California Press. For an alternative explanation, see S. Krech III, ed. 1981. *Indians, Animals and the Fur Trade: A Critique of Keepers of the Game*. The University of Georgia Press, Athens.

[12] Richard B. Lee and Richard Daly. 1999. *The Cambridge Encyclopedia of Hunters and Gatherers*, p.388. Cambridge University Press, Cambridge.

[13] Masakazu Osaki. 1984. 'The social influence of change in hunting technique among the Central Kalahari San' in *African Study Monographs* 5, 49–62.

[14] John Marshall. 1974. *Bushmen of the Kalahari*, National Geographic television film.

[15] Richard Katz. 1982. *Boiling Energy – Community Healing Among the Kalahari Kung.*

Harvard University Press, Cambridge, Massachusetts. Other insightful references into contemporary Bushman society are Sandy Gall. 2001. *The Bushmen of Southern Africa – Slaughter of the Innocent*. Chatto & Windus, London; Elizabeth Marshall Thomas. 1989. *The Harmless People* (Revised Edition). Vintage books, New York; and Edwin N. Wilmsen. 1989. *Land Filled with Flies – A Political Economy of the Kalahari*. University of Chicago Press, Chicago. A short overview of the contemporary condition set in the context of other indigenous foragers is provided in Robert K. Hitchcock. 1999. 'Indigenous peoples' organizations and advocacy groups', and in Richard B. Lee and Richard Daly (eds.). 1999. *The Cambridge Encyclopedia of Hunters and Gatherers*, pp. 480–486. Cambridge University Press, Cambridge.

[16] Pippa Skotnes. 1999. *Heaven's Things – A Story of the /Xam*, p.19. University of Cape Town Press, Cape Town.

Chapter 13

[1] Subsequently the enlightened management plan was abandoned and replaced by another hastily put together to support the government's attempts to relocate the Bushmen from the Central Kalahari Game Reserve. This ultimately succeeded in 2002 when Molathwe and all the others in Molapo and other Bushman settlements were forced to leave. Fortunately there was the option of legal redress. In December 2006 after a protracted hearing, the High Court of Botswana held that the Bushmen had a legal right to live on their land, and that their eviction by the government was 'unlawful and unconstitutional'. It also ruled that the government had acted illegally in depriving the Bushmen of their licences to hunt in the Central Kalahari. However, as Justice Phumaphi observed: 'this judgment does not finally resolve the dispute between the parties but merely refers them back to the negotiating table'. Government has subsequently taken the view that the judgement only applies to the small number of original applicants named on court papers. Harassment continues.

In May 2007, Roy Sesana handed a letter to the British Prime Minister at 10 Downing Street in which he pleaded for help and justice. It finished as follows: 'We hope that you will talk strongly to the Botswana government so that they know they will not have your support in the future for human rights abuses that they are still carrying out on the Bushmen. We also need your strong support in order to stop the government harassing us (which they are still doing), to help us to go home (as our government will not help us) and to let us hunt our lands (as our government will still not let us do this, despite the court judgment). Without our land and without our hunting we will not survive.'

[2] Doug Williamson and his wife Jane lived for three years in the camp at Deception Pan shortly after it was vacated by Mark and Delia Owens. Some of their adventures and observations can be found in: Mort Rosenblum and Doug Williamson. 1987. *Squandering Eden: Africa at the Edge*. The Bodley Head, London.

[3] They also prayed to certain stars, particularly to the morning star and the Southern Cross which they called the 'fire shoe'. Dorothea F. Bleek. 1928. *The Naron: A Bushman Tribe of the Central Kalahari*, pp.26,27. Cambridge University Press, Cambridge.

Chapter 14

[1] Ian Parker is an African wildlife manager and author of *Oh Quagga!*, a highly amusing and perceptive book about people and animals in which he discusses the intelligent use of space as a way to manage intractable differences in approaches to wildlife management.

Chapter 15

[1] Mort Rosenblum and Doug Williamson, *ibid*.
[2] A summary of the wildebeest migrations and conservation problems is given in: D.

Williamson. 1999. 'The future of antelope migrations in a changing physical and socio-economic environment' in UNEP/CMS. ed. 'Proceedings of the Symposium on Animal Migration (Gland, Switzerland, 13 April 1997)' in *CMS Technical Series Publication No. 2*, Bonn/The Hague. There is a fuller account of the die-off in D. Williamson and B. Mbano. 1988. 'Wildebeest mortality during 1983 at Lake Xau, Botswana' in *African Journal of Ecology*, 26, 341–344.

[3]   Bonifica 1992. *Initial Measures for the Conservation of the Kalahari Ecosystem.* Final Report to the Botswana Government and Commission of the EC.

[4]   Ronald Barry and Peter Mundy. 1998. 'Population dynamics of two species of hyraxes in Matobo National Park' in *African Journal of Ecology*, 36, 221–233.

[5]   The painting is reproduced in C.K. Cooke. 1974. *A Guide to the Rock Art of Rhodesia.* Longman Rhodesia (Pvt) Ltd., Salisbury.

Chapter 17

[1]   Salisbury was renamed Harare shortly after independence in 1980.

[2]   The lifetime of the homemade collars turned out to be over three years, much longer than those in the catalogues at that time.

Chapter 18

[1]   In the Ndebele language, *Ntaba Yamanqe* translates as the mountain of vultures. A mountain or hill is called *intaba*. Every noun starts with i (or u in the case of people) but the i can be omitted. A vulture is called *ilinqe*. The *ya* means 'of' and the *ma* makes it plural, giving either *Intaba Yamanqe* or *Ntaba Yamanqe*. On maps the hill has sometimes been given the anglicised spelling, Thaba Mangwe or Ntabamangwe.

Chapter 19

[1]   P.R. Guy. 1976. 'The feeding behaviour of elephant (*Loxodonta Africana*) in the Sengwa area, Rhodesia' in *South African Journal of Wildlife Research* 6, 55–63.

[2]   Some ecologists have even suggested that elephants deliberately push over trees in order to create rich coppiced feeding. See H. Jachmann and R.H.V. Bell. 1985. 'Utilization by elephants of the Brachystegia woodlands of the Kasungu National Park, Malawi' in *African Journal of Ecology* 23, 245–258.

[3]   G.D. Anderson and B.H. Walker. 1974. 'Vegetation composition and elephant damage in the Sengwa Wildife Research Area, Rhodesia' in *Journal of Southern African Wildlife Management Association* 41:1–14.

[4]   Jeremy Gavron. 1993. *The Last Elephant: An African Quest.* Harper Collins.

[5]   P. Glover. 1963. 'The elephant problem at Tsavo' in *East African Wildlife Journal* 1, 30–38.

[6]   R.M. Laws. 1969. 'The Tsavo research project' in *Journal of Reproductive Fertility.* suppl. 6, 495–531.

[7]   R.M. Laws. 1970. 'Biology of African elephants' in *Sci. Prog., Oxf.* 58, 251–262.

[8]   D. Sheldrick, 1973. *The Tsavo Story.* Collins, London.

[9]   T. F. Corfield. 1973. 'Elephant mortality in Tsavo National Park' in *East African Wildlife Journal* 11, 339–368.

[10] C.A. Spinage. 1994. *Elephants.* T & A.D. Poyser, London; Amanda Barrett. 2001. 'The generation gap' on *BBC Wildlife*, November 2001.

[11] Helmut Buechner, personal communication. W. Leuthold. 1996. 'Recovery of woody vegetation in Tsavo National Park, Kenya (1970–1994)' in *African Journal of Ecology* 34, 101–112.

[12] Barbara McKnight. 2000. 'Changes in elephant demography, reproduction and group structure in Tsavo East National Park (1966–1994)' in *Pachyderm* 29, 15–24.

[13] Recovery of vegetation at Tsavo is documented in Amar Inamdar. 1996. 'The ecological consequences of elephant depletion' in *D.Phil thesis*, University of Cambridge.

[14] G. Caughley. 1976. 'The elephant problem – an alternative hypothesis' in *East African Wildlife Journal* 14, 265–283.

[15] In fact the causation is probably the other way round: prairie dogs and Brandt's vole prosper chiefly on range that has already been overgrazed by livestock.

[16] Taken from a lecture given in April 1963, now published in R.P. Feynman. 1998. *The Meaning of It All.* Allen Lane, The Penguin Press.

[17] D.H.M. Cumming. 1981. 'The management of elephants and other large mammals in Zimbabwe' in *Problems in Management of Locally Abundant Wild Mammals*, pp.91–118. Edited by P.A. Jewell and S. Holt. Academic Press, London. See also: R.H.V. Bell. 1981. 'An outline of a management plan for Kasungu National Park, Malawi' in *Problems in Management of Locally Abundant Wild Mammals*, pp.69–89. Edited by P.A. Jewell and S. Holt. Academic Press, London.

[18] At the time, 80 Zimbabwean dollars was worth about £1 UK or 1.5– 2 US dollars, a significant sum in rural areas.

Chapter 20

[1] Communal Area Management Programme for Indigenous Resources (CAMPFIRE) offers a framework by which rural communities can take control of their own wildlife resources, turn a profit and secure some meat.

[2] G. Copway. 1850. *The Traditional History and Characteristic Sketches of the Ojibway Nation.* Charles Gilpin, London.

[3] C. Martin. 1991. *The Rainforest of West Africa: Ecology-Threat-Conservation.* Birkhäuser, Basel.

[4] C. Spinage. 1994. *Elephants.* T. & A.D. Poyser, London.

[5] Julian Derry, personal communication.

[6] Jane Dyson, personal communication. A fair appraisal of CAMPFIRE is provided in Russell Taylor (2009). Community based natural resource management in Zimbabwe: the experience of CAMPFIRE. *Biodiversity and Conservation* 18: 2563–2583.

[7] Adam Smith (in *The Wealth of Nations*) held to the idea, with some misgiving, that 'an invisible hand' would convert the pursuit of self-interest, so apparent in the throughput economy of the west, into a publicly beneficial practice. After a two-year struggle to find some other conclusion, he wrote that if each individual pursues his own advantage (in the marketplace) he is *'led by an invisible hand to promote an end which was no part of his intention'* and as a result of such guidance, society ends up with social consequences that are beneficial.

[8] Jared Diamond. 2007. 'Easter Island Revisited' in *Science* 317: 1693–1693.

Chapter 21

[1] K. McComb, C. Moss, S.M. Durant, L. Baker and S. Sayialel. 2001. 'Matriarchs as repositories of social knowledge in African elephants' in *Science* 292, 491–494.

[2] C. Moss. 1988. *Elephant Memories: Thirteen Years in the Life of an Elephant Family.* Elm Tree Books, London.

[3] D. Sheldrick. 1973. *The Tsavo Story.* Collins and Harvill Press. See also: Jeremy Gavron. 1993. *The Last Elephant: An African Quest.* Harper Collins.

[4] D.H.M. Cumming, *et al.* 1997. 'Elephants, woodlands and biodiversity in southern Africa' in *South African Journal of Science* 93: 231–236.

[5] R.P. Feynman. 1998. *The Meaning of it All.* Allen Lane, The Penguin Press.

[6] The exclosure is described in K.M. Dunham. 1994. 'The effect of drought on the large mammal populations of Zambezi riverine woodlands' in *Journal of Zoology, London* 234, 489–526.

[7] The Addo Elephant National Park was proclaimed in 1931 to protect a local elephant population. At this time several small 'botanical reserves' were fenced off with the aim of excluding elephants in order to preserve a segment of the succulent Kaffrarian thicket in an unaltered state. Further information can be found in the following references: B.L. Penzhorn, P.J. Robbertse and M.C. Olivier. 1974. 'The influence of the African elephant on the vegetation of the Addo Elephant National Park' in *Koedoe* 17, 137–158; D.G. Barratt and A. Hall-Martin. 1991. 'The effect of indigenous browsers on valley bushveld in the Addo Elephant National Park' in *Proc. 1ˢᵗ Valley Bushveld/Subtropical Thicket Symp.* Edited by P.J.K. Zacharias, G.C. Stuart-Hill and J. Midgley. Grassland Society of Southern Africa, Howick.

Chapter 22

[1] R. Hoare. 2000. 'Humans and elephants in conflict: the outlook for coexistence' in *Oryx* 34, 34–38.

[2] Bushman territories averaged 780 km² in the central Kalahari or approximately 14 km² per person: G.B. Silberbauer. 1981. *Hunter and Habitat in the Central Kalahari Desert.* Cambridge University Press, Cambridge.

[3] J.M. Orpen. 1874. 'A glimpse into the mythology of the Maluti Bushmen' in *The Cape Monthly Magazine* 9:139–156.

[4] By way of example, of the 524 European bird species assessed in 2004, some 226 were given unfavourable conservation status, an increase of five per cent from the 1994 assessment. In BirdLife International 2004. 'Birds in Europe: Population Estimates, Trends and Conservation Status'. BirdLife International, Cambridge, UK (BirdLife Conservation Series No. 12).

[5] Millennium Ecosystem Assessment. 2006. *Ecosystems and Human Well-being: Current State and Trends.* Island Press, Washington DC.

[6] Such a science is already in its infancy, as illustrated by the collection of papers in R. Woodroffe, S. Thirgood and A. Rabinowitz (eds.). 2005. 'People and Wildlife: Conflict or Coexistence?' Cambridge University Press, Cambridge.

[7] D.R. Griffith. 2008. 'The ecological implications of individual fishing quotas and harvest cooperatives' in *Frontiers in Ecology and the Environment* 6: 191–198.

[8] The importance of an ecological conscience in the development of a conservation ethic is highlighted by Aldo Leopold. 1949. *A Sand County Almanac and Sketches Here and There.* Oxford University Press, Oxford.

Chapter 23

[1] Kevin Dunham, personal communication.

[2] K.M. Dunham. 1990. 'Fruit production by *Acacia albida* trees in Zambezi riverine woodlands' in *Journal of Tropical Ecology* 6, 445–457.

[3] With apologies to Robert Burns and his immortal poem, 'To a Mouse'.

[4] Readers are cautioned against approaching wild elephants in this way. Whilst elephants are remarkably tolerant for the most part, on occasion they can be extremely dangerous, especially if frightened at close quarters. In their book, *Among the Elephants,* (William Collins, London, 1975), Iain and Oria Douglas-Hamilton describe their four years living in the midst of wild elephants. They give a rare glimpse of the respectful relations that can develop between people and elephants.

Chapter 24

[1] The skull was discovered in 1959 at Olduvai Gorge; the hominid is now known as *Australopithecus boisei.*

[2]   Essentially the same point is eloquently made by E.O. Wilson. 1984. *Biophilia*, Harvard University Press.

[3]   R.J. Blumenschine and J.A. Cavallo. October 1992. 'Scavenging and human evolution' in *Scientific American*, 90–96.

[4]   This idea was tabled by Mary Leakey and two wildlife ecologists who spent many years working in the Serengeti ecosystem. It was presented in a letter to *Nature*: A.R.E Sinclair, M.D. Leakey and M. Norton-Griffiths. 1986. 'Migration and hominid bipedalism' in *Nature* 324, 307–308.

[5]   Lucy is the name given to the 3.2-million-year-old skeleton of an *Australopithecus afarensis* female discovered in 1974 in the Hadar region of Ethiopia's Afar Triangle by Don Johanson and Tom Gray.

[6]   C. Carbone, J.T. du Toit and I.J. Gordon. 1997. 'Feeding success in African wild dogs: does kleptoparasitism by spotted hyaenas influence hunting group size?' in *Journal of Animal Ecology*, 66: 318–326.

[7]   In very arid regions, even single off-road journeys leave a near-permanent scar on the landscape. However, the cheetah biologists in Serengeti have found that single tracks on the short grass plains disappear in time, whilst multiple-use tracks leave a permanent mark. Consequently, scientists working in the area tend to choose their own route across the plains. Avoiding previous tracks only works as a conservation measure when there is little vehicle traffic. Once commercial tourism is developed, it becomes necessary, sadly, to create permanent tracks and to stick to them.

[8]   The body size of *Australopithecus afarensis* was markedly dimorphic with females estimated from fossilized remains to weigh 30 kilograms and males an impressive 65 kilograms. This is not much greater than the maximum sizes recorded for olive baboons (*Papio anubis*) whose females and males weigh up to 30 and 50 kilograms, respectively.

[9]   J. Kingdon. 1993. *Self-Made Man and His Undoing*. Simon & Schuster, London.

[10] It has been suggested that the early East African specimens of *Homo erectus* should be called *H. ergaster*. Whether this putative species was the first hominid to migrate out of Africa is still debated, as discussed in R. Dennell and W. Roebroeks. 2005. 'An Asian perspective on early human dispersal from Africa' in *Nature* 438: 1099–1104.

[11] George B. Silberbauer. 1981. *Hunter and Habitat in the Central Kalahari Desert*. Cambridge University Press, Cambridge.

[12] The Cheetah Conservation Foundation in Namibia has been training Anatolian sheep dogs to guard livestock against cheetahs, leopards, baboons, jackals and other predators, and promoting this as an alternative to the eradication of predators on farms using poisoned bait.

[13] Pippa Skotnes. 1999. *Heaven's Things: A Story of the /Xam*. University of Cape Town Press, Cape Town.